Consultant editor: Lizzie Boyd

Typeset in Century Schoolbook

PRINTED IN SPAIN

ISBN 0 276 42095 0

Opposite: Early summer in the kitchen garden arrives with
sweet-tasting peas and the first crop of juicy rhubarb.

Overleaf: An autumn harvest that includes strings of firm,
sun-ripened onions more than repays the hours spent
in the kitchen garden.

PUBLISHED BY THE READER'S DIGEST ASSOCIATION LIMITED
LONDON NEW YORK MONTREAL SYDNEY CAPE TOWN

Originally published in partwork form
by Eaglemoss Publications Limited

SUCCESSFUL GARDENING

FRUIT & VEGETABLES

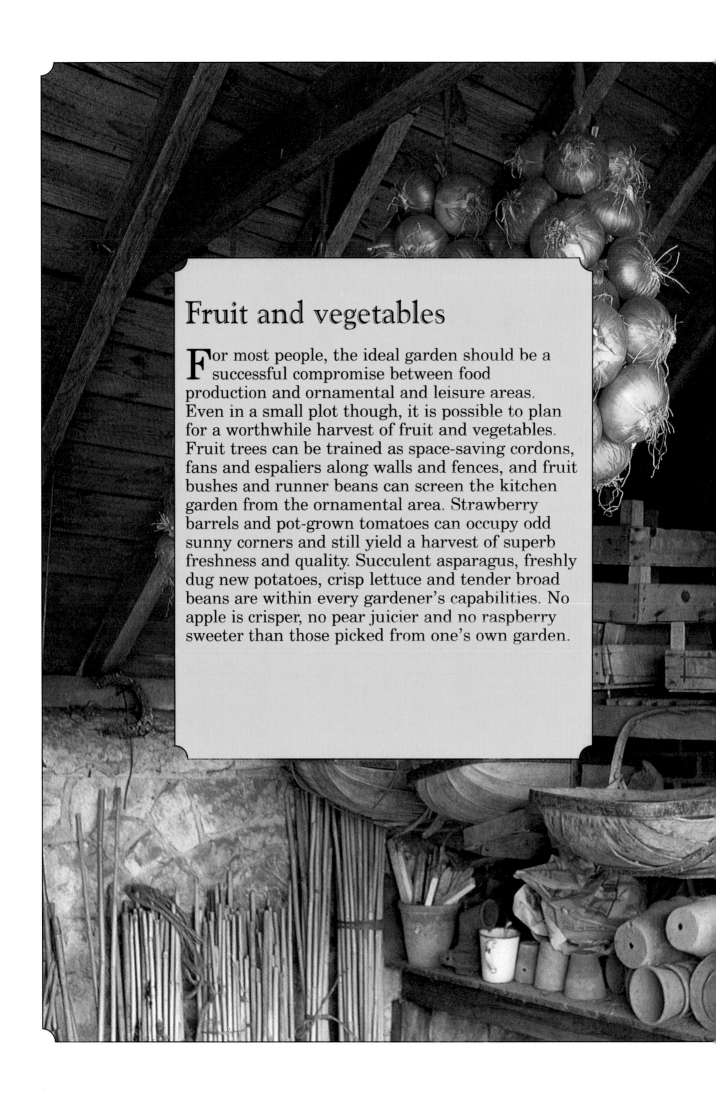

Fruit and vegetables

For most people, the ideal garden should be a successful compromise between food production and ornamental and leisure areas. Even in a small plot though, it is possible to plan for a worthwhile harvest of fruit and vegetables. Fruit trees can be trained as space-saving cordons, fans and espaliers along walls and fences, and fruit bushes and runner beans can screen the kitchen garden from the ornamental area. Strawberry barrels and pot-grown tomatoes can occupy odd sunny corners and still yield a harvest of superb freshness and quality. Succulent asparagus, freshly dug new potatoes, crisp lettuce and tender broad beans are within every gardener's capabilities. No apple is crisper, no pear juicier and no raspberry sweeter than those picked from one's own garden.

CONTENTS

Top fruit

Soft fruit

Vegetables

Espalier-grown apples Wall-trained fruit trees are ornamental, easy to tend and take up little space.

Top fruit

Few gardeners have space for a fruit orchard, but even a small garden can yield good crops of a variety of fruits if they are chosen to suit its particular size and style. Fruit trees occupy the ground for several decades and their roots and branches spread over a wide area; they cast too much shade to be grown in the vegetable garden, but they can be grown as specimen trees near the lawn – fruit blossom is a cheerful sight in spring. If there is room in the garden for only one fruit tree, make sure it is a self-fertile variety.

Many fruit trees – apples, pears and plums for instance – are grafted on to particular rootstocks which have predictable effects on the eventual size of the trees and how they will crop. Fruit trees come in different forms, the largest of which is the bush tree; dwarf pyramids are suitable for more restricted areas, while cordons are the most economical in terms of space. They are grown obliquely against a wall and consist of one main stem, with short fruiting side spurs. Fan-trained trees, too, take up little ground space and are the preferred form for apricots and peaches.

Espaliers are good choices for small gardens – they can be trained against walls and fences and are particularly attractive when grown as low screens on post and wire supports. Fruit trees grafted on to dwarf rootstock can even be grown in patio containers, and you can also buy family trees, which have been grafted with two, three or four different varieties of apples or pears, and which provide a long cropping season of different flavours and keeping qualities.

Most fruit trees are supplied by nurserymen as two- or three-year-olds, with the initial training already completed. In the first few years after planting, a framework of main branches should be established through hard pruning in order to achieve a proper balance between new growth and fruit production. Thereafter, little or no pruning should be necessary.

PRUNING TOP FRUIT

**Apples, pears, plums, cherries and other
fruit trees need regular pruning to achieve a balance
between new growth and continued fruitfulness.**

The pruning of top fruit trees is carried out in two main stages – training a young tree to the shape required, and regular pruning once the framework has been established. Training methods are basically identical for all top fruits – apples, apricots, cherries, nectarines, peaches, pears and plums – but after the initial years, the annual pruning regime varies from fruit to fruit.

As one of the main aims of pruning is to regulate the crop and improve the quality on established trees, pruning also depends on a tree's particular growth habit.

Pruning apples and pears

Apple and pear trees are trained and pruned in much the same way, although pears will tolerate harder pruning. They also produce fruiting spurs more readily, which need more thinning, in early summer.

The method of pruning depends on the shape of the trees. Bush apple trees for garden planting are grafted on to a dwarfing rootstock (M26), which is also the most satisfactory type for pyramids, cordons, fans and espaliers. Pears are grafted on quince rootstock. A very dwarfing stock (M27) is used for container-grown fruit trees with an average height of 1.2m (4ft).

Winter pruning encourages growth by directing energy on growth buds rather than on fruit buds. Pruning in mid to late summer, however, promotes the formation of fruit spurs.

When pruning a fruit tree, you must be able to distinguish between a fruit bud (which will produce blossom and then fruit) and a growth bud (which will produce leaves and eventually develop into a new shoot). Fruit buds are large and round, while growth buds are smaller and lie flatter on the stem. Growth buds develop into fruit buds on tip-bearing varieties.

Spurs are short stems, often in groups of two or three, on which fruit is formed. A leader (which is the leading shoot of a branch) must be distinguished from a lateral (which is a side-shoot from a branch or the main stem). Laterals can be trained to form a new branch or pruned to develop fruiting spurs.

Trees bought from a nursery are usually partly trained and may be up to four years old. Find out the tree's age when you buy it so that you can continue its training.

Ideally, a tree should not be allowed to bear fruit in the first year after planting, although one or two fruits are permissible. A bush tree on a vigorous rootstock takes five years before it sets fruit.

The time a tree takes to reach its full bearing capacity will depend on the variety, rootstock and method of pruning. Trees on dwarfing and semi-dwarfing rootstocks begin cropping in either the third or fourth year.

Training bush trees Grow bush trees approximately 3-4.5m (10-15ft) apart, depending on the rootstock (dwarfing or semi-dwarfing). If you buy a one-year-old (maiden) tree for training, cut the stem back to 45-60cm (1½-2ft) high, just above a bud, after planting in late autumn or winter.

The buds or small shoots just below the cut will grow out the following summer. There may be

◀ **Pruning apple trees** On established bush trees, good crops of uniform fruits are ensured by light pruning in winter. Aim to keep the centre of the tree open by removing crossing and crowded branches or by shortening them to form fruiting spurs.

APPLE AND PEAR TREE SHAPES

Apple and pear trees are grafted on to rootstocks of proven vigour and cropping qualities. For general garden planting, dwarfing and semi-dwarfing rootstocks are the best choices, and the trees will start to yield in the third or fourth year after planting. Most top fruits need a nearby pollinator of another variety that flowers at the same time, and therefore bush trees need considerable space. Dwarf pyramids are suitable for more restricted gardens, and fans, cordons and espaliers can be trained against walls, fences or on post and wire supports.

◀ **Bush trees** need plenty of space.

▼ **Dwarf pyramids** spread no more than 1.5-1.8m (5-6ft).

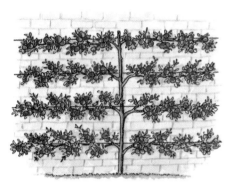

Espaliers are trained with an upright main stem and several horizontal tiers tied to strong wire supports.

Fans are trained flat against a wall on a main stem of about 60cm (2ft). Main branches and extension shoots are tied to angled canes until established.

Cordons can form low screens. They have single or multiple stems at an angle of 45°.

only three or four, perhaps more. Choose three or four to form the first branches. They should be evenly spaced round the stem with none pointing towards the supporting stake. Rub out any unwanted buds or young shoots with your thumb.

Though more expensive, it may be easier for the beginner to buy two-, three- or four-year-old trees from a nursery, and so avoid the initial training.

Year two A two-year-old bush tree in winter will have three or four branches that developed during the previous summer. Cut back each of the branches to an outward-pointing bud – if the branches are thick and vigorous,

cut them back by half. If they are thin and weak, cut them back by two-thirds. Rub out any inward-pointing buds below the cuts with your thumb.

Year three By the third winter, a number of lateral shoots will have grown out from the branches. Choose some of these laterals to form, with the first branches, the tree's framework. They should all point outwards and their tips, after pruning, should be at least 45cm (1½ft) apart.

Cut all main branches back to an outward-pointing bud, shortening new laterals on each branch by one-third if the branch is growing vigorously or by half if it is of average growth. If growth is

weak, shorten the new laterals by two-thirds.

Each of the laterals not chosen to form the main branches should be cut back to four buds from the base – they will form future fruiting spurs. Cut off any side-shoots – feathers – on the main stem flush with the stem. After this third year of pruning, the basic shape of the tree is fully established.

Pruning established trees The subsequent pruning of a bush tree depends on whether it is a spur- or a tip-bearing variety.

Spur-bearing varieties, such as 'Cox's Orange Pippin', 'James Grieve' and 'Ellison's Orange' which bear their fruits on short

GROWTH AND FRUITING BUDS ON APPLE AND PEAR TREES

Spurs are short lateral growths, often in twos or threes, on which fruit is produced.

Fruit buds are large, plump and rounded; they first produce blossom and later fruit.

Growth buds are small, pointed and flatter than fruit buds; they will produce leaves or new shoots.

PRUNING AN ESTABLISHED SPUR-BEARING BUSH APPLE OR PEAR TREE

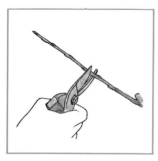   

Branch leaders should be cut back by half of their new growth in winter. Cut back strong ones by one-third, and weaker ones by two-thirds.

One-year-old shoots from a main branch bear only growth buds. Leave these unless they are extension shoots on older laterals in need of shortening.

Two-year-old shoots bear fruit buds. Prune by cutting hard back to two fruit buds on weak growth; leave more buds to develop on stronger laterals.

Three-year-old shoots have spurs. Prune back to the lowest fruiting spur to encourage new replacements. The cycle of growth then starts again.

SPUR-BEARING BUSH TREE   TIP-BEARING BUSH TREE

PRUNING AN ESTABLISHED TIP-BEARING BUSH APPLE OR PEAR TREE

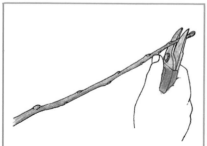  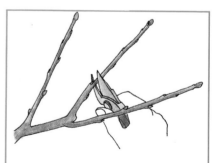

Branch leaders that are crowded should be pruned in winter. Cut the fruit bud at the tip back to a lower growth bud, forcing new tip-bearing shoots to grow out.

Untipped shoots – with no fruit bud at the tip – should be cut back to just above the highest fruit bud. Alternatively, prune back to four growth buds from the base.

Tip-bearing shoots – with a fruit bud at the tip – should not be pruned unless they are crowded. Thin them out by pruning back to two fruit buds from the base.

PRUNING A NEGLECTED BUSH APPLE OR PEAR TREE

An apple or pear tree that has been neglected for some years can sometimes be brought back to fruitfulness by a systematic programme of pruning, fertilizing and spraying against pests.

Neglected trees are either too vigorous and produce fruits well out of reach, or they become weakened, with reduced crops of small fruits. Tall trees can be pruned back gradually over three or four winters. Entirely remove all dead, broken and diseased branches, and high branches from the centre, cutting them cleanly back to the main trunk. Prune outer, tall-growing branches right back to the lower ones, and thin out small laterals to 45cm (1½ft) apart.

Restore weak-growing trees to vigour by reducing the length of long spur systems in winter. Cut out the weakest spurs and leave the plumpest fruit buds, which will produce larger fruits. Begin feeding the trees from mid winter.

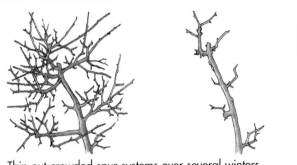

Thin out crowded spur systems over several winters. Remove the weakest ones entirely and reduce others in size. The remaining spurs with plump buds should be 23-30cm (9-12in) apart.

spurs, are pruned each winter by the method known as the renewal system. The aim is to produce new growth each season to replace those that have already borne fruit. It is based on a three-year cycle.

A growth bud sends out a shoot during its first summer. In the second summer this shoot produces fruit buds. And in the third summer, the fruit buds form spurs and bear fruit that same summer and in the following summers.

During its second summer, a shoot not only produces fruit buds but also new growth from its tip, so that a two-year-old shoot includes some one-year-old extension growth. In the same way, a three-year-old shoot has two-year-old and one-year-old extension growth.

Under the renewal system, a number of two-year-old and three-year-old shoots are cut back in winter. This keeps the centre of the tree open, allowing good air circulation. It also prevents over-cropping and overcrowding, improves fruit quality, and makes way for new growth.

There is no rule governing how

many shoots to prune out and how many to leave. Use your own judgement to maintain a balance between new growth and crops. Try to prevent the tree becoming overcrowded with branches and entirely cut out any crossing branches and dead or diseased wood; allow sufficient new fruit-bearing shoots to form.

Do not prune one-year-old shoots growing out from a main branch. However, you cannot avoid cutting away some one-year-old extension growth when cutting back two-year-old and three-year-old shoots. When choosing shoots for pruning, trace back to older wood from one-year-old tips.

On trees with weak growth, cut selected two-year-old shoots hard back to two fruit buds. On stronger trees leave more buds. Cut back selected three-year-old shoots to the lowest fruiting spur. Growth buds on the spur will produce new shoots the following season, and the cycle of growth will start again.

In the early years, branch leaders should be shortened by one-third if the branch is growing vigorously, by half if it is of average growth,

and by two-thirds if it is weak. When branches are fully grown (about 2.5m/8ft long), prune them in winter in exactly the same way as laterals.

Tip-bearing varieties are fewer in number. They include 'Bramley's Seedling', 'Worcester Pearmain' and 'George Cave', and produce some of their fruit buds on the tips of the shoots and some on spurs. The cycle of growth is the same as for spur-bearing trees, but many one-year-old shoots produce a fruit bud at the tip.

Tip-bearing trees need comparatively little pruning. Once a year, in winter, prune back shoots without a fruit bud at the tip. Cut just above the highest fruit bud, if there is one, otherwise cut back to four or five growth buds from the base of the shoot.

Shoots that have a fruit bud at the tip should not be pruned unless they are crowded – that is, if the tips are less than 30cm (1ft) apart. Thin them out by pruning some back to two buds from the base, preferably above a fruit bud, if there is one.

Prune branch leaders by removing the fruit bud at the tip,

PRUNING A TWO-YEAR-OLD PYRAMID PLUM

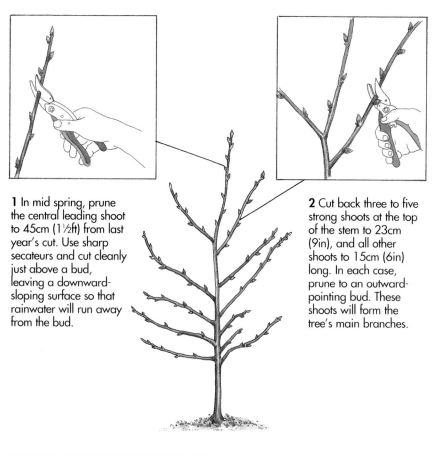

1 In mid spring, prune the central leading shoot to 45cm (1½ft) from last year's cut. Use sharp secateurs and cut cleanly just above a bud, leaving a downward-sloping surface so that rainwater will run away from the bud.

2 Cut back three to five strong shoots at the top of the stem to 23cm (9in), and all other shoots to 15cm (6in) long. In each case, prune to an outward-pointing bud. These shoots will form the tree's main branches.

PRUNING A THREE-YEAR-OLD PYRAMID PLUM

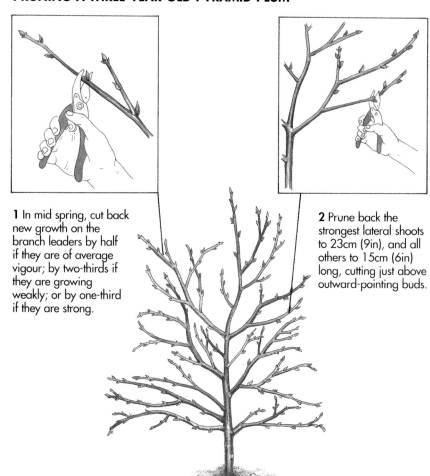

1 In mid spring, cut back new growth on the branch leaders by half if they are of average vigour; by two-thirds if they are growing weakly; or by one-third if they are strong.

2 Prune back the strongest lateral shoots to 23cm (9in), and all others to 15cm (6in) long, cutting just above outward-pointing buds.

cutting back to a healthy growth bud. This induces some of the lower growth buds to break and produce more tip-bearing shoots. They will improve the yield in subsequent years.

Pruning sweet cherries
Sweet cherries are generally very vigorous and fan-trained trees can span 4.5-6m (15-20ft), while bush tree cherries reach up to 10m (30ft) high. However, new dwarfing rootstocks have made it possible to restrict the growth of bush trees to a height of about 2.1m (7ft), with good yields at an early age. Most varieties are also available as fans.

Fan-trained cherries For the first three years after planting a young cherry tree for training against a wall, little pruning is needed apart from building up the framework. In mid spring, rub out all the new shoots growing towards or away from the wall, but leave the tips of the leading shoots unpruned.

After the framework of branches has been established, pruning should continue to be light as sweet cherries have more spurs and fewer laterals than apples.

In early summer rub out the current year's shoots growing directly towards or away from the wall. Pinch out the tips of the remaining shoots in early or mid summer when they have produced five to six leaves.

When the branches reach the top of the wall or support system, cut them back to a weak lateral shoot, or bend the shoots horizontally and tie them in place along the wires. This will slow down growth and encourage new shoots to break.

In early autumn, cut back the shoots pinched out in summer to three or four fruit buds. Also cut out any dead wood.

On older trees, tie new shoots into the fan shape in early or mid summer where room is available. Some may be needed to replace old shoots.

Bush tree (standard) cherries
Prune trees lightly in spring after the bud-burst stage. Once the tree has started to fruit (in the second or third year after planting), thin it out to let in light and air. Cut back older shoots to just above one-year-old laterals. Thin out the outer spread occasionally, where new growth develops.

PRUNING AN ESTABLISHED PYRAMID PLUM

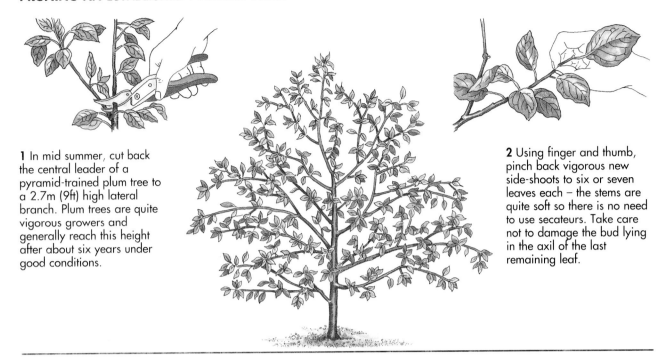

1 In mid summer, cut back the central leader of a pyramid-trained plum tree to a 2.7m (9ft) high lateral branch. Plum trees are quite vigorous growers and generally reach this height after about six years under good conditions.

2 Using finger and thumb, pinch back vigorous new side-shoots to six or seven leaves each – the stems are quite soft so there is no need to use secateurs. Take care not to damage the bud lying in the axil of the last remaining leaf.

Pruning acid cherries

As with sweet cherries, acid cherries can either be grown as bush trees (standards) or as fans. Fan-trained acid cherries can be grown against any wall – even a north-facing one.

Prune fan-trained acid cherries like fan peaches (see pages 14-15), in early spring. Acid cherries fruit on spurs grown the previous summer. Thin out the branches on established bush trees as for sweet cherries, cutting out non-producing shoots to one-year-old laterals, but leaving those more than three years old.

Pruning plums

Free-standing plum trees, damsons and gages are usually grown in a pyramid shape, very similar to a dwarf pyramid apple tree, but slightly taller (approximately 2.7m/9ft) and much wider (2.5-3m/8-10ft).

Pyramid plum trees are more irregular in outline than dwarf pyramid apples, because plums generally grow more vigorously and so it is often quite difficult to maintain a perfectly regular shape. After the basic framework has been fully established, plums need less restrictive pruning than apple trees.

Pyramid-training Plums, damsons and gages are supplied grafted on to St. Julian A rootstock. To train young maiden trees into a pyramid shape, cut back the stem to 1.5m (5ft) above ground in mid spring after planting, slicing just above a bud. Cut off flush with the stem any young branches which are lower than 45cm (1½ft) from the ground.

If the newly planted tree is much less than 1.5m (5ft) in height, allow it to continue growing for at least another year before training it.

On a two-year-old plum tree, cut back the central leader in mid spring to about 45cm (1½ft) from last year's cut. Again, make the cut just above a bud.

Cut back three to five of the strongest side-shoots at the top of the stem to 23cm (9in), pruning to outward-pointing buds. Cut back all other side-shoots to 15cm (6in). Since lower growth tends to be

PRUNING A FAN-TRAINED PLUM

1 At the beginning of mid summer, pinch out the tips of all side-shoots which are not needed as branches as soon as they have produced six or seven leaves. Prevent shoots from growing towards or away from the wall by rubbing out the offending buds in spring before they begin to develop.

2 At the end of summer, after the crop of plums has been harvested, shorten by half those shoots that were pinched back earlier in the season.

ESTABLISHING A FAN-TRAINED PEACH

1 In late winter, before growth begins, cut back both the side branches to 30-45cm (1-1½ft), making each slanting cut just above a growth bud. Secure the canes to the wires at about 40° and tie the branches to these.

2 During the summer after planting, tie in the shoots that have grown from each bud. Allow two well-spaced shoots to grow upwards from each branch, and one from the lower side. Tie these to canes and rub out any other buds.

weaker, it should be cut back harder to encourage even growth. Allow these side-shoots to grow on to form the tree's first main branches.

From the third year onwards, until the plum tree reaches full height, cut back the central leader to about 45cm (1½ft) above last year's cut in mid spring. Cut back the branch leaders according to their vigour – by one-third of new growth if they are of average growth, or by two-thirds if they are weak.

Cut back the strongest laterals from main branches to 23cm (9in) long, and the remainder to 15cm (6in) long. Always make the cut above an outward-pointing bud.

Once a plum tree has reached 2.7m (9ft) – when it is about six years old – keep it at this height by cutting back the central leader to a strong lateral in summer. You may need to do this every second or third year, depending on the rate of growth.

Prune established plum trees only in mid summer – winter pruning can result in die-back or silver leaf infection. If the mature tree is fruiting regularly, prune as little as possible, since fruit is borne on the previous season's shoots as well as on spurs on old

wood. Merely pinch back vigorous new side-shoots to six or seven leaves from the parent stem.

Thin out any overcrowded branches as necessary, cutting flush with the parent stem. Also cut away any dead wood. If branch leaders grow exceptionally long, cut them back to a strong main lateral shoot. Aim to keep branches to a maximum length of 1.2-1.5m (4-5ft).

Fan-trained plums are treated like fan-trained peaches (see opposite) until the third year from planting, but delay pruning until early spring when growth begins. Unlike peaches, plums fruit on both old wood and on shoots produced the previous season.

After the third summer, when the framework is built up, rub out all buds pointing towards or away from the wall as soon as growth starts in spring. At the beginning of mid summer, when side-shoots that are not needed as branches have produced six or seven leaves, pinch out their tips.

After the crop has been picked, shorten by half those shoots that were pinched back. Do not allow any shoots to grow strongly upwards, as they may rob lower branches of nourishment. If one is needed to fill up a space or replace an old branch, tie it to a wire.

Cut out any unwanted shoots flush with the wood from which they sprout. Also remove any dead, diseased or damaged wood.

A neglected plum tree can sometimes be reclaimed in the same way as a neglected apple, but the work must be carried out in summer.

Pruning apricots
Train fan and bush apricot trees like apples until the framework is built up, but prune in early spring as growth begins. Then prune fan apricots like plums, and bush tree apricots like acid cherries.

Pruning peaches/nectarines
Both fan-trained and bush tree peaches will grow in any situation other than a frost pocket or site exposed to cold winds. But they do best in a warm, sunny position, with the fans preferably against a wall which faces south or south-west.

Nectarines are grown in the same way as peaches, but they need a warmer situation and should be grown only as fans.

Fan-trained peaches/ nectarines are pruned in early spring as growth begins. Peaches and nectarines produce side-shoots off the current year's growth. Pinch these side-shoots out one bud from the base.

From the fourth spring after planting a maiden tree, when it has 24-32 rib branches, pruning is dictated by the tree's growth habit, as peaches and nectarines fruit mainly on last year's shoots.

When growth starts in the fourth spring, rub or pinch out any buds or shoots pointing towards or away from the wall. From the remaining buds, select only the good ones on each side of a rib spaced at about 15cm (6in) intervals, and rub out all others except the bud at the tip.

During the fourth summer these buds will produce laterals that will fruit the following summer, and the bud at the tip will grow on as a rib leader.

In the fifth spring, at least two growth buds will have emerged at the base of last year's laterals. Allow one to grow on as a replacement, but remove any others when they are 5-7.5cm (2-3in) long.

Let the tips of fruit-bearing laterals grow on in order to draw the sap and help develop the fruit. If space is limited, pinch them back to four leaves when they have made six leaves. Pinch off any side-shoots that grow from them.

In autumn or early winter, after fruit picking, cut back each of the laterals that has borne fruit to its replacement, and tie in the replacement with soft string.

Repeat this process of disbudding, pinching back, cutting out old shoots and tying in replacements every year.

Bush tree peaches are pruned in late spring. On maiden trees cut back the central leader to about 60cm (2ft) above the ground.

Leave the top three or four buds or side-shoots below the cut to form the first branches. Remove all the side-shoots lower down.

In the following years, remove any crossing branches, cutting flush with the parent branch.

Remove any shoots from the main trunk below the lowest branch, flush with the trunk. Peaches are prone to die-back, so cut back any branch that is dying at the tip to a healthy side-shoot.

On established bush trees, cut out any branches drooping to the ground and older branches as their fruit-bearing capacity diminishes.

PRUNING A MATURE FAN-TRAINED PEACH

1 In mid spring, pinch back growth buds on last year's laterals (those with flowers) to one leaf, leaving one bud to provide a replacement shoot.

2 In late spring, thin out new laterals on the upper and lower sides of the rib branches to 15cm (6in) apart. These will fruit the following year.

3 Also in late spring, if space is limited, pinch back fruit-bearing laterals to four leaves, unless they are needed as replacement shoots.

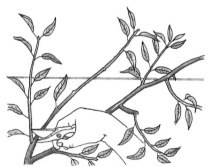

4 After harvesting, cut out fruited laterals to the replacement shoots, unless they are needed as part of the framework. Tie in the replacements.

APPLES

**Crisp and tasty home-grown apples are good
money-saving crops and a greater choice of varieties can be
grown than are found in supermarkets.**

All apple trees are grafted on to rootstocks of varying performance, ranging from very vigorous types for standard and half-standard trees to dwarf rootstock for bush and pyramid trees, and very dwarf rootstock for pot-grown apples. The eventual height and spread of a tree depends on the rootstock, the particular variety and the type of soil, but standards and half-standards are the types of tree usually grown in orchards and are not recommended for general garden planting.

Bush trees, which average a height and spread at maturity of 3-3.5m (10-12ft), are good choices for gardens with plenty of space; they carry heavy yields and one well-grown tree can produce 36-45kg (80-100lb) of fruit annually.

Where space is more restricted, dwarf pyramid trees, planted 1.5-1.8m (5-6ft) apart, are better choices, as are trees grown in trained or restricted form as they occupy the least ground space. The yields from such trees are smaller than from free-growing trees, and they also require more attention.

Family trees are also available – they have three or four different apple varieties grafted on to one rootstock. These will have been selected for simultaneous blossoming, but the tree will still provide a succession of fruit.

Popularly, apples are divided into cookers and eaters (dessert apples), but there is no precise distinction. Although some varieties are used mainly for cooking, they can also be enjoyed for their quite sharp taste if eaten raw. Similarly, some dessert apples can be used for cooking.

The first apples are ready for picking and eating in late summer. With careful storage of late-maturing fruit, home-grown apples can be enjoyed until the end of the following spring.

Pollination

Most apple trees cannot pollinate themselves, and so it is necessary to plant at least two varieties that blossom at the same time for cross-pollination to take place. Catalogues list apple varieties as belonging to groups 1, 2 or 3, indicating flowering as taking place in early, mid or late spring. A few varieties, including 'Bramley's Seedling', are such poor pollinators that a third variety is needed to fertilize the tree chosen as pollinator.

▲ **Apple harvest** Established and well-tended trees will yield heavy crops of dessert or cooking apples for anything up to 50 years.

Site and soil

Apples thrive in inland areas, but do not grow well in coastal areas exposed to salt-laden winds. In cold northern gardens and in low-lying local frost pockets, spring frosts are likely to destroy the blossom, especially on early-flowering varieties.

An open, sunny, but sheltered site is best. Most soils are suitable except those that are waterlogged or high in lime. Well-drained but moisture-retentive, slightly acid soil is the ideal.

In early to mid autumn, fork well-rotted manure or compost into the soil at the rate of a bucketful per sq m/yd. Apply 75g per sq m (3oz per sq yd) of a general fertilizer before planting.

Buying apple trees

Nurseries and garden centres offer one-, two- or three-year-old trees. Apple trees in their first year are cheaper than older trees because they need training and pruning into shape. Two or three-year old trees, although slightly more expensive, may be better buys. They will have been partly trained to a particular shape by the nurseryman, and they will start cropping earlier.

Make sure the nurseryman knows what position and what type of soil the tree will be given before he advises you on the variety and rootstock you should choose.

PLANTING

▲ Dig a hole large enough to hold the roots of the tree when they are well spread out. Drive in a stake and plant the tree close to it with the graft union 10cm (4in) above soil level.

Planting an apple tree

The best time for planting is during frost-free weather between late autumn and early spring.

Dig a hole big enough to take the roots of the tree when they are well spread out. When planting a bush tree, drive in a supporting stake and plant the tree against it. Make sure that the graft union between the rootstock and the scion will be at least 10cm (4in) above soil level. Plant bush trees 1.8-5.5m (6-18ft) apart, depending on the vigour of the rootstock. Space dwarf pyramid trees 1.5-1.8m (5-6ft) apart.

When planting trees against a wall, position them 23cm (9in) away from the base of the wall. Attach strong horizontal wires, at 30cm (12in) intervals, against which to train cordons, espaliers and fans. Space cordons ¾-1m (2½-3ft) apart, espaliers and fans up to 3.5m (12ft) apart. In order for cordons and espaliers to be grown as free-standing screens, construct a supporting framework of stout posts and wires before planting.

Looking after the trees

Until the trees have become established, water them during dry spells and mulch them in spring with manure or garden compost to help the soil retain moisture.

In the second winter after planting, begin an annual feeding routine. Apply 25g per sq m (1oz per sq yd) of sulphate of potash. Every third year, add 50g (2oz) of superphospate to that dressing.

In early spring apply 25g per sq m (1oz per sq yd) of sulphate of ammonia. Increase this to 50g per sq m (2oz per sq yd) for cooking varieties and for all apple trees grown in grass.

Keep down weeds by shallow hoeing or hand weeding. For training and pruning apple trees see pages 8-11.

Apple trees are hosts to a number of serious pests and diseases. They are controlled by a systematic spraying programme based on the stage of flower bud development (see below) and on regular winter applications of tar-oil wash to destroy aphids, scale insects and apple suckers.

Thinning the crop

Bearing a heavy crop of fruit can put a strain on a tree and result in a harvest of poor-quality fruits. Thinning the fruits in early summer ensures that the remaining apples grow to full size.

Heavy thinning is rarely needed on cordons, espaliers, fans and dwarf pyramids. On large bush trees, however, the fruit should be well spaced out.

Start to thin the crop in early summer, removing any badly shaped or damaged fruits and the central apple of each cluster. Use a pair of scissors to cut the stalk, or hold it between two fingers and press the apple away with your thumb. Never pull fruit off since this can damage the spur (short side branch bearing fruit).

By mid summer there is a natural drop of fruit. But if there is still a plentiful crop afterwards, thin again to leave one apple on each spur for trained trees – on bush trees, dessert varieties should be spaced 10-15cm (4-6in) apart and cooking apples 15-23cm (6-9in) apart.

Harvesting

Early apples are ready for picking from late summer to early autumn. They should be eaten as soon as possible because they don't keep. Mid-season and late varieties should be picked before they are ripe in early to mid autumn and allowed to ripen in store. Apples are ready for har-

SPRAYING PROGRAMME

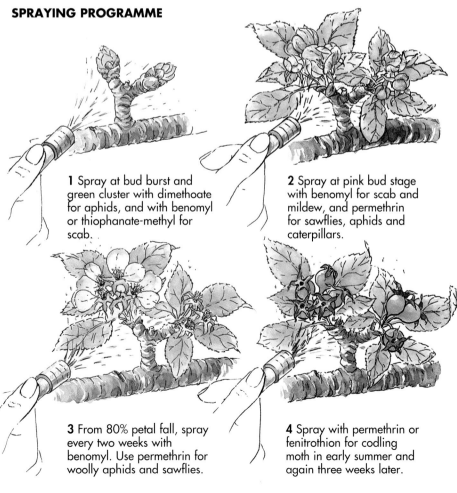

1 Spray at bud burst and green cluster with dimethoate for aphids, and with benomyl or thiophanate-methyl for scab.

2 Spray at pink bud stage with benomyl for scab and mildew, and permethrin for sawflies, aphids and caterpillars.

3 From 80% petal fall, spray every two weeks with benomyl. Use permethrin for woolly aphids and sawflies.

4 Spray with permethrin or fenitrothion for codling moth in early summer and again three weeks later.

vesting when, with a gentle twist, they part easily from the spurs.

For reaching fruit high on a bush tree use an apple picker – a net on a long pole. Push the frame of the net against the stalk – if the apple is ready it will drop into the net. Handle apples with care – they bruise easily.

Place the apples in a cool, well-ventilated room or shed for a couple of days. Then sort them out for storing, putting any which are even slightly damaged (without a stalk for instance) or diseased to one side for immediate use.

Storing

Store mid-season varieties separately from late varieties. They are ready for eating at different times – mid-season varieties from mid autumn to early winter, and late varieties from mid winter to mid spring. If stored together, the gases given off by earlier apples can hasten the ripening of the later ones.

There are several different ways of storing apples. They can be wrapped in pieces of oiled paper or in small squares of newspaper (to keep them dry, and prevent them touching each other). Wrap them loosely – don't make an airtight seal. Place two or three layers of wrapped apples in a well-ventilated box and store in a dark and cool place.

Apples can also be kept in plastic bags – make small punctures in the bag so that the gases given off by the apples can escape.

Polystyrene trays are also ideal. They are available from garden centres. Place the apples in the moulded trays and stack these on top of each other in a dark and cool place.

Pests and diseases

The most common pests of apples are aphids, codling moths, apple sawflies, caterpillars of the winter moth, capsids, red spider mites and woolly aphids. Regular spraying and winter washes should eliminate most of these.

The main diseases are apple canker, brown rot, magnesium deficiency, powdery mildew and scab. Good cultural practices and correct pruning are essential.

▶ **Thinning apples** By reducing the number of apples from each spur, the remainder grow to uniform size. Heavy crops put a strain on fruit trees.

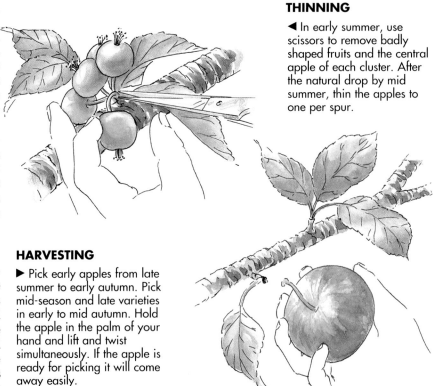

THINNING

◀ In early summer, use scissors to remove badly shaped fruits and the central apple of each cluster. After the natural drop by mid summer, thin the apples to one per spur.

HARVESTING

▶ Pick early apples from late summer to early autumn. Pick mid-season and late varieties in early to mid autumn. Hold the apple in the palm of your hand and lift and twist simultaneously. If the apple is ready for picking it will come away easily.

VARIETIES TO CHOOSE

Varieties in the same pollination group (A,B,C) blossom at about the same time. Two trees that blossom simultaneously are necessary for cross-pollination.

Varieties are grouped according to when the apples are ready for eating.

Early

'Discovery' – dessert, crisp, sweet and juicy; some scab resistance; tip-bearing; eat late summer to early autumn; B.

'George Cave' – dessert; sweet aromatic flavour; regular cropper; eat late summer; A.

'Grenadier' – cooker; firm flesh, acid flavour; regular heavy cropper; resistant to scab; use mid summer to early autumn; B.

'Merton Knave' – dessert; crisp white flesh, sweet flavour; eat late summer to early autumn; C.

Mid-season

'Egremont Russet' – dessert; sweet flavour; some scab resistance; eat mid autumn to early winter; A.

'Golden Noble' – cooker; tender flesh, acid flavour; use early autumn to mid winter; C.

'James Grieve' – dessert; tender, juicy, good flavour; prone to canker; eat early to mid autumn; A.

'Lane's Prince Albert' – cooker; crisp juicy flesh, acid; use mid autumn to mid winter; C.

'Lord Lambourne' – dessert; crisp, moderately sweet; some resistance to scab; eat mid autumn; A.

'Worcester Pearmain' – dessert; crisp, sweet; mildew resistant; tip-bearing; eat early to mid autumn; B.

Late

'Bramley's Seedling' – cooker; use late autumn to early spring; partly tip-bearing; needs two pollinators from group B.

'Cox's Orange Pippin' – dessert; excellent flavour; susceptible to scab, mildew and canker; eat late autumn to early winter; B.

'Golden Delicious' – dessert; crisp, sweet and juicy; eat early winter to spring; C.

'Howgate Wonder' – cooker; crisp texture; regular cropper; use autumn to mid winter; C.

'Idared' – dessert and cooker; crisp, juicy; regular cropper; eat early winter to mid spring; A.

'Grenadier'

'Discovery'

'Merton Knave'

'Egremont Russet'

'Worcester Pearmain'

'Cox's Orange Pippin'

'Golden Delicious'

'Golden Noble'

'Howgate Wonder'

'Idared'

'Lane's Prince Albert'

'Bramley's Seedling'

APRICOTS

**Although both sun and shelter are needed
for these early flowering fruit trees, good crops of fruit
are possible from fan-trained apricots.**

The problem with growing apricots in Britain is that they are very early flowering. Blooms appear as early as February when few insects are about to assist pollination. Apricots also need plenty of sun in summer and early autumn to do well. Therefore they can only be grown under glass – which generally isn't practical – north of the River Trent and are only successful in southern gardens if grown in a sheltered position on a south-facing wall. Avoid low-lying valley positions where frost pockets occur.

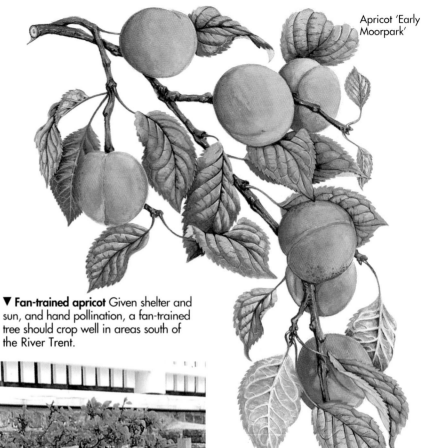

Apricot 'Early Moorpark'

Cultivation

Apricots are fussy in that they need a well-drained, moisture-retentive and slightly limy loam. If the soil is heavy, line the base of the planting hole with a layer of

▼ **Fan-trained apricot** Given shelter and sun, and hand pollination, a fan-trained tree should crop well in areas south of the River Trent.

rubble to assist drainage. Add lime to acid soil according to the supplier's instructions and the level of acidity of the soil. Mix the returned soil with half as much again of bulky organic matter and grit at 3kg per sq m (7lb per sq yd). Apricots will never do well in extremely heavy subsoil.

Buy two- or three-year-old trees – they can be expected to begin fruiting at four years old. Choose trees grafted on to a dwarfing rootstock such as St. Julien A or Pixy, which are less vig-

PLANTING

A layer of rubble at the base of the planting hole improves drainage and helps to break up heavy soil. Add grit and bulky organic matter to the soil; dress with lime if the ground is acid.

Apricot 'New Large Early'

VARIETIES TO CHOOSE

'Alfred' – juicy; ripens mid/late summer; biennial.

'Early Moorpark' – large pale orange fruit; strong growth when young; ripens mid summer.

'Farmingdale' – moderate vigour; somewhat resistant to die-back; ripens in mid summer.

'Goldcot' – recent introduction; good cropper and hardier than most other apricots.

'Moorpark' – old favourite; large fruit; heavy cropper; ripens late summer; prone to die-back.

'New Large Early' – large juicy fruit; crops well; suitable for a small garden; ripens mid summer.

orous than others and won't grow too large. One fan-trained tree, when established, will spread 3.5m (12ft) wide and reach a height of 2.5m (8ft) or more depending on the height of the wall and pruning. Apricots are self-fertile and do not need another pollinator.

Plant from late autumn to early spring, setting the tree to the same depth as the soil mark on the stem and about 15cm (6in) away from the wall or fence. Mulch with compost and water in well. Keep the ground clear of weeds.

Every year in late winter, apply a top dressing of bonemeal at the rate of 75g per sq m (3oz per sq yd) and sulphate of potash at 25g per sq m (1oz per sq yd). Spread these dressings over the entire rooting area of the tree, which is equivalent to the ultimate spread of the branches.

Every third year omit the bonemeal and replace it with a 7.5cm (3in) thick layer of well-rotted compost or manure.

In winter protect the tree from frost with a double thickness of 2.5cm (1in) nylon mesh or plastic netting draped over the branches.

When the flowers are fully open, use a camel-hair brush to transfer pollen from one flower to another to ensure that the fruits set.

In mid to late spring thin the small fruits to 10cm (4in) apart – this helps the remaining fruits to develop. If thinning is neglected, some varieties tend to bear fruit every other year only (biennial-bearing). In early summer apply a dressing of sulphate of ammonia at the rate of 25g per sq m (1oz per sq yd) to moist soil and

water it in. Water the tree well in dry spells to ensure that the swelling of the fruit is not checked.

Fan-training
Before planting fix horizontal wood supports or training wires securely to the wall or fence at about 23cm (9in) intervals.

After planting the tree, tie in the young branches in an even fan formation to canes fixed to the supports. For a three-year-old tree, tie in four leading branches on each side of the main trunk. In late winter shorten each leader by one-third, pruning to a downward-pointing bud (about 45cm/1½ft of stem should remain).

In mid or late summer select and tie in three extra shoots from each pruned leader – pinch out all remaining shoots. Tie these extra shoots to canes fixed on the supports, training them to face outwards to fill the space on the wall. Allow these laterals to grow to 45cm (1½ft), then pinch out the growing point. These laterals will bear fruit the following summer.

The following spring rub out

any buds pointing towards or away from the wall and prune the leaders by one-quarter. Early in mid summer pinch out the tips of side-shoots six leaves from the base. After cropping, cut back these laterals by half.

Apricots carry the best fruit on short spurs on two- and three-year-old wood. Every four to six years cut out older shoots which have fruited to make room for young replacement shoots. Some lateral fan-trained branches will also need to be cut back. Tie in replacement shoots; don't cut them back until the second season.

Fully ripe apricots have a good colour and part easily from the spurs. Depending on the variety, they are ready for harvesting from mid to late summer. They will keep for up to a month if stored in a cool, well-ventilated place.

Pests and diseases
The major pests are aphids and red spider mite; spray with a systemic insecticide. Diseases include silver leaf, brown-rot and die-back; prune out affected shoots.

CHERRIES

**Cherry trees bear beautiful spring flowers and sweet
or acid juicy fruit in summer. They can be grown as free-standing
bush trees or fan-trained against a wall.**

There are two kinds of cherry – sweet cherries are eaten fresh as a dessert fruit, and sour or acid ('Morello') cherries are used for cooking, bottling and making jam.

Both kinds need very deep, well-drained soil, preferably alkaline, although sour cherries will thrive on less fertile soils than sweet cherries. The two types are cultivated differently. Sweet cherries are ready for picking from mid summer to early autumn, and sour cherries in late summer or early autumn.

Sweet cherries are very vigorous, and as bush or standard trees can grow up to 10m (30ft) high or more. Until the fairly recent introduction of dwarfing rootstocks the sweet cherry was much too vigorous for an average-sized garden. Rootstock such as Colt and other more dwarfing rootstocks have made it possible to grow sweet cherries as fans against a wall about 2-2.5m (6-8ft) high. They can also be trained as pyramids when they will reach a height of about 2m (7ft).

Older varieties of sweet cherries require cross-pollination and at least two varieties must be grown for pollination to take place. It takes several years for such newly planted trees to fruit.

New sweet cherry varieties on dwarfing rootstocks are generally self-fertile and do not need a pollinating partner. They often begin fruit-bearing in the second year after planting.

If you already have a sweet cherry in your garden, prune and feed it annually. Drape netting over it in early summer to prevent birds from eating the crop.

Acid cherries are less vigorous than sweet cherries, and can be grown either as bush trees or as fans. As each tree is self-fertile only a single tree is needed, although crops are better if a second tree of a different variety is grown nearby. Sour cherry will also pollinate sweet cherry. Even though birds are less attracted to acid cherries, it is still advisable to net them.

sweet cherry

'Morello' acid cherry

Planting an acid cherry tree

A fan-trained tree grown against a wall will attain a span of 4.5-6m (15-20ft), less on dwarfing rootstock. A similar distance is needed between bush trees. A deep, well-drained soil gives the best results; aspect is not all that important and 'Morello' can be grown against north-facing walls.

Plant between mid autumn and mid spring. When planting a bush tree, drive a supporting stake in the hole and tie the tree to it. Unless secured, the tree will tend to rock in high winds, loosening the roots and delaying the development of the upper framework.

Planting a sweet cherry tree

Older varieties of sweet cherry trees grow vigorously; fan-grown trees will span 4.5-6m (15-20ft), so plant them 6-8m (20-26ft) apart, against a sheltered wall facing south or west.

Sweet cherries grown on Colt rootstock should be planted 4.5m (15ft) apart for fans and bushes, and 4m (13ft) for pyramids trained in the open garden. Sweet cherries on dwarf rootstock can be planted closer.

Nurserymen will advise on suitable rootstocks and possible pollinators.

Cultivation

In mid winter, feed annually with 15g per sq m (½oz per sq yd) of sulphate of potash over an area roughly equivalent to the spread

▲ **Sweet and sour cherries** Birds are the greatest threat to cherry crops, sweet cherries being the most favoured. Wall-trained trees are easier to protect with netting than trees grown in open ground.

of the top growth. Follow with a thick mulch of well-rotted manure or garden compost. In early spring, apply 25g per sq m (1oz per sq yd) of sulphate of ammonia. Every third year, apply 75g per sq m (3oz per sq yd) of superphosphate. Thoroughly water the ground during dry spells.

Pruning acid cherries

In the first year, train maiden bush forms by retaining about four of the strongest side-branches 90-100cm (3-3½ft) above the ground and cutting the remainder off flush with the stem. Cut the main stem back to just above the top side-shoot, and prune each retained side-shoot back to one-third of its length. Do this in early spring before the buds start to develop. During the next two springs, prune the new side-shoots on the retained shoots by half.

Fan-trained cherries are usually bought with the fan already started; further early training is identical to that for peaches (see pages 14-15).

Established acid cherries fruit only on wood that developed during the previous summer. Pruning should therefore be aimed at stimulating plenty of new growth each year to produce renewal shoots. Annual feeding in spring is also essential.

In spring, rub out side-shoots on fan trees that are growing towards the wall, and either tie in or remove outward-growing shoots. Tie in young shoots that are growing parallel with the wall. Thin out the remainder so that they are spaced about 7.5cm (3in) apart, and tie them in as they grow.

In late summer, after fruiting, cut back the fruited shoots to young replacement shoots, and also a proportion of three-year-old shoots. Prune both sides of the fan equally to keep the tree in balance.

Bush trees need similar if less severe treatment. After fruiting, cut out about a quarter of the fruited shoots, cutting back to just above strong new growth. As the tree ages, take out a few four-year-old branches, again just above new growth.

Pruning sweet cherries

Fan-trained sweet cherries are

▶ **Fan-trained cherries** Acid cherries flower in mid to late spring. They need pruning twice a year, in spring and in late summer after harvesting.

PRUNING FAN-TRAINED SWEET CHERRIES

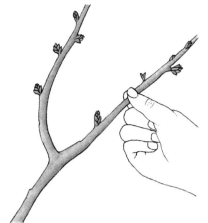

1 In mid spring, rub out with your finger and thumb any side-shoots which grow towards or away from the wall; leave the leading shoots to grow on unpruned.

2 Within a few weeks, when the remaining shoots have five or six leaves, carefully pinch out the growing tips of all laterals, other than branch leaders.

3 When leaders reach the top of the wall, shorten them by pruning back close to a side-shoot; or bend them over horizontally and fasten them to the top wire.

4 In early autumn, cut back shoots that were pinched back earlier, reducing them to three or four fruit buds. At the same time cut away dead, damaged or diseased shoots.

trained in the same way as peaches (see pages 14-15). Once the framework is present, pruning and training in spring consists of rubbing out all new shoots growing towards the wall; do not prune the leaders that will become part of the main framework. In early to mid summer, pinch out the growing tips of all new shoots, except those needed to fill a space, after they have produced five or six leaves. Sweet cherries fruit on new as well as older spurs.

When leading shoots have reached the top of the wall, shorten them to just above a weak lateral shoot, or bend them over horizontally and fasten to the top wire. All the new shoots should be tied to fit into the fan shape.

In early autumn cut away any dead wood and shorten the shoots that were pinched out in the summer to three or four buds.

On bush sweet cherries, remove dead or diseased branches, and any that rub against one another. Do this after picking or in early winter and paint the cuts with a proprietary sealing compound to keep out silver-leaf infection.

In the first spring after planting bush cherries grown on dwarfing rootstock, select three or four well-spaced side-shoots for the framework. Cut them back by half to outward-facing buds. By the following spring, there should be between six and nine well-spaced laterals. Prune lightly, leaving them unpruned if there is enough room. But cut out upright sub-laterals in the centre, and any sub-laterals competing with the main laterals back to three buds.

Harvesting and storing

Sweet cherries do not keep and should be eaten soon after harvesting. Use scissors to cut off the fruit clusters of all cherries; pulling can wound the spurs and allow diseases to enter the fruit.

Acid cherries can be frozen or used in preserves and wine.

Pests and diseases

Apart from birds, the pests most likely to attack cherries are aphids and caterpillars; spray with a systemic insecticide and apply a winter wash. The more troublesome diseases are bacterial canker, chlorosis, honey fungus and silver leaf. They are more likely to occur on neglected and badly pruned trees.

Acid cherry 'Morello'

Sweet cherry 'Merton Glory'

VARIETIES TO CHOOSE

Sweet cherries

'Cherokee' ('Lapins') – self-fertile; large dark red fruit; high yields, resistant to splitting; late summer.

'Early Rivers' – large black fruit from early summer; reliable; vigorous; pollinate with 'Merton Glory' or 'Noir de Guben'.

'Frogmore Early' – yellow cherry; generous crops; pollinate with 'Stella'.

'Merton Bigarreau' – black; large fruit; mid summer; pollinate with 'Merton Glory'.

'Merton Glory' – early; large yellow-flushed crimson; pollinators are 'Merton Bigarreau' and 'Morello'; early summer.

'Noir de Guben' – large, dark red; resistant to canker; pollinate with 'Merton Glory' or 'Early Rivers'; early/mid summer.

'Stella' – self-fertile; excellent cropper; large, dark red almost black fruit; mid summer; good pollinator for other sweet cherries.

Acid cherries

'Morello' – large, dark red juicy fruit with bitter-sweet flavour; suitable only for cooking and preserves; ripens late summer to early autumn; self-fertile and needs no pollinator; will pollinate sweet cherry trees. Can be grown as a bush, or fan-trained against walls or free-standing post and wire supports.

Sweet cherry 'Noir de Guben'

CRAB APPLES

**Ornamental crab apples have beautiful
spring blossom and autumn colours, and also provide
tangy fruits for jelly-making.**

◄ **Crab apples** Much used as pollinators in commercial apple orchards, crab apples are also suitable for family gardens. They make handsome specimen trees, stunning with their spring blossom, vivid autumn leaf colours and their large, useful crops of small, brilliantly coloured fruits.

The crab apple is a genuinely dual-purpose tree whose ornamental fruit makes excellent jams, jellies and wines. Crab apples remain piquant even after cooking – perfect as tart accompaniments for rich meats and poultry. Their tangy flavour makes them superior to the cultivated apple for jelly and wine-making.

Apart from its attractive and useful fruits, the crab apple tree also has delightful white or pink blossom; some varieties also have fine autumnal colour. Nurseries stock a variety of crabs sold purely for their ornamental value, but edible varieties – which have every bit as good blossom as ornamental ones – are often cheaper.

The crab apple is generally self-fertile and some varieties – such as the upright and compact, yellow-fruited 'Golden Hornet' – are good pollinators of dessert apples.

Soil and site

Crab apples fruit very heavily – the small rounded or conical apples grow in clusters on long stalks like cherries. Even a dwarf tree will provide about 10kg (22lb) of fruit when established.

Some varieties grow too large to warrant space in small gardens, but many are sold on dwarfing rootstock – good nurserymen will advise according to the amount of space available. The average height of a standard-trained tree is 4.5-6m (15-20ft) by 5-6.5m (16-21ft) wide, but if grafted on to a dwarfing rootstock both height and spread at maturity are reduced.

Crab apples grow in any fertile, well-drained soil. A dressing of well-rotted manure or garden compost dug in a few weeks before planting helps to get a tree started, but no feeding is needed after that.

Planting

Plant trees while they are dormant – from autumn to early spring. It is essential that the ground is neither waterlogged nor frozen. They grow best in an open and sunny position.

The day before planting, soak the roots in water for 12-24 hours. Trim off any broken or excessively long roots with secateurs. Take out a planting hole large enough to hold the tree with its roots fully spread out. Dig the hole deep enough to set the tree so that the soil mark on the stem is level with the ground.

The tree needs support for the first few years, so drive a strong stake into the hole. Place the tree in the hole and gently spread the roots out. Position the main stem about 10cm (4in) from the stake. Fill the hole with fine soil, shaking the tree vigorously to help the soil settle and to fill any air pockets under the roots. Firm the soil carefully with your feet. Continue to fill in with soil and firm it until level with the surrounding soil.

Ensure that the graft union between stock and scion is at least 10cm (4in) above soil level. (The union shows as an elbow-like protrusion.) Spread a mulch of well-rotted organic matter around the tree. Secure to the stake with ties.

Keep the soil well watered if the weather is dry in the spring after planting. Pruning is not necessary except to remove dead wood and any diseased and crossing branches – do this in winter.

Harvesting

The apples ripen in early to mid autumn. Although fruits of some varieties may stay on the tree all winter, they are best picked as soon as they are ripe when the swelling is completed and colouring has ceased to change. If you have some to spare, leave them on the tree for decoration – birds will gradually remove them for you.

Varieties

The white-flowered 'John Downie', with its large, conical, orange and scarlet fruits, is one of the most widely planted crab apples. Other ornamental and high-yielding varieties include the striking red-flowered 'Floribunda', white-blossoming 'Golden Hornet', and 'Red Siberian Crab', which bears drooping clusters of red cherry-like fruits. Some nurseries also stock crab apples grafted with two or more different varieties.

Pests and diseases

Crab apples suffer from the same pests and diseases as other types of apples, but to a lesser extent.

Crab apple 'Golden Hornet'

FIGS

**Figs are a rare delicacy and delicious as
fresh dessert fruit. They can be grown outdoors against a
south-facing wall in sheltered garden soil.**

Figs come from the Mediterranean countries, and can be grown in Britain in the south and west, though they require more attention than most fruits. They *can* be grown under glass north of the River Trent, but they take up considerable space.

Even in the south and west, figs do best against a south-facing wall which will capture maximum sun and warmth.

Figs harvested in summer are formed during the previous year, and are present on the trees during the winter as embryo fruits next to the terminal growth buds on young shoots. It is these shoots and the tiny fruits which require protection during cold weather as they are easily killed off by a harsh winter.

Site and soil preparation
Fig trees for garden planting are generally supplied as two- or three-year-olds – only one tree is necessary as figs fruit without pollination and fertilization.

The root system must always be restricted to stop the tree from producing excessive, unfruitful wood. Dig a hole about 1m (3ft) square and 1m (3ft) deep against

◄ **Fresh figs** Picked straight from the tree, figs are at their sweetest and juiciest. They take two years to reach harvesting size, surviving most winters outdoors if given adequate protection. The most common varieties are 'Brown Turkey' and 'White Marseilles'.

a wall and line the sides with bricks, concrete or stone slabs.

To prevent the development of long tap roots, spread a 30cm (12in) layer of brick rubble in the bottom of the hole. Then fill it with two parts of good, but not rich, garden soil mixed with one part of mortar rubble and 1kg (2lb) of bonemeal.

Fig trees can also be grown in 38cm (15in) pots of potting compost. Sink the pot in the ground, with the rim just above ground level to reduce loss of moisture. Each winter, dig around the pot with a sharp spade and remove any roots that have grown through the drainage holes.

Cultivation
Plant in early spring. Make a hole in the prepared bed just big enough to take the roots spread out; cover with soil and firm the ground. Mulch lightly with well-rotted manure or garden compost.

In spring, after new growth has begun, start training the tree. It can be grown in bush form, like apples, but succeeds better as a fan trained against a sunny sheltered wall. Cut the main central

◄ **Fan-trained fig** Even in sheltered southern gardens, fig trees do best against south-facing walls which will soak up all available sunlight. The 'ribs' with their immature fruits need winter protection – drape them with covering material supported by training wires.

stem hard back to leave two strong lateral branches – one to the left and one to the right. Fix lengths of wire to the wall before tying each lateral branch to a cane and attaching these to the wire at an angle of about 45°.

When all danger of frost has passed, cut the stems back to 40cm (16in). If the stem has side-shoots, reduce these by about a quarter to stimulate the growth of more laterals. During the summer tie in the new shoots.

In subsequent years, by early summer, pinch the side-shoots back to five leaves from their base. Early in the season, rub out crossing shoots and any growing towards the wall.

Once the framework is established, cut two or three branches back by half in autumn or early winter to encourage new, young shoots; otherwise the tree will become bare low down. Fruiting occurs on two-year-old shoots, with one-year-olds constantly coming along to replace them.

By early autumn, thin the fruit and protect the remainder by tying bracken, spruce branches or ferns over the shoots, or by loosening the branches from their supports, bunching them together and covering them with straw or canvas. Gradually remove the protection in spring.

Feeding is unnecessary during the three years the framework is being built up. In subsequent years, mulch with manure or garden compost at the rate of a bucketful per sq m/yd in spring.

Harvesting

Figs must ripen while still on the tree – usually between late summer and mid autumn. The fruit is ripe when it hangs down, the stalk softens and the skin shows signs of splitting; a drop of moisture (nectar) may appear in the 'eye'.

Pests and diseases

Figs are generally free of pests. Diseases liable to attack are coral spot on the shoots and grey mould on ripening fruits.

Fig canker – when the bark cracks and lesions appear on branches – sometimes occurs when a fungus enters through wounds or cut twigs, particularly during the growing season. Prune out diseased branches, cutting back into clean and healthy wood, and paint with wound-sealer.

TRAINING AND PRUNING

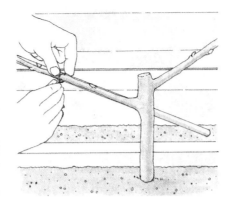

1 In spring after growth has begun, cut back the main stem to leave two strong lateral branches which will form the first two ribs of the fan. Fix wires across the wall or fence. Tie each lateral branch to a cane and fix the canes to the wires at an angle of about 45°.

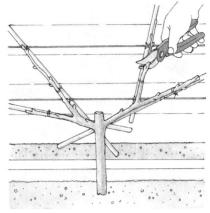

2 When all danger of frost has passed, prune the two main laterals back to 40cm (16in). Cut any side-shoots on the laterals back by a quarter. This stimulates the growth of yet more side-shoots – train them fanwise along additional canes as they grow out.

3 In subsequent years, pinch side-shoots back to at least five leaves before mid summer. This encourages new fruit-bearing shoots to form – train them in to the fan shape where there is room. Also entirely pinch out any shoots growing towards or away from the support.

4 Before autumn remove all immature figs that have grown larger than peas during the summer – they will not survive the winter. The smallest fruitlets that are left near the end of the shoots, and which survive the winter, will mature for harvesting the following year.

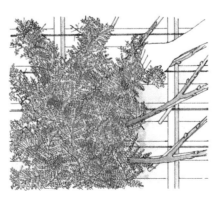

5 Protect the fig tree in winter by carefully tying spruce or fern branches in a loose framework over the shoots. Alternatively, detach the fig branches from their supports, bunch them together and cover them completely with either straw or canvas fixed to the wires.

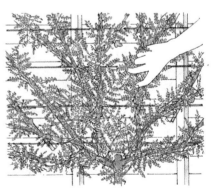

6 In mid to late spring, gradually expose the fig tree to normal weather conditions. Remove the protective covering of straw, canvas, fern or spruce branches in stages, freeing the shoot tips and young fruits only after all danger of frost has entirely passed.

NUT TREES

**Nut trees are ornamental as well as productive,
with hazels cropping several years before walnuts. The
harvest is usually shared with the squirrels!**

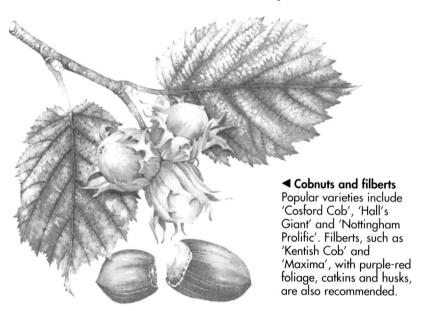

◄ Cobnuts and filberts
Popular varieties include
'Cosford Cob', 'Hall's
Giant' and 'Nottingham
Prolific'. Filberts, such as
'Kentish Cob' and
'Maxima', with purple-red
foliage, catkins and husks,
are also recommended.

HAZEL NUTS
Hazel is the common name given to trees of the genus *Corylus*, which includes cobnuts and filberts. A little confusingly, it is the cobnut which is usually sold as a 'hazel nut' while the most popular filbert variety is called 'Kentish Cob'. This only serves to illustrate that the differences between the nuts are minor – small variations in size and slight subtleties of flavour. Both nuts have the same culture. If you want only one tree, a single cobnut crops better than a single filbert.

Site and soil
Even if pruned into bush form, a mature hazel stands 1.8m (6ft) high and has a spread of 3.5m (12ft); if you have the space it is worth planting for its beautiful pale yellow catkins in spring, and for its substantial crops of protein-rich nuts in autumn.

Hazels do equally well in full sun or partial shade, and preferably sheltered from north and east winds. They are ideal as lawn shrubs. Any well-drained soil is suitable, including chalky soils.

Cobnuts and filberts are self-fertile and are usually supplied as two-year-old shrubs with the main stem pruned back to 45cm (1½ft) to encourage side-shoots. First crops can be expected two years from planting.

Cultivation
Plant in mid to late autumn. Unless already done, prune the main stem back to 30-45cm (1-1½ft) after planting.

In the first summer the shrub will produce numerous side-shoots. During winter, choose three or four of the strongest shoots, evenly spaced, nearer the top than the base. Prune them hard back to 20-25cm (8-10in) and remove all others completely.

During the following one or two winters repeat this pruning process, reducing all new shoots by half, until the shrub has the required number of branches. Thereafter cut the new growth at the ends of the branches hard back each winter until the shrub has reached the required height; every winter prune all extension growth back to this height.

Once the shrub begins to bear catkins, delay pruning until pollen has been shed, then cut back all the shoots that bore nuts in the previous season to two or three buds.

In late summer, thin out any shoots crowding the centre. Chop away basal suckers with a spade.

The cobnut has soft yellow catkins, while filbert catkins range from yellow-green to red. Fertilization occurs when pollen from the large clusters of male catkins is blown by the wind on to the smaller female flowers.

Feeding
Every three years in mid winter apply a general fertilizer, such as Growmore, at the rate of 75g per sq m (3oz per sq yd). In spring or autumn apply a mulch of rotted manure or garden compost at the rate of one bucketful per sq m/yd.

Harvesting
Towards the end of summer the calyx (husk) around each nut will turn brown and shrivel before exposing the brown nut inside, ready for picking.

Leave the nuts to dry out in a warm place for a few days, then dehusk them if necessary. Store them in containers in a cool place for up to six months.

Pests and diseases
The main threat to the crop is the squirrel. There is no simple defence against them.

Hazel nuts are also subject to attack by nut weevils – grubs hatch inside the husk and eat the kernels. Dust or spray trees in early summer with HCH and repeat three weeks later. Honey fungus is the principal disease.

Hazel nut 'Kentish Cob'

WALNUTS

The English or common walnut, (*Juglans regia*) is a majestic tree which is ideal for parks and large gardens, reaching a height of about 8m (25ft) after 20 years and a final height of 18-30m (60-100ft).

The walnut tree bears separate male and female flowers in late spring; the tiny green female flowers appear in small clusters, while the yellowish-green male flowers grow as catkins, about 5-10cm (2-4in) long.

Nuts are produced after about 15 years, but nurseries supply grafted trees, such as 'Broadview' and 'Buccaneer', which fruit at an earlier age and produce fine-quality nuts. Unlike the species itself, such selected varieties are entirely self-fertile.

Cultivation

The walnut grows well on any deep, fertile and well-drained soil. However, an open position with as much shelter as possible while the tree is young is best because both the young growth and the flowers are highly susceptible to frost damage.

For fruiting purposes, buy three- or four-year-old grafted trees of named varieties of the common walnut, identified by its smooth bark (on older trees this becomes deeply fissured). They are usually supplied as full or half-standards with the head partly formed.

The black walnut (*Juglans nigra*) from the United States is another suitable fruiting tree; it is fast-growing, with deeply furrowed bark. The large nuts are usually borne in pairs.

Two months before planting, lightly fork in ground lime if the soil is acid. In early autumn clear away perennial weeds over an area 1.2-1.5m (4-5ft) square. Fork in a compound fertilizer, such as Growmore, at the rate of 75g per sq m (3oz per sq yd).

Dig a hole which is deep and wide enough to accommodate the roots when they are fully extended. Then drive in a double stake so that it reaches just below the lowest branches of the tree. Plant the tree at exactly the same depth as at the nursery – look for the soil mark – being very careful not to damage any of the roots. Tie the tree to the stake and water thoroughly.

Pruning

In the early years prune the lower side-shoots back to establish a strong, clean trunk that will show off the whitish bark. When the tree is about eight years old, prune side-shoots off completely, flush with the trunk.

While you can still reach the crown, make sure that the tree develops a balanced head by pruning it like a round-headed shrub. Once the head has been formed, little regular pruning is required. Cut out any dead, badly placed or crowded branches in late summer and protect the cuts with a wound-sealing paint. Avoid any pruning between mid winter and mid spring as severed stems tend to bleed profusely.

To bring a young grafted tree to fruit early, keep it small by using a dwarfing technique. During the growing season after planting, pinch out the tips of the strongest shoots just above the fifth or sixth leaf, but leave the shoots on which the catkins are borne unpruned. Continue pinching out every year in summer while the tree is still young.

Only grafted trees benefit from such pruning treatment. A dwarfed tree will take about eight years to produce nuts – and a tree which is not dwarfed can take as long as 10-15 years to bear its first crop.

▲ **Walnuts** Nuts are rarely produced in large quantities before trees are 15 years old. However, grafted and dwarfed trees will often fruit after eight years. The nuts are enclosed in husks which turn brown when ripe and can stain skin and clothes.

Harvesting the crop

When the husks turn brown in autumn, shake the tree or wait until the nuts fall. Always pick them as soon as they ripen and before the squirrels are able to get to them.

Spread the nuts out on a dry surface until the husks shrivel and fall off; if necessary, use a stiff wire brush to clean the shells of the husks which can stain skin and clothing.

Store the cleaned nuts in their shells in boxes filled with sand or in tins. They will keep for up to three months, but thereafter lose their flavour.

Walnuts can also be picked before they are fully ripe when they are easily removed from the still soft husks. They are delicious pickled in vinegar.

Pests and diseases

Leaf blotch shows as yellowish blotches on foliage and sometimes causes defoliation. Little can be done to a mature tree, though mancozeb or copper fungicide may help young trees.

PEACHES AND NECTARINES

**Luscious and juicy, peaches and nectarines
are among the most popular fruits. Outdoors they
need sunny and sheltered conditions.**

Peaches and nectarines will thrive only in sunny, sheltered positions. They usually do best when fan-trained against a south-facing wall or fence. If this is not possible, one facing west or south-west may be suitable. Nectarines, a smooth-skinned variety of peach, are slightly less hardy and succeed only in warm sheltered spots.

Both peaches and nectarines do well under glass, but they do take up a large amount of space in a greenhouse, though in a lean-to greenhouse they can be fan-trained against the rear wall.

Peaches and nectarines are self-fertile (each flower can be fertilized from another on the same tree), and so a second pollinating tree is not needed.

Peaches require well-drained soil. If the soil is heavy, dig a trench 1.8m (6ft) long, 1m (3ft) wide and 1m (3ft) deep along the wall where the tree is to be trained. Line the bottom of the trench with broken bricks or old mortar, cover with chopped turf and then fill with high-quality loam. Add nitro-chalk at a rate of 25g per sq m (1oz per sq yd) to improve flowering and fruiting.

Before planting, secure horizontal wires 15cm (6in) apart to vine eyes along the fence or wall.

Peach 'Peregrine'

Nectarine 'Lord Napier'

▲ **Peaches and nectarines** These sweet and delicious fruits can be grown outdoors in warm sunny gardens, preferably as fans trained against a sheltered wall. Given good growing conditions, they usually begin to crop in the fifth summer after planting.

Cultivation

Plant peaches and nectarines between mid autumn and mid winter. Space fans 3.6-4.5m (12-15ft) apart; bush trees 4.5m (15ft) apart.

Dig a hole deep and wide enough to accommodate the spread-out roots and plant the trees to the same depth as at the nursery. Set the stems of fan-trained trees about 23cm (9in) from the wall and angle them slightly inwards.

In mid winter each year feed with 25g per sq m (1oz per sq yd) of sulphate of potash. Every third year add 50g per sq m (2oz per sq yd) of superphosphate. In early spring top-dress with 25g per sq m (1oz per sq yd) of nitro-chalk, and mulch with either garden compost or manure.

Pollination is necessary to ensure a fruit crop. If the flowers open before there are sufficient insects around, artificial pollination

THINNING AND HARVESTING

1 Thin fruits when they are the size of marbles. Reduce clusters to a single fruit and remove all fruits growing towards the wall and any that are short of growing space. Thin later to 23cm (9in) apart.

2 Peaches and nectarines are ready for harvesting when they yield to gentle pressure. Always pick the fruits carefully by gripping them in the palm of the hand and twisting them off the spurs.

is always essential. Dab each flower with a camel-hair brush daily at midday. Protect the flowers against night frosts by covering outdoor trees with small-mesh netting. Remove the mesh during the day to allow insects to reach the flowers.

Water the ground thoroughly throughout the growing season. The ground near walls dries out very quickly in hot weather and needs large quantities of water.

Thin peach fruits when they are about the size of marbles. Reduce clusters to single fruits, and remove all fruits growing towards a wall or any that lack space in which to develop.

Thin peaches to a final spacing of 23cm (9in) when they are the size of golf balls. Thin nectarines to 15cm (6in) apart.

Pruning

During the first four years after planting a peach or nectarine tree, pruning is directed towards building up a fan-shape of branches. The trees fruit on laterals of the previous year, and annual pruning consists of disbudding in spring, pinching back in summer and cutting back laterals in autumn (see pages 14-15).

Harvesting and storing

Peaches and nectarines are ready for picking when the flesh around the stalks yields to gentle pressure. Pick fruits carefully by gripping them in the palm of your hand and twisting gently.

Pests and diseases

Pests likely to attack peaches and nectarines are aphids, caterpillars and scale insects; spray with a systemic insecticide. Common diseases include bacterial canker, brown rot, chlorosis, honey fungus, peach leaf curl, powdery mildew, shot-hole and silver leaf; in all but severe cases, copper fungicide should be effective. Split stone occurs on poor dry soils deficient in lime.

VARIETIES TO CHOOSE

Peaches
'Amsden June' – green-white skin flushed red; yellow flesh; reliable cropper.

'Duke of York' – large fruits with greenish-yellow flesh; ripens mid summer.

'Peregrine' – crimson, smooth-skinned fruits with yellowish-white flesh; ripens late summer.

'Rochester' – medium-sized yellow fruits streaked with red; yellow flesh; ripens late summer.

Nectarines
'Lord Napier' – large oval fruits with pale green flesh; ripens mid to late summer.

PRUNING BUSH TREES

1 Mature bush peach trees need regular pruning. In late spring, cut out older branches from the centre and remove any branch which crosses another, cutting it flush with the parent branch.

2 Damaged and diseased branches should also be removed in late spring. Cut them back to just above a healthy side-shoot to encourage new growth.

Peach 'Peregrine'

Peach 'Rochester'

PEARS

**In good years, pear trees will begin to crop
a couple of years after planting, and every spring there's
the delight of beautiful white blossom.**

Wherever apples will grow, pears will grow too, but they need slightly better conditions. Since the blossoms open earlier than apple blossom, they should be planted in a less exposed position; and they need frequent watering in times of drought.

Few pears are self-fertile, so to be certain of fruit you should plant two different varieties which will flower at the same time. Pear varieties are not grown on their own roots but are grafted on to quince rootstocks; the graft union between the rootstock and the grafted shoot (scion) is always visible.

Like apples, pear trees come in two forms – those grown in open ground (bush and dwarf pyramids) and those trained against a wall or fence, such as cordons, espaliers and fans. The latter three can also be grown as free-standing screens supported by a framework of strong rustic poles.

Which you choose depends on the quantity of fruit you want and on the amount of space available. Bush trees yield heavy crops, but need plenty of room; dwarf pyramids and trees trained in restricted forms are more suitable for small gardens but yield less fruit.

You can also buy family trees, which have three or four different pear varieties grafted on to one rootstock. These are especially suitable for very small gardens, with room for only one tree. The varieties will pollinate each other, and the tree should have a long fruiting season.

Yields will probably vary from year to year, depending on the severity of spring frosts and the amount of rainfall. As a rough guide, expect 18-23kg (40-50lb) from a bush tree; 10-12kg (20-25lb) from a three-tier espalier; 3-5kg (7-11lb) from a dwarf pyramid, and 1.5-2.5kg (3-5lb) from an established cordon.

▶ **Dessert pears** By choosing a selection of early, mid-season and late varieties, it is possible to have pears ready for picking and eating from late summer through to Christmas and into early spring.

▲ **Fan-trained pears** These are suitable for growing against a fence, wall or post and wire supports. Before planting, calculate the eventual spread of the trees, as crowding could stunt new growth.

Site and soil

Plant pears in a sunny, sheltered position. They grow well inland, but dislike the salt-laden winds of coastal areas. In the north, spring frosts are likely to destroy the blossom of early varieties.

The soil should preferably be deep and loamy and retain moisture well in summer. However, avoid waterlogged sites. On free-draining, shallow and sandy soils, increase the water-holding capacity by double-digging in autumn and incorporating well-rotted strawy manure or garden compost in the bottom spit at the rate of two bucketfuls per sq m/sq yd. A week before planting, fork in 75g per sq m (3oz per sq yd) of a general compound fertilizer.

Buying pear trees

Most nurseries and good garden centres offer a choice of one-, two- and three-year-old trees. Trees in their first year (maidens) are cheaper than older trees, because they need training – a job best left to the nurseryman. It is worthwhile buying two- or three-year-old trees of bush and cordon

▶ **Pear espaliers** Ideal where space is restricted, espaliers grow a number of tiers, or horizontal branches. The main stem is stopped when it reaches the top of its support.

forms; and espaliers should preferably have at least two tiers of branches and fan trees four ribs.

A three-year-old tree should fruit within two or three years of planting, depending on its position and the weather.

Specialist fruit nurseries will advise on suitable pear varieties and rootstocks for particular soils and situations.

Planting a pear tree

Plant pear trees in frost-free weather between late autumn and early spring. A late autumn planting gives the best start.

Space bush trees 3.5-4.5m (12-15ft) apart, depending on the rootstock; dwarf pyramid trees 1.2-1.5m (4-5ft) apart; and cordons 75cm-90cm (2½-3ft) apart. If you have room to place espaliers or fan-trained trees side by side on a wall or fence, calculate their eventual width before planting: as a general rule, espaliers and fans should be set 3.5-4.5m (12-15ft) apart. Allow at least 23cm (9in) between the wall and the planting hole to give the roots plenty of room in which to spread.

Dig a hole big enough to accommodate the roots of the tree when they are well spread out. For a bush tree, drive a stake at least 60cm (2ft) deep into the soil and plant the tree against it, securing it with strong plastic strap ties.

Plant to the same depth as the tree was set in the nursery, judging by the soil mark on the stem. Make sure that the graft union between the rootstock and the scion is at least 10cm (4in) above soil level. Spread the roots out evenly, so that the tree will be well balanced, and return the soil over the roots, firming it well in. Water thoroughly after planting.

Cultivation

Water well during dry spells, especially during the first growing season. Mature pear trees are also intolerant of drought and should be watered well during prolonged dry weather.

Mulch the root area in early spring with coir or well-rotted garden compost or manure.

Each mid winter, apply 25g per sq m (1oz per sq yd) of sulphate of potash. In late winter, follow this up with 25-40g per sq m (1-1½oz per sq yd) of sulphate of ammonia.

Every third year, add 40-50g (1½-2oz) of superphosphate to the sulphate of ammonia dressing.

Spraying

A number of pests and diseases affect pear trees, attacking either the foliage or the developing fruit. Where damage is known to be severe, institute a spraying programme tailored to bud development. Begin spraying at bud-burst and continue until the blossoms are fully open. Do not spray when the blossom is open, or you may harm pollinating insects.

Don't spray on windy days. Over-spraying will do more harm than good, so follow the manufacturer's instructions carefully.

Spray at bud-burst and green cluster stage with permethrin for aphids and with benomyl or thiophanate-methyl for scab. Follow with a second application when the buds begin to show white.

After about 80 per cent of the petals have fallen, spray every two weeks with benomyl. Spray with permethrin for codling moth in early summer and again three weeks later.

Every third year in the dormant period, between early and late winter, apply tar-oil wash to kill winter eggs of aphids.

Pruning and training

Pear trees, in bush or restricted form, are trained and pruned in the same way as apples (see pages 8-11). Established bush pear trees can be cut back harder than apple trees, so always remove overcrowded branches, particularly in the centre of the tree, during winter pruning.

Summer pruning of cordons, espaliers and dwarf pyramids is earlier than for apples. Start when the summer growth matures – usually in early to mid summer in the south of Britain, but later in the north. Cut back the lateral shoots made during the current season, not the leading branches.

As a pear tree matures it will produce fruiting spurs (short fruit-bearing side-branches) more freely than apple trees do. Thin these out in winter.

Thinning the crop

Pears generally need less thinning than apples, but a heavy crop of fruit can put a strain on any tree's resources, resulting in fruits of

PRUNING AND THINNING

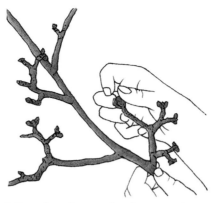

1 Guard against overloading a tree's cropping capacity by rubbing fruit buds from the spurs in spring, leaving only one or two buds on each spur.

2 Summer pruning of laterals on trained trees should be done as soon as the summer growth matures (by mid summer). Cut back to three leaves.

3 Thin the fruit after the natural drop by mid summer, when the immature fruits have just started to turn downwards. Aim for no more than two fruits per spur.

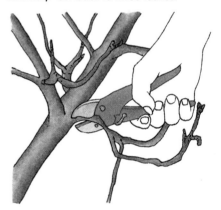

4 Prune out weak and crowded branches from late autumn to late winter, cutting them back flush with the main branches. Keep the centre of the tree open.

poor quality. Pears should be well spaced out on large bush trees; cordons, espaliers, fans and dwarfs rarely need thinning beyond the natural fruit drop.

By mid summer, there is a natural drop of fruit. After this, remove any badly shaped or damaged fruits still on the tree, along with the central pear of thick and crowded clusters.

Never pull the fruit off, since this may damage the spur. Instead, hold the fruit firmly but lightly and cut the stalk with a pair of scissors.

Harvesting and storing

Most varieties of pear ripen off the tree. Harvest early varieties by cutting the stalk close to the spur when the fruit is mature in size but still hard.

Pick mid-season fruits (for eating in mid or late autumn) and late varieties (for eating from early winter) when the stalks can be twisted away easily from the branch without tearing the spurs.

Store pears in a cool room or shed at a temperature of 2-4°C (36-40°F). Lay them on trays or shelves in a single layer, making sure that they don't touch each other. Check them frequently: when they begin to soften slightly and change colour near the stalk, bring them into the warmth at 16°C (61°F) for a couple of days to finish ripening. Don't store any damaged or diseased fruit – even a slightly bruised pear can cause others to go bad and perhaps ruin the whole crop.

Pests and diseases

Pears are affected by many of the same pests and diseases as apples, although they tend to be more resistant. The most common pests are aphids, caterpillars, codling moths, red spider mites, pear leaf blister mite, pear sucker and tortrix moths.

The main diseases and disorders are boron deficiency, brown rot, fireblight, honey fungus, scab, splitting and stony pit.

'Conference'

'Louise Bonne of Jersey'

'William's Bon Chrétien'

'Doyenné du Comice'

'Fertility'

'Joséphine de Malines'

'Winter Nelis'

VARIETIES TO CHOOSE

Varieties are grouped according to when the pears are ready for eating. Dessert varieties are also suitable for cooking, provided they are still firm and not fully ripe.

Early
'William's Bon Chrétien' – pick late summer to ripen in early autumn; one of the best-flavoured early autumn pears, but keeps only a short time; pollinated by 'Conference' and 'Joséphine de Malines'.

Mid-season
'Conference' – pick early autumn for eating mid to late autumn; a regular and heavy cropper; sweet, creamy white flesh, very juicy; excellent for bottling; pollinated by 'William's Bon Chrétien' and 'Joséphine de Malines'.

'Doyenné du Comice' – pick early mid autumn for eating from late mid autumn through winter and early spring; excellent flavour and good for bottling; needs a sheltered position with rich soil and regular mulching; pollinated by 'Fertility' and 'Winter Nelis'.

'Fertility' – pick early autumn for eating mid autumn; a heavy cropper; round, juicy fruits; pollinated by 'Doyenné du Comice' and 'Winter Nelis'.

'Louise Bonne of Jersey' – pick early autumn for eating in mid autumn; also stores well; strong, upright growth; large, greenish-yellow fruit; self-fertile, can also be pollinated by 'Joséphine de Malines'.

Late
'Glou Morceau' – pick in mid autumn and keep for eating mid winter; crops heavily to carry medium-sized fruits on compact trees; moderate vigour; pollinated by 'Doyenné du Comice'.

'Joséphine de Malines' – pick in late autumn to ripen at a temperature of 16°C (61°F) from early to mid winter; a good late pear; pollinated by 'Conference', 'Louise Bonne of Jersey' and 'William's Bon Chrétien'.

'Winter Nelis' – pick in mid autumn to ripen at a temperature of 16°C (61°F) in early winter; moderate growth, heavy cropper; cooker/dessert; sweet, scented flavour; pollinated by 'Doyenné du Comice'.

PLUMS, GAGES AND DAMSONS

**Plums are well worth making space for in
the fruit garden – under good conditions they will yield
rich harvests for up to fifty years.**

Plum trees are vigorous and usually prolific, giving good harvests from established trees though yields vary according to the size of the tree and the variety, and may plummet if the flowers are damaged by spring frosts. All plums fruit on one-year-old and two-year-old shoots.

Gages, a sweet-flavoured type of dessert plum, are less hardy than other plum varieties.

Because of their vigour, plum trees are grafted on to dwarfing rootstocks such as St Julian A or Pixy, which ensure earlier fruiting and smaller trees.

Some plums are self-fertile, but others need a nearby pollinator. Bush trees can have a spread of 4.5m (15ft) or more at maturity. In small gardens, dwarf pyramid forms which can be kept manageable with annual pruning, or fan-trained types take up less space.

Site and soil

Plums and gages grow best in full sun and wind-shelter. Avoid frost pockets, because the trees flower early in spring.

Plum trees succeed in most well-drained soils – the ideal is a fairly heavy clay loam with a pH between 6.0 and 6.5. Top-dress very acid soils after planting with enough carbonate of lime (chalk) to bring the soil up to the pH value given above.

plum

▲ **Dessert plums** Excellent as fresh fruits, most varieties of plums and gages are also good for bottling and cooking.

gage

A single self-fertile tree should produce enough fruit for the average family. An established pyramid may yield 13.5-34kg (30-75lb) in a single season, according to variety and rootstock. If planting more than one tree, space them 2.5-3.5m (8-12ft) apart.

A fan-trained tree will produce on average 7-11kg (15-25lb) of plums when fully grown, even more in a good year. Plant fans 4.5-5.5m (15-18ft) apart.

Bush trees will produce an average of 23-45kg (50-100lb) when fully established. Plant them 3.5-4.5m (12-15ft) apart.

Planting and pruning

Plant plum trees at any time from late autumn to early spring – the earlier the better. Prepare an area 1m (3ft) square in early autumn, thoroughly clearing away all weeds and forking in well-rotted garden compost or manure, at one bucketful per tree, or two bucketfuls on light soil. Fork in a balanced

SUPPORTING, THINNING AND HARVESTING PLUMS

1 Plum tree branches are often brittle and may snap under a heavy weight of fruit; support them with props (using cloth to prevent chafing of the bark) or tie them to stakes.

2 Thin a heavy crop of plums at the beginning of early summer. The final thinning (after the natural early summer drop) should be to 5-7.5cm (2-3in) apart, or one in each cluster.

3 Plums ripen from mid summer to late autumn, depending on the variety and locality. Pick cooking varieties before they are fully ripe but leave dessert plums and gages to ripen on the trees.

▲ **Fan-trained plum** The white blossom appears in early spring. If few insects are around, it may be necessary to pollinate by hand, transferring pollen from one flower to another with a brush.

fertilizer just before planting, at the rate of 75g per sq m (3oz per sq yd).

Take out a hole slightly wider than the spread of the roots. Plant the tree at the same depth as it was in the nursery, indicated by the soil mark on the stem.

Bush and dwarf pyramids need staking. Put the stake in position first, then place the tree against it and secure it with tree ties.

Before planting a fan tree, secure horizontal training wires 15cm (6in) apart to vine eyes along the fence or wall, placing the lowest one 38cm (15in) above the ground. Allow for a final height of 1.8-2.4m (6-8ft). Position the stem about 23cm (9in) from the wall, sloping it slightly towards the wall while you replace the soil.

Spread out the ribs of the fan evenly and tie them to the support wires with soft string.

Apply sulphate of ammonia and sulphate of potash annually in late winter or early spring, at the rate of 40g and 15g per sq m (1½ and ½oz per sq yd) respectively, covering the entire root area. Every third year add a dressing of superphosphate at the rate of 50g per sq m (2oz per sq yd). Also mulch with well-rotted garden compost or manure in early to mid spring at the rate of a bucketful per sq m/yd.

Be careful not to disturb the roots when weeding or the tree will throw up suckers. If suckers do appear, pull them up rather than cutting them off.

Training plum trees

Most plums, gages and damsons are supplied as two-year-old bush trees on dwarfing rootstock. For training and pruning into fan, pyramid or bush shapes, see pages 12-14.

Once the basic framework has been established, plum trees should need little structural pruning. Cut out dead wood and crowded and crossing shoots every year, and cut a few of the side-shoots back to encourage younger fruiting growth. Do all this as soon as possible after the fruit has been picked, and before leaf-fall. Winter pruning encourages the serious silver leaf disease.

Thinning

Plum-tree branches are often brittle and may snap under a heavy weight of fruit; to guard against this happening, start thinning a heavy crop at the beginning of early summer. The final thinning should be to 5-7.5cm (2-3in) apart or one in each cluster – delay thinning until after the natural early summer drop.

Support and protection

If the branches are still overladen after thinning, support them with either clothes-line props or forked branches or by tying them to sturdy stakes driven into the ground.

Protect wall-grown trees from frost at blossom time by draping them with hessian or bird netting. Trees grown in the open may also be draped with netting or hessian, if practicable; this will also protect the buds and fruit from birds.

Harvesting and storing

Plums ripen from mid summer to late autumn, depending on variety and locality. Pick them before they are quite ripe for cooking, bottling or freezing; leave dessert plums on the tree for as long as possible before picking. Pick the stalk along with the fruit.

If the weather is particularly wet, pick gages before they are quite ripe, otherwise their skins may split.

Pests and diseases
Plums and gages may be attacked by aphids, caterpillars, fruit tree red spider mites, wasps and plum sawfly. Spray with a systemic insecticide before and after petal fall. They are particularly vulnerable to bacterial canker, brown rot, honey fungus, scald and silver leaf. Treat with a copper fungicide during winter.

DAMSONS
The smallest-fruited variety of plum, damsons succeed in areas with heavier rainfall and less sun than plums will tolerate and where gages would not survive. The small fruits are richly flavoured and suitable for cooking, bottling and wine-making.

Planting and cultivation
Damsons grow in most soils but do best in deep, well-drained heavy loams. Most damson varieties are self-fertile but if more than one tree is to be grown, set bush and fan-trained forms 3.5m (12ft) apart, and pyramids 2.5m (8ft) apart.

Plant damson trees like plums, from mid autumn to spring, staking bush and pyramid types.

Damsons grown on dwarfing rootstock need feeding, especially on light soils. Feed as for plums, spreading the fertilizer evenly over the root area and leaving it to be washed in by rain.

Training and pruning
Damsons, like all plums, can suffer from silver leaf disease. To substantially reduce the chances of an outbreak, never prune damsons in winter and protect all cuts with a bituminous wound-sealing paint.

A pyramid plum tree grafted onto a dwarfing rootstock is probably the best overall choice for an average-sized garden. After planting, prune and train pyramids and fan-shaped forms in the same way as other plums (see pages 12-14).

Damsons are vigorous growers and need hard pruning in their formative years. Once the basic framework is established, when the trees are about 1.8m (6ft) high, little annual pruning is needed – damsons fruit on both old and new wood. Bush trees eventually become compact and crowded and the old wood in the centre may need thinning out; do this in mid spring.

Thinning and harvesting
Start thinning a particularly heavy crop by early summer. Curl your finger around the stalk and snap off the fruit with your thumbnail, leaving the stalk behind on the tree. Thin again after the natural fall until the fruits are approximately 5cm (2in) apart, leaving at least one fruit in each cluster.

When harvesting, carefully pick the fruit by the stalk to avoid bruising. The stalk will snap and come away with the fruit. Pick damsons when they have completely finished swelling.

Pests and diseases
Damsons are affected by exactly the same common pests and disorders as plums.

▲ **Damson 'Merryweather'** Ripening in early to mid autumn, this reliably heavy cropper yields large, deliciously juicy black fruits.

▼ **Damson blossom** Flowering in mid to late spring, damson blossom is rarely damaged by frost. The trees are ultra-hardy and usually yield heavy crops, even in exposed gardens.

DAMSON VARIETIES

'Farleigh's Damson' – round, small fruit; black with a hint of blue; ripens early autumn; partly self-fertile but needs a pollinator to guarantee a heavy crop.

'Merryweather' – large, black, fine-flavoured fruit; reliable, heavy cropper; ripens early/mid autumn; self-fertile.

'Shropshire Prune' – medium, tapering, blue-black fruit; very juicy; ripens mid autumn; prolific cropper; self-fertile.

PLUM VARIETIES

Self-fertile

'Ariel' – medium, oval, yellow-green fruits sometimes flushed pink; golden flesh; regular, heavy cropper; dessert.

'Czar' – medium, round to oval, dark purple fruits with yellow-green juicy flesh, maturing late summer; heavy, reliable cropper; cooker.

'Early Transparent Gage' – medium, pale yellow fruits with red dots, maturing in late summer.

'Laxtons Gage' – medium-large, golden-yellow fruits, maturing late summer; heavy yielder; dessert.

'Marjorie's Seedling' – large, purple fruits, maturing mid autumn; partially self-fertile; regular cropper; for cooking, bottling and dessert.

'Pershore Yellow' – medium, golden-yellow, oval fruits with yellow flesh; reliable cropper; hardy and prolific; good for jam and cooking.

'Purple Pershore' – medium, purple-blue fruits, maturing late summer; good for cooking; heavy yielder.

'Victoria' – medium-large bright red fruits, maturing early autumn; too heavy cropping in some years; good for bottling, jam and dessert; susceptible to silver leaf.

'Warwickshire Drooper' – large yellow fruits, maturing early autumn; good for cooking and as dessert plum.

Cross-pollinators

'Cambridge Gage' (Green Gage) – small, yellow-green fruits, flushed with red; dessert gage, also for cooking and bottling; heavy cropper; pollinated by 'Marjorie's Seedling' or 'Victoria'.

'Early Laxton' – very early, end of mid summer; medium, yellow-red fruits; dessert or cooking plum; pollinated by 'Victoria'.

'Early Rivers' – small, compact tree; round purple-blue fruits with yellow flesh, maturing late summer; pollinated by 'Victoria'.

'Kirke's Blue' – large, purple-black dessert plum, maturing early autumn; pollinated by 'Early Transparent Gage' or 'Czar'.

Cooking plum 'Marjorie's Seedling'

Dessert plum 'Ariel'

Gage 'Early Transparent Gage'

Dessert plum 'Victoria'

39

Harvest basket Incomparable in flavour and freshness, home-grown soft fruits are real money-savers.

Soft fruit

Soft fruit, produced on bushes, canes and low-growing plants, include currants, gooseberries, blackberries, raspberries and strawberries. This chapter also covers grapes and melons, and rhubarb which is often grown as a permanent crop in the vegetable plot. Soft fruits can easily be incorporated into the vegetable plan, space permitting. As they occupy permanent sites, they do not interfere with crop rotation and can make attractive screens between the ornamental and the kitchen garden.

Berry fruits start cropping sooner after planting than top fruits and generally give a better return for the space they occupy. On the other hand, they have a shorter life-span; under good growing conditions, bush fruits can be expected to crop for 10-15 years and cane fruits for 10 years. The yield and vigour of strawberries decreases rapidly, and the plants should be renewed at least every four or five years.

No shop-bought produce can compare in flavour and freshness with home-grown soft fruit, but they demand regular attention in order to ensure healthy and heavy crops. Pruning and feeding are mandatory chores every year, and the gardener is engaged in a constant battle with birds and other predators. If you have only a few canes or bushes, protect them with a temporary cover of fine-mesh plastic netting supported on stakes or canes. Put the covering in place before the birds begin to gorge on the ripening fruit. Wall-trained cordons and espaliers can be protected in the same way, with netting fixed to battens attached to the wall. The ideal, though rather more expensive, way of protecting soft fruit is with a permanent fruit cage. For durability, it should be constructed from stout timber frames clad with either wire netting or plastic mesh.

PRUNING SOFT FRUIT

**Pruning cane fruits is simply a matter of
cutting out fruited stems and tying in replacement shoots.
Bush fruits need more careful treatment.**

PRUNING CANE FRUITS

Cane fruits are slender deciduous shrubs with sturdy fruit-bearing stems. They include raspberries, blackberries, loganberries and the lesser known hybrid berries, such as boysenberries, tayberries, young-berries and wineberries.

The flexible stems are too weak to support themselves and must either be trained to wires tensioned between posts, or tied to wires against a wall or fence. Every year after fruiting, the canes are cut out at ground level to make room for the new shoots that will carry next year's crop. Cane fruits will crop for 10 years.

Pruning raspberries

Some raspberry varieties bear fruit in mid summer on the previous year's shoots; others fruit in early or mid autumn on the current season's shoots. In both cases, canes that have produced fruit must be replaced annually by new canes.

To make training and harvesting easy, raspberry canes are best grown in straight rows and supported on wires stretched between wooden stakes or posts. The height of the posts and wires depends on the type of raspberry.

If there is not enough space for rows of raspberries trained on wires, canes can be trained up single posts. Train four or five canes up a post, such as a sturdy fence post standing 1.8m (6ft) out of the ground. Tie the canes to the post with strings or wire loops. Several posts will be needed to crop enough raspberries for the average family, but these can be dotted around the garden wherever space permits.

First-year pruning Immediately after planting raspberry canes, cut each stem down to just above a healthy growth bud 30cm (1ft) above ground level – it is important to prevent fruiting in the first year so that the plant can build up its strength for subsequent years.

As the canes grow, tie them in with garden string to the support wires. Rub out any flowers.

Subsequent years Allow the canes to bear fruit in the second year after planting. In early autumn, when summer-fruiting types have been picked, untie all the old canes that have fruited and cut them down to just above ground level.

Select up to eight of the strongest new canes on each plant and tie them to the wires or other supports. Cut out all unwanted new canes at soil level in the same way as for old canes.

Vigorous raspberries tend to produce sucker canes directly from their roots and these spring up between the rows, getting in the way of weeding, training and harvesting. Eliminate suckers by pulling them away from the roots using a tearing action. Wear gloves to protect your hands from the scaly, often rather prickly, stems. Do not sever sucker canes with secateurs as any buds left intact at the base will soon start growing.

In late winter, cut back all summer-fruiting canes extending

◄ **Raspberry canes** The best crops are borne on stems of the previous season, and exposed to full sun and good air circulation. Space the canes evenly along the rows and tie them to wires.

PRUNING AND TRAINING RASPBERRIES

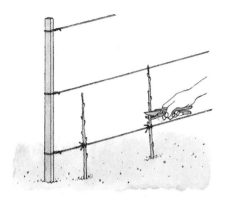

1 After planting new raspberry canes in autumn, or winter to early spring, cut down each cane to 30cm (1ft) above ground. Use secateurs and cut cleanly just above a healthy bud. Tie the cane to the bottom wire.

2 In the first spring, new canes appear from ground level. Allow them to grow on, but cut out the original cane at ground level. No fruit will form during the first year while the plants are developing strong canes and roots.

3 During summer and early autumn, secure the new canes to the wires as they develop, using garden string, wire rings or plastic raffia. Keep the canes well apart in the row, allowing about 10cm (4in) between each one.

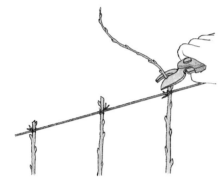

4 In late winter or early spring, before new growth begins, cut off the tips of all canes above a healthy bud, to encourage vigour in the lower buds. Trim the tallest canes to just above the top wire.

5 In subsequent years, cut down to the ground all canes which have borne fruit. Do this as soon as possible after the last harvest. Also remove any spindly new growth at ground level, leaving up to eight new canes per plant.

6 Tie the selected new canes to the horizontal wire supports, and remove any sucker shoots which are growing directly from the roots in the pathways between rows. This is best done by pulling away with a tearing action.

above the top wire to a bud just above it. This will reduce wind damage and encourage stronger growth from the lower buds.

With autumn-fruiting raspberries, pruning is easier still. Simply cut all canes to the ground in late winter. The new stems which will bear fruit that autumn appear from ground level soon afterwards. Tie them to the wires as they grow in summer.

Pruning blackberries
In the wild, blackberries scramble through hedgerows, using their profuse thorns to gain support. Cultivated blackberries, including thornless varieties, are best grown on a support system of posts and wires. The best fruits are borne on shoots produced in the previous season, and fruited canes should therefore be pruned out at the end of each growing season and replaced by new one-year-old shoots.

Blackberry canes are very long and it is difficult to separate them from other stems without breaking them or getting yourself entangled in the thorns. They are best trained in a fan shape on wires against a fence or wall in such a way that the new growing shoots are kept well away from last year's growth which bears this year's fruits. This makes harvesting and replacement training easier and also helps to prevent the spread of disease.

Immediately after planting, cut back the canes to 23-38cm (9-15in) above ground level, pruning just above a healthy bud. In subsequent years, cut out all the old canes as soon as their fruit has been picked in autumn, severing them at ground level with either secateurs or long-handled pruners (see the illustrations on page 44).

Wear gardening gloves to protect your hands from the thorns. Thornless varieties are easier to handle.

On fan-trained blackberries, untie the current year's shoots from their temporary positions and tie them in to replace the old, cut-down shoots. Nylon string is better than ordinary garden string for this purpose.

Loganberries and other hybrid cane berries are trained and pruned like blackberries.

PRUNING BUSH FRUITS
Bush fruits – currants and gooseberries – differ from cane fruits in forming compact bushes with a mixture of old and new shoots. However, they also differ from each other in the way the fruit is borne. Black currants, for example, produce their best fruit on young wood of the previous season, while red and white currants, whether grown as bushes or cordons, bear the finest crops on spurs on old wood. Gooseberries fruit on new wood as well as on spurs of older wood. Pruning in each case is aimed at

TRAINING BLACKBERRIES

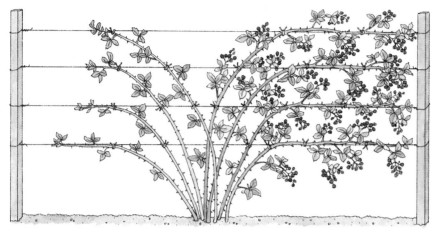

1 The main requirement of any training system for blackberries, loganberries and hybrid berries is to keep the current year's stems clear of the fruiting canes – once they get entangled it is difficult to harvest the crop and carry out the correct replacement pruning later on.

Given enough space, blackberries are best grown against strong galvanized wires stretched tautly between posts. Tie fruiting canes in one direction and canes of the current season in the opposite direction. Attach one cane only to each wire, using nylon string or wire rings. Fruit will be borne on alternate halves of the support system each year.

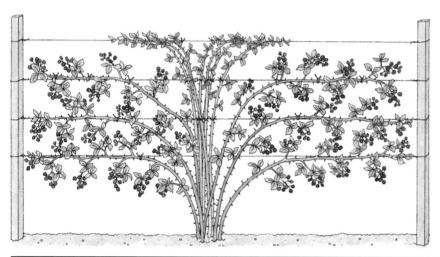

2 Fan-trained blackberries, with fruiting canes spread evenly along the wires in both directions, give the flower and fruit clusters the maximum amount of space and light available, and the berries are also much easier to pick.

The new canes, which will carry next year's blackberry crop, are trained upwards between the fan-trained fruiting canes and tied in temporarily to the top wire. After harvesting is completed in late autumn, cut out the fruited canes at ground level and untie the new canes. Tie them into position along the wires, and repeat this replacement system annually.

encouraging the healthy growth of fruit-bearing shoots.

In addition, fruit bushes are pruned to prevent overcrowding of the branches, especially those in the centre of the bush – sunlight must reach as many of the fruiting branches as possible, and air must circulate freely between them. Fruit clusters which are shaded by surrounding foliage, and so do not dry out thoroughly after rain or morning dew, are more liable to infection from disease. Most fruits ripen much faster and more uniformly in sunlight than in shade, although black currants are more tolerant of poor light than other fruit crops.

The particular growth habit of a fruit bush influences the best method of pruning. For instance, gooseberry varieties range from spreading bushes, in which the branches often tend to droop, to upright bushes or trained cordons. Spreading bushes are therefore pruned to upward-pointing buds and upright varieties and cordons to outward-pointing buds. For in-between varieties, always prune to outward-pointing buds.

Birds – especially bullfinches and pigeons – do a lot of damage to fruit bushes in winter by pecking the dormant growth and fruit buds. Where this is a problem, delay winter pruning until the buds begin to swell in late winter. Always prune back to undamaged buds.

Use sharp secateurs for making pruning cuts to small, young branches, and use long-handled pruners or a small pruning saw for coarser, older wood.

Pruning black currants

Cut newly planted black currant bushes down to about 2.5cm (1in) above ground level, cutting just above a bud. This means that the bushes will yield no fruit in the first summer – instead their energy will go into producing vigorous new growth that will provide a crop during the second summer after planting.

In the autumn of the first growing season, cut any weak shoots back to one bud within 5cm (2in) of ground level. By the second autumn after planting, the bush should have developed considerable new growth. Remove a few – no more than a quarter – of the two-year-old shoots entirely, sacrificing their new extension wood. This will stimulate the development of new shoots.

Black currant bushes produce the majority of their fruit on the previous season's young wood, so the actual aim of pruning is to remove some older, darker wood annually to encourage the new shoots to grow.

Young wood is either extension shoots from the older branches or new shoots springing from or near the base. A good balance between old and new wood must be kept, and some of the older wood must be retained for extension growth.

Prune an established bush after picking the fruit or during the autumn months. Remove some older wood to make way for younger shoots. On regularly pruned bushes, no wood should be older than four years.

A neglected bush with congested growth needs hard pruning

to induce new shoots. First cut out entirely any shoots either drooping to the ground or so low that the fruit will be soiled. Next, cut out older wood from the centre of the bush to let in light and air.

Cut out the oldest of the remaining wood – this is distinguished by its dark colour. Clear away all debris from the base of the bush.

Pruning red and white currants

After planting a one-year-old bush, cut each branch back to four buds from the main stem, above an outward-facing bud.

In the second winter, cut out any branches that spoil the overall shape flush with the stem. Shorten branch leaders by two-thirds of new growth if growth is weak, or by half if growth is strong, cutting to outward-pointing buds. Prune side-shoots to one bud to promote spurs.

In the third and fourth years, leave some laterals to grow into branches where there is room, so that the established bush has eight to ten main branches on a 15-23cm (6-9in) leg. Otherwise, prune the laterals back to spurs each year. Cut branch leaders back by half the new growth in the third winter. In the fourth winter, remove a quarter of new growth. After that, prune by about 2.5cm (1in) yearly. Keep the centre of the bush open, and as the oldest branches become too spreading or unproductive, cut them out entirely to be replaced by strong new shoots.

On newly planted cordons, select the strongest shoots – or two shoots for a double cordon –

and cut the remainder back to the base. Thereafter, winter-pruning consists of shortening the leading shoots by one third and cutting all laterals back to one bud. Stop the leading shoots of cordons when they reach 1.8m (6ft) high.

Bush and cordon-trained red and white currants need to be pruned in summer as well as winter, beginning when they are two years old. In each case, prune by mid summer, reducing all lateral shoots to three to five leaves, cutting just above a leaf joint.

Pruning gooseberries

After planting, prune a one-year-old bush in autumn or winter, or as late as bud-burst in late winter if birds are likely to damage the buds. Choose the best three or four shoots and cut them back above a bud to about a quarter their length. Cut out all other shoots flush with the main stem.

When pruning, firm in with your heel plants which have been lifted and loosened in the ground by frosts.

During the first summer after planting, the branch framework should be clear. In mid summer, shorten any unwanted lateral shoots to leave about five leaves. Leave the leaders unpruned.

In the second winter, choose six to eight of the strongest shoots. Cut the new growth on these shoots back by half if they are growing strongly, or by two-thirds if growth is weak. Remove all dead, damaged or diseased wood. Cut back all other shoots to one bud from their base.

Aim to produce a goblet-shaped bush with an open centre. This not only encourages the highest yields, but makes picking the fruits much easier – the sharply spined branches are difficult and painful to deal with once they have become congested and contorted by inadequate pruning.

On established bushes, cut back branch leaders by half their new growth in winter. To encourage spur formation, shorten the strongest side-shoots to 7.5cm (3in) of new growth, and weaker ones to 2.5cm (1in). Remove weak shoots entirely, cutting them flush with the branch.

If a branch has drooped to the ground, choose a new shoot as a replacement and cut the drooping branch back to the source of the new shoot. Prune the replacement

branch by at least half. Keep the centre of the bush open.

In summer shorten all side-shoots to five leaves, cutting just above a leaf joint. Do not shorten the branch leaders.

PRUNING A TWO-YEAR-OLD GOOSEBERRY BUSH

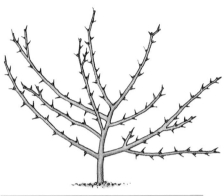

Reduce new growth by half on six to eight of the strongest shoots.

PRUNING AN ESTABLISHED GOOSEBERRY BUSH

Summer-prune established bushes by cutting side-shoots back to five leaves from the base.

PRUNING A ONE-YEAR-OLD GOOSEBERRY BUSH

Shorten three or four well-spaced shoots by three-quarters in winter. They will form the main framework.

BLACKBERRIES

**Prolific and easy to grow,
blackberries are ideal fruit for training
against a wall or fence.**

Cultivated blackberries are much larger and juicier than the wild kind. They flourish in any moisture-retaining, well-drained soil and will even tolerate slightly impeded drainage. However, soil preparation and some training are necessary for really good yields.

Blackberries are self-fertile, so you can grow just a single plant if space is limited. They should ideally be trained against a wall or fence. Three plants should provide more than enough berries for the average family.

Site and soil
Grow blackberries where they will be in the sun for at least part of

the day. They do best in a slightly acid soil. Enrich limy soil with garden compost, coir or other organic matter a few months before planting – this will also help to retain moisture during dry weather. Thin, dry soil should be improved in the same manner.

Cultivation
Late autumn is the best time for planting, but any time from then until early spring is suitable. Dig a hole wide and deep enough to

▼ **Fruit trellis** Trained up a trellis arbour, a thornless blackberry is decorative as well as productive, though picking the top berries can be difficult.

cultivated
blackberries

accommodate the roots, which should be well spread out. After planting, firm the soil with your feet, then cut back each cane to 23cm (9in) from ground level, just above a bud.

Blackberries can be trained along wires or up posts, but a wire system is the easiest to manage. Secure the wires to a wall with vine eyes, or stretch them between strong end posts. Use 10-12 gauge wires, setting them 30cm (1ft) apart, the first 90cm (3ft) above ground, up to a height of 1.8m (6ft).

Set the blackberry clumps at least 2.5m (8ft) apart; very vigorous varieties need 3.5-4.5m (12-15ft) of space between each plant.

The one-way system of training is the simplest, although not very

TRAINING BLACKBERRIES

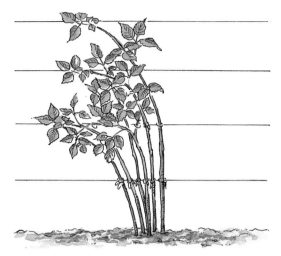

1 Blackberries can be trained along wires or up posts, but the wire system exposes more canes to sun and air and makes harvesting easier. The one-way system is simpler than fan-training – in the first year, train all fruiting branches in one direction along the wires. Train the longest cane straight up until it reaches the top wire.

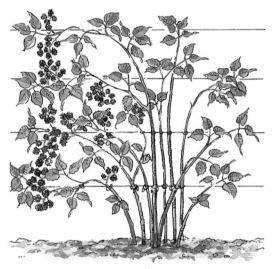

2 Train the current season's canes in the other direction along the wires, in the same way as before. Separating the current season's wood from that of the previous year helps to prevent disease from spreading. It also helps to keep the canes tidy and easier to manage. Tie the branches firmly to the wires, using tree ties or ordinary garden string.

3 After gathering the season's fruit, cut the fruiting canes down to soil level. The new canes are then ready to fruit the following year; afterwards they should be cut down to the ground in their turn. Keep training the branches to alternate sides for healthy stock.

Blackberry 'Himalaya Giant'

economical on space. By this system, the young branches are all trained in one direction along the wires, to one side of the plant, and the following year's growth is trained in the opposite direction (see also pages 43 and 44).

Feed the canes regularly in spring with general compound fertilizer at a rate of 50g per sq m (2oz per sq yd). Watering is usually unnecessary, except during prolonged dry spells.

After gathering the fruit, cut the fruited canes down to soil level each year, and tie in the replacement canes.

Propagation

You can increase blackberry canes by layering the tips of new (current season) branches, between mid summer and early autumn. Take out a hole approximately 10cm (4in) deep near the plant, bend down a shoot and plant its tip firmly in the hole.

The tip should have rooted by late autumn: the following spring, sever the young plant from its parent, with about 25cm (10in) of stem. Cut just above a bud, remove the new plant and set it in its permanent site.

Harvesting and storing

Pick fruit when it is ripe (black), even if you don't need it immediately; this will help later fruit to reach a good size. The fruit deteriorates quickly after picking.

Pests and diseases

Blackberry plants are often attacked by raspberry beetle, and may suffer from cane blight, cane spot, chlorosis, crown gall, grey mould, honey fungus and virus disease.

BLACK CURRANTS

**Hardy and long-living bush fruits, black currants
are also easy to grow. With good management they will yield
heavy crops for up to fifteen years.**

Black currants are one of the most versatile fruits in the kitchen – the dark, acid berries are used for desserts, jam-making and medicinal drinks.

Site and soil preparation
Black currants grow best in an open sunny position, although they will tolerate partial shade. Avoid planting in cold, exposed sites or frost pockets.

Any well-drained, moisture-retentive soil is suitable, and black currants thrive in well-manured ground. Before planting, work in a generous dressing of well-rotted farmyard manure or good garden compost.

Planting
When buying young plants from a nursery or garden centre, insist that they are certified as being disease free. Reversion is a serious virus disease for which there is no cure; it is transmitted by gall mites.

Plant black currant bushes any time between mid autumn and early spring as long as the soil isn't frozen – it is best done in autumn. Take out holes large enough to accommodate the roots comfortably when well spread out. Set the plants 2.5-5cm (1-2in) deeper than they were growing at the nursery – use the soil mark on the stem as a guide. Set the bushes 1.5-1.8m (5-6ft) apart.

After planting, cut the stems back to just above the second bud from soil level. This prevents any fruit-bearing shoots in the first year, but ensures stronger bushes. Mulch with a 5cm (2in) layer of well-rotted manure, garden compost or leaf-mould.

Looking after the crop
To help retain moisture in the soil, replace the mulch of rotted manure, garden compost or leaf-mould every year in early spring; use two buckets per sq m/sq yd.

In mid winter, apply sulphate of potash at the rate of 25g per sq m (1oz per sq yd). Every third year, add 50g per sq m (2oz per sq yd) of superphosphate. In early

▲ **Black currants** The best crops are produced on spurs on shoots of the previous season, although older stems continue to bear fruit. Well-balanced bushes consist of a proportion of older shoots from which fruit-bearing extension shoots grow. Aim to keep the centre of the bush open so that air can circulate.

PRUNING BLACK CURRANTS

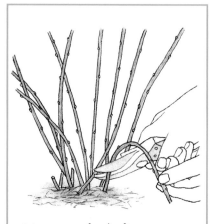

1 In autumn after the first growing season, cut any weak shoots back to 5cm (2in) above ground to induce stronger vigour from the base.

2 By the second autumn, new growth should have developed. Remove up to a quarter of two-year-old shoots from the centre.

spring, apply 50g per sq m (2oz per sq yd) of sulphate of ammonia.

Avoid disturbing the shallow roots when weeding with a fork or hoe. After hard frosts, check that the bushes have not been lifted – if they have, firm them in with your feet. Water the plants regularly during dry periods. Prune annually in autumn (see also pages 44-45).

Harvesting

Pick black currants when they are fully ripe – a week or two after they have turned black.

Propagating black currants

Black currants root easily from cuttings taken in mid autumn. Select healthy, well-ripened shoots of the current year and cut them off just above a bud.

Cut away the unripened wood at the top of the shoot just above a bud and trim the base below a bud to give cuttings 23cm (9in) long.

Insert the cuttings in a 20cm (8in) deep trench outdoors; they should have rooted and be ready for planting in their permanent positions in autumn.

Pests and diseases

The main pests of black currants are aphids and leaf midge; spray with dimethoate in spring, before flowering, and if necessary again afterwards. Gall mites, which show as 'big buds' that fail to develop, should be treated with a fungicide as the flowers open.

In addition to reversion, American gooseberry mildew, grey mould, honey fungus and leaf spot may occur.

PRUNING AN ESTABLISHED BLACK CURRANT BUSH

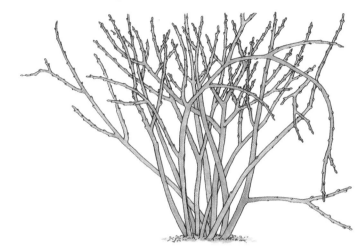

1 Every autumn prune out old stems to make room for new. No wood should be older than four years.

2 Cut neglected bushes back to the ground to induce new growth. Cut out lax shoots and the oldest wood.

VARIETIES TO CHOOSE

Early varieties
'Blackdown' – good cropper; sweet flavour; medium to large-sized berries; resistant to mildew.

'Tsema' – vigorous and spreading; long trusses of medium-sized berries.

Mid season varieties
'Ben Lomond' – good cropper; acid flavour; flowers late; resistant to pests

'Ben Sarck' – small and compact; heavy yields of large sweet berries;

largely resistant to mildew.

'Blacksmith' – reliable cropper; large sweet fruits.

'Wellington XXX' – long-established, popular; crops well; sweet fruits.

Late varieties
'Baldwin' – very rich in vitamin C; acid flavour; vigorous plants.

'Jet' – acid fruit in very long trusses; heavy cropper.

Black currant 'Tsema'

Black currant 'Blacksmith'

Black currant 'Jet'

BLUEBERRIES

Blueberry bushes are ultra-hardy and will provide luscious fruit for many years if planted in acid soil.

blueberry 'Berkeley'

The blueberry (*Vaccinium corymbosum*), often called the highbush blueberry to distinguish it from dwarf carpeting species of vaccinium, is an American relative of the British bilberry or whortleberry (*V. myrtillus*). It bears clusters of white flowers, occasionally tinged pink, in late spring, followed by blue-black berries.

The sweet berries, up to 2cm (¾in) across, become covered with a silvery waxy bloom as they begin to ripen to dark blue. Good when fresh, the berries also bottle and freeze well.

The attractive rich green foliage is deciduous and in most varieties turns deep red in autumn. The shrubs are often grown for their ornamental value.

Site and soil preparation

The blueberry is a member of the heather family and needs moist, but free-draining, deep acid soil in a sunny or slightly shaded place sheltered from wind. It will not succeed in neutral or alkaline soils.

A few weeks before planting, prepare the site by digging a hole about 45cm (1½ft) square for each bush. Break up the subsoil, and mix damp peat substitute with the topsoil in equal amounts. Do not use manure – it will burn the roots. Fill the hole with the mixture and give it time to settle.

On alkaline soil, grow blueberries in tubs or large pots filled with lime-free compost.

Planting

Cropping depends partly on the weather and soil conditions, and partly on the age of the bushes. One bush should provide 2.5-5kg (5-10lb) of fruit, the higher yields coming from mature shrubs. To ensure cross pollination, with subsequent high fruit production, plant at least two bushes, preferably of different varieties.

Plant two- or three-year-old bushes, setting them 1.5m (5ft) apart in the prepared ground during late autumn to early spring, and mulch with forest bark or wet sawdust to a depth of 15cm (6in). Blueberry shrubs are obtainable from specialist fruit nurseries and are usually container-grown. A mature bush may grow 1.8m (6ft) tall and 1.5m (5ft) wide.

Cultivation

Each year in early spring apply a balanced compound fertilizer at the rate of 50g per sq m (2oz per sq yd), mixing it lightly with the mulch. At the end of mid spring apply sulphate of ammonia at the rate of 25g per sq m (1oz per sq yd). The mulch should be moist at the time fertilizers are applied.

During the first two winters after planting, prune out any diseased, damaged or prostrate stems. In the third winter, and annually thereafter, cut out all weak stems and cut back old wood to the base or to vigorous new side-shoots. Prune to encourage the formation of new growth annually. Blueberries bear fruit on the tips of the previous season's growth. For the first two growing seasons, rub out flower buds in spring to prevent fruit from forming while the shrubs build up their strength.

Blueberries are surface rooting,

◄ **Highbush blueberries** Beginning to crop in their third year, blueberries bear fruit at the shoot tips. The berries are green at first but eventually turn slate-blue. They are ready for picking when they are soft and covered with a waxy bloom.

so weed by hand to avoid damaging or disturbing the roots. An annual mulch in spring helps to prevent weeds and also conserves soil moisture.

Blueberries grown in large pots or tubs need generous amounts of rainwater during the growing season and a potash-high liquid fertilizer every ten days from the start of flowering to the beginning of berry ripening.

Harvesting
Depending on the variety, the berries can be picked from mid summer to early autumn. They do not all ripen at once so go over the clusters a number of times. Ripe berries are light to dark blue with a waxy bloom.

Pests and diseases
Blueberries are generally free of pests and diseases, but protect the flower buds and the ripening fruit from birds with netting.

VARIETIES TO CHOOSE

'Berkeley' – vigorous; large, sweet fruit; crops late summer.

'Bluecrop' – vigorous; height and spread 1.5m (5ft); consistently good cropper; large, sweet berries ripen in the early part of late summer.

'Coville' – vigorous; broad bush to 1.5m (5ft); large, light blue fruit appear in long clusters in early autumn; good yields.

'Earliblue' – vigorous bush; moderate yields of large, light blue berries from mid summer.

'Herbert' – vigorous and upright to 1.2m (4ft) high and 1.4m (4½ft); large, mid blue berries; ripen late summer; exceptionally good flavour.

LAYERING

1 In early autumn select a long shoot and cut a tongue slightly into the heartwood where it can be bent to reach the ground.

2 Peg down the shoot with wire staples and if necessary tie the tip to a cane support. After one or two years, sever the plant and set in a permanent site.

TAKING CUTTINGS

1 Take semi-ripe shoots with a heel in mid summer. Remove the soft growing tip and dip the heel in a hormone rooting powder.

2 Insert the cuttings in a proprietary potting compost in a cold frame. Spray frequently with water until well rooted. Then plant out.

PRUNING

Blueberries need no pruning for the first two years after planting. After that, prune each winter to encourage new growth – fruit is borne on the previous year's shoots. Weak, damaged, or dead wood should be cut out and old wood should be cut back to the base or to vigorous new side-shoots.

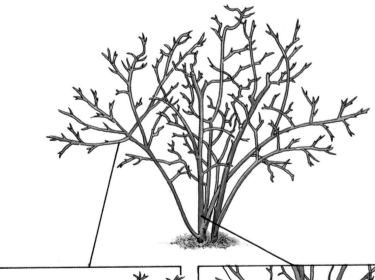

1 In winter cut back branches that have fruited and become twiggy to a vigorous new shoot. Remove cross branches.

2 Cut back one to four of the oldest shoots to a strong new shoot, or to soil level if there are plenty of new basal shoots.

CRANBERRIES

**Traditionally used as a garnish for
turkey, cranberries are heathland fruits that succeed
only in acid and boggy conditions.**

Cranberries, along with plum pudding, tend to vanish from our diet the moment Christmas lunch is cleared away. Yet the use of these piquant berries features in many recipes for tarts and puddings. The cranberry's robust, tangy flavour and firm texture also go well with strong-tasting foods, and suit meat, game and poultry – turkey, in particular.

There are two species of cranberry. The common or small cranberry (*Vaccinium oxycoccos*), with small, rounded, leathery leaves and a ground-hugging habit, grows wild on the heathlands of northern England and Scotland and thrives in acidic peat bogs. It bears small, red juicy fruit on stems about 7.5cm (3in) tall.

The cultivated fruit sold at most supermarkets is the American cranberry (*Vaccinium macrocarpon*), a slightly larger species that is grown commercially only in the USA. The red berries are about 2cm (¾in) wide.

You can grow common cranberries from heathland cuttings, but the berries are smaller than those of the American species. Varieties from *V. macrocarpon* are more suitable for garden cultivation. Such high-yielding varieties will

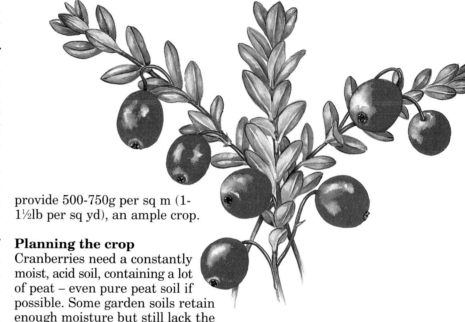

provide 500-750g per sq m (1-1½lb per sq yd), an ample crop.

Planning the crop
Cranberries need a constantly moist, acid soil, containing a lot of peat – even pure peat soil if possible. Some garden soils retain enough moisture but still lack the pH value of 3.2-4.5 and the high percentage of peat that cranberries thrive on.

As few gardens can provide such conditions, either grow the plants in pots of suitably mixed acid compost or make up a site in a sunny spot.

Dig a trench two spades deep and 45cm (1½ft) wide for one row of plants – 60cm (2ft) wide for two. Fill the bottom with a layer of drainage material about 10cm

▲ **Cranberries** Growing wild in wet areas such as the Lake District, native cranberries are smaller than the imported US fruit found in supermarkets in late autumn and winter.

(4in) deep and cover with a sheet of perforated plastic – use a skewer to puncture holes in it. Fill the remainder of the trench with a mixture of two parts peat to one part medium-light acid soil,

CREATING A BOG BED

1 Choose a sunny spot and dig a trench about two spades deep. Vary the width according to the number of rows to be accommodated. Cover the bottom with a layer of hardcore about 10cm (4in) deep.

2 Spread a sheet of hard-wearing polythene and perforate it with a skewer. Lay the sheet in the trench, making sure it covers the side walls to prevent sideways drainage.

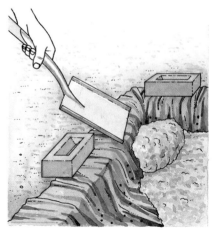

3 Keep the sheet in place with bricks and fill up the trench with a mixture of two parts peat to one part medium-light soil or three parts peat to one part coarse sand – all parts by volume.

or three parts peat to one part coarse sand (parts by volume).

Planting

Plant one- or two-year-old divisions, seedlings or rooted cuttings about 30cm (1ft) apart in rows spaced at the same distance, in late autumn or winter when the ground is soft. Secure any straggly growth to prevent the plant being lifted out of the ground before it has had time to become fully established. If you peg down the long shoots, cranberries will root at the leaf joints, so increasing their sturdiness and size.

Immediately after planting water the bed, preferably with a sprinkler attachment, until the peat mixture is thoroughly soaked. To prevent the peat surface becoming dry, cover after watering with a 2.5cm (1in) layer of coarse lime-free sand; this will also help the stems root.

The following spring, dress with a balanced compound fertilizer at 15g per sq m (½oz per sq yd), and repeat at monthly intervals until the middle of summer. Water it in lightly if it doesn't rain soon after application, so the dressing doesn't sit on the leaves and branches of the plants.

In mid spring each year, dress the soil with a high-potash compound fertilizer at 20g per sq m (¾oz per sq yd), sprinkled on as before.

In early spring, prune any creeping stems in order to confine

PLANTING AND PRUNING

1 Plant cranberries during suitable weather in late autumn or spring. Peg down any straggly growth and water the bed until thoroughly soaked. Cover with a layer of coarse, lime-free sand.

2 In early spring prune out creeping stems to confine the plants to the bed. Remove tall, upright stems along with any dead wood. Keep the bed saturated throughout the year.

the plants to the limits of the peat bed. Remove any upright fruiting shoots which are old, weak or crowding the centre.

Water is vital throughout the year; the bed should always be saturated. After a dry winter water heavily in early spring, and throughout summer and autumn.

Propagation

New plants can be raised by layering shoots in early autumn; they are usually ready for severing and planting out after one or two years. Strong plants can also be divided and replanted between autumn and winter.

Harvesting

Although the berries don't all mature at once – they are deep red when ripe – it is better to pick them all at the same time, as the berries are close to the ground and difficult to detach.

Harvest during early and mid autumn. The berries keep for up to three weeks in a cool, dry place – eight to twelve weeks in a fridge, and for several months in a freezer. Use any spare fruit to make delicious cranberry jelly.

Pests and diseases

Cranberry plants are usually disease and pest free.

Common cranberry

GOOSEBERRIES

Dessert and culinary gooseberries are easy to grow as bushes or cordons and produce excellent crops for many years.

Gooseberries have been grown in British gardens since the Middle Ages and are a traditional ingredient of many dishes. The juicy, sharp-tasting fruits are used unripe in cooking and as dessert fruits when fully ripe.

Plants can be grown as bushes or cordons – double and triple cordons are much more common than single ones. Bushes are frequently grown on a 'leg' – a 20cm (8in) clear length of main stem below the branches. This prevents suckers from growing out and keeps the fruit clear of the soil. A mature, well-tended gooseberry bush will yield up to 4-5kg (8-10lb) of fruit, and a cordon about 1-2kg (2-4lb).

Site and soil preparation

Gooseberries do equally well in semi-shade or full sun. Choose a site protected from cold winds and frosts, which could damage the flowers. Where possible grow

▲ **Gooseberries** Ranging widely in colour from green to white, yellow or red and in flavour from very sharp to particularly sweet, gooseberries are in season from late spring until the end of summer.

gooseberries in a fruit cage or under netting.

Any moist, well-drained soil is suitable, but the best results are obtained on deep, well-manured loam free of perennial weeds.

Before planting, work liberal quantities of compost into the soil – at least a bucketful per sq m/yd. Then apply sulphate of potash at the rate of 25g per sq m (1oz per sq yd).

Planting

Buy two- or three-year-old plants and plant them between mid autumn and early spring. Set bushes 1.5m (5ft) apart, single cordons 38cm (15in) apart, double cordons 60cm (2ft) apart and triple cordons 1m (3ft) apart. Leave 1.5m (5ft) between rows.

Cordons are best grown against a fence or wall. Staple or nail three horizontal support wires to the fence or wall at 30cm (1ft) intervals. Tie a cane to the wires at an angle of 45° and secure the cordon to the cane with string. The cane can be removed when the cordon reaches the top wire.

TAKING GOOSEBERRY CUTTINGS

In mid autumn, choose well-ripened current year's shoots and cut off just above a bud. Trim the top above a bud and the base below a bud. Root the cuttings 15cm (6in) apart in a V-shaped trench 20cm (8in) deep, with the top four buds above soil level.

Mid season 'Whinham's Industry'

Late 'Whitesmith'

Looking after the crop

In winter, firm any bushes that have been loosened by frost.

At the end of winter (but not in the first year after planting), feed the plants with sulphate of potash at the rate of 20g per sq m (¾oz per sq yd), and apply a mulch of well-rotted compost or manure. In early spring, apply one tablespoon of sulphate of ammonia per sq m/sq yd. Every third year, add two tablespoons of superphosphate to each sq m/yd. Kill any weeds with a contact weedkiller, or hand-weed with a small fork.

If there is any chance of frost on spring nights, protect the blossom by covering the plants with fine-mesh netting. Remove the

THINNING OUT

Start thinning gooseberries on heavy-cropping branches in late spring. Thinning can be carried out in stages until the fruits are spaced 7.5cm (3in) apart; the unripe fruits can be used in cooking.

VARIETIES TO CHOOSE

Early varieties
'May Duke' – red; dessert, or cooking when green in late spring.

Mid season
'Careless' – most popular gooseberry; large, pale green, smooth-skinned; reliable cropper.

'Leveller' – yellow; dessert or

cooking; good cropper; susceptible to mildew.

'Whinham's Industry' – red; dessert or cooking; suitable for heavy soils.

Late
'Whitesmith' – pale green; dessert or cooking; tolerates shade.

covering during the day so as not to discourage pollinating insects.

Remove any suckers that appear from the stem or roots. Water during hot weather.

Pruning

Cut gooseberry bushes back in winter (see page 45) or when the buds have started to swell. In addition, prune mature plants in early summer, pruning side-shoots to five leaves from the base.

On cordons, allow the leaders to grow unpruned but cut back new growth at the tip in late spring once they have reached the top wire.

Prune back mature laterals to three leaves in mid summer and side-shoots to one leaf. Any secondary growth produced thereafter should be cut back to one bud in autumn. One or two laterals can grow on and be trained in parallel to the main stem.

Raising new plants

In mid autumn, take cuttings 30-38cm (12-15in) long from straight shoots of well-ripened current year's wood – cut just above a bud. If the top 2.5-7.5cm (1-3in) of the cutting is soft and unripened, cut it off above a bud; if it is brown to

the tip, leave it. Trim the lower end just below a bud.

Choose a sheltered but not shaded site and take out a 20cm (8in) deep trench in which to root the cuttings 15cm (6in) apart.

The cuttings should be ready for digging up and setting in their final position the following winter. Remove them carefully with a fork. Cut off flush with the stem any shoots growing from buds buried below ground and any shoots on the bottom 10-12cm (4-5in) of stem. Plant the cuttings as for nursery-bought bushes.

Harvesting

Start picking gooseberries for cooking when they are about 1½cm (½in) in diameter. Do not pick fruit for eating raw until it is soft and fully ripe.

Pests and diseases

The most common pests of gooseberries are aphids, capsid bugs and sawfly caterpillars.

The most serious disease is American gooseberry mildew; prune to keep bushes open, cut out diseased shoots and spray with a fungicide after harvesting. Grey mould, leaf spot and rust may also be troublesome.

GRAPES

**In southern England luscious grapes
can be grown outdoors in sunny sheltered sites.
Elsewhere they must be grown under glass.**

Vines have been grown in Britain for many centuries – outdoors in sheltered areas by the Romans and medieval monks, and indoors under glass on large country estates in the 18th and 19th centuries.

Success with growing grapes, for dessert fruits or wine-making, depends on two factors – locality and cost. South of a line from Pembroke to The Wash, grapes can be grown in the open on wire supports, against sunny south-facing walls or fences, or in a cold greenhouse. In sheltered places north of this line, grapes may be grown against a south-facing wall if given protection with glass or plastic to aid ripening. However, they succeed better in a greenhouse with some heat in late spring and early autumn.

Black grapes require more warmth and a longer growing season than white and red grapes.

Planning an outdoor crop

Choose a sheltered position in full sun for growing grapes in the open in the south. Avoid frost pockets and sites in even partial shade. A gentle slope facing south or south-west is ideal.

For vines on a wall or fence choose a site facing south, south-west or south-east. Wall-grown vines succeed in areas too cold for growing grapes in the open. The extra warmth radiating from the wall makes the grapes sweeter and better flavoured.

Preparing the soil Vines grow best in a sandy, gravelly soil that warms up quickly in the sun, but they will succeed in any type of soil if the drainage is good.

Two or three months before planting, prepare the ground by forking in well-rotted manure or garden compost at the rate of a bucketful per sq m/yd. Add a general fertilizer such as Growmore at the same time, at the rate of 75g per sq m (3oz per sq yd).

Putting up supports To grow vines in a row, set support posts 1.5m (5ft) high at 2.5-3m (8-10ft) intervals. The end posts should be at least 6.5cm (2½in) in diameter

▶ **Grape varieties**
Modern varieties – white, red or black – have been bred specifically to succeed in British climates. Some have highly ornamental autumn foliage.

and intermediate posts about 5cm (2in) in diameter. Allow 1.5m (5ft) between rows.

Staple a single strand of 12 gauge galvanized wire to the posts 45cm (1½ft) from the ground.

Loosely twist two strands of wire together and staple them to the posts 75cm (2½ft) from the ground, with another length of twisted wire 45cm (1½ft) above this. Training the fruiting shoots through the twisted double wire saves tying in individual shoots.

Planting An established vine in the open will produce at least 10 bunches of grapes – about 2.5kg (5lb) in a good year. A cordon on a wall may produce 7-10kg (15-20lb) or more, depending on the amount of wall covered. Start with just two or three vines and add more later if you have space.

Vines are bought as one-year-old plants – often the named variety is grafted as a scion on to a vigorous rootstock. Plant at any time while the vine is dormant – preferably mid autumn, though early spring may be safer in cold districts as the risk of prolonged severe frost is usually over.

Dig a wide hole for the roots to spread evenly and deep enough for the vine to be at the same level as in the nursery – look for the soil mark on the stem.

Plant the vines 1.2m (4ft) apart. Just before planting, drive a stout cane into the soil, with 1.8m (6ft) left above soil level – this will provide a support for tying in replacement shoots in subsequent years.

Allow only one strong shoot to grow in the first year. Tie this to the support cane; pinch out all other shoots at one or two leaves.

Training In the late autumn following planting, the vine will be ready for training – use the double Guyot system, the simplest way of growing vines in the open.

By this method grapes are grown on laterals from stems produced the previous year; at the same time

GROWING OUTDOOR GRAPES

1 Staple a single wire to support posts 45cm (1½ft) from the ground, and two loosely twisted strands 75cm (2½ft) and 1.2m (4ft) from the ground.

2 To support replacement shoots, drive a stout cane into the hole before planting the vine, leaving 1.8m (6ft) above ground. Tie the cane to the wires.

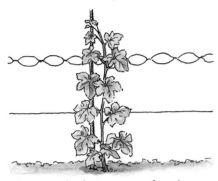

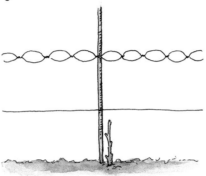

3 During the first summer after planting, tie the strongest vine shoot to the cane support. Pinch out all other shoots to one or two leaves.

4 After leaf fall cut the vine down to three or four buds. Cover with bracken or straw as a protection against prolonged and severe frost. Remove by early spring.

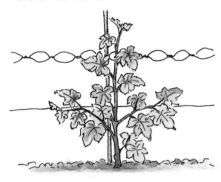

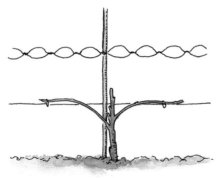

5 In the following summer, allow the three strongest shoots to grow. Tie them to the support cane and pinch out all other shoots.

6 In late autumn tie two of the shoots along the bottom wire. (Stop growth when the space is filled.) Cut the third central shoot back to three buds.

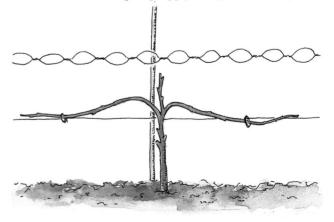

7 Next summer train the fruiting laterals from the two horizontal stems through the twisted wires. In late summer cut tips of laterals back to two or three leaves above the top wire. Remove sub-laterals. Tie in replacement stems.

8 In late autumn cut right back the horizontal stems that have carried fruit. Tie two replacement shoots to the bottom wire, and prune the remaining central shoot back to three buds. These buds will provide the following year's shoots.

replacement stems are trained for fruiting the following year.

After leaf-fall cut the vine down to three or four buds. The following summer, allow the three strongest shoots to grow on, pinching out all others.

In late autumn tie two of the shoots along the bottom wire, one to the left and one to the right. Cut the third shoot back to three buds. Stop growth of the two shoots when they fill the available space.

The following summer train the fruiting laterals from the two horizontal stems through the double wires. In late summer cut the tips of the laterals back to two or three leaves above the top wire and remove all sub-laterals completely, cutting them back to their point of origin.

Tie three replacement shoots to the support cane as they grow, and pinch back laterals growing from them to one leaf in late summer.

In late autumn, completely remove the two horizontal stems carrying the laterals that have fruited. Tie two replacement shoots to the bottom wire (one to the left and one to the right, as before) and cut back the third to three buds.

Repeat this horizontal training each year. Restrict the crop to four bunches per vine in the first fruiting year – the third year after planting – and six in the second, then allow full cropping.

General cultivation Keep the ground well watered, especially in the first year after planting. Dress generously every spring with coir, well-rotted garden compost or spent mushroom compost.

In winter apply a general fertilizer at the rate of 50g per sq m (2oz per sq yd) along each side of the row. In spring apply magnesium sulphate

(Epsom salts) as a top-dressing at 50g per sq m (2oz per sq yd).

Wall-grown grapes

Train grapes on a wall or fence on a single cordon, or rod. Fix support wires to the walls 30cm (1ft) apart, and held 12.5cm (5in) from the wall with vine eyes. Prepare the soil and plant the vines as in the open; set the vines 1.2m (4ft) apart and 23cm (9in) away from the wall.

Plant between late autumn and late winter, then cut the rod back to two buds from ground level. In the following growing season leave the strongest rod untouched; pinch out the growing points on any others when about 10cm (4in) long. Pinch out subsequent sub-laterals to one leaf, and all flowers as they appear.

In early winter, as soon as the leaves have fallen, cut back the vine by two-thirds. As growth develops in spring, let the topmost bud grow on as the new extension leader. Thin laterals if necessary by pinching them out when they are 2.5cm (1in) long. The aim is to produce fruit-bearing laterals alternately on opposite sides of the stem.

If the vine is growing strongly, two laterals on each side can be allowed to fruit. Pinch out these laterals at two leaves beyond the embryo bunch of grapes. Stop unfruited laterals when they reach 60cm (2ft). In early winter, shorten the leader by one-half. Cut back each lateral to about 2.5cm (1in), leaving two buds. Repeat this training of the single-stem cordon every year as an annual routine.

GREENHOUSE VINES: PINCHING OUT

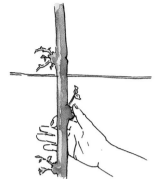 

1 In early to mid spring, as the buds swell, select the strongest shoot from each spur and rub out the others with your thumb.

2 Two weeks after rubbing out unwanted buds, stop the shoots with the longest flowering trusses at two leaves beyond the bunch. Pinch out the others at the fourth or fifth leaf, and sub-laterals at the first. Tie laterals to supporting wires.

Greenhouse grapes

The minimum size of a greenhouse suitable for growing grapes is about 2.5m (8ft) long, 2m (7ft) high to the ridge and 1.5m (5ft) high to the eaves.

Greenhouse grapes are usually grown like those trained against walls – as single-stem cordons.

First decide whether to plant the vine inside the greenhouse or set it in an outside border and train it indoors through an aperture. Although you have less control over the management of a vine in an outside border, watering is easier.

Soil preparation Two months before planting prepare the soil by digging a hole about 60cm (2ft) deep and at least as wide, keeping the topsoil and subsoil separate. Line the base with a 15cm (6in) deep drainage layer of straw. Mix the piles of soil with two buckets of rotted organic matter and 250g (8oz) bone meal, and return, using the subsoil first, followed by the topsoil. Plant the vines in late autumn.

Installing supports Set up support wires 30cm (1ft) apart and held 45cm (1½ft) from the roof by vine eyes screwed into the glazing bars or secured at the gable ends.

Single-stem cordons should be set 1.2m (4ft) apart. The number of vines you plant will depend on the length of the greenhouse.

General greenhouse cultivation

For the first two or three years after planting, train the cordon as for wall-grown vines. For an established vine, keep to the following annual routine.

Late autumn – early winter Prune the previous summer's lateral shoots back to one bud. After pruning, scrub the rods gently with tar-oil winter wash, diluted according to the manufacturer's

GREENHOUSE VINES: POLLINATING AND THINNING

1 When the flowers open, which is generally around late spring, assist pollination by stroking gently along the flower trusses with a very soft camel-hair brush.

2 As the grapes begin to swell – usually in mid summer – start initial thinning by carefully removing some of the grapes from the inside of each bunch. Take care not to bruise the remaining fruit.

3 Spread the final thinning gradually over seven to ten days. With a free-setting variety remove half the grapes. Leave more on the shoulders to give the bunches a good shape.

Outdoor grape 'Müller Thurgau'

Choose early ripening grapes for cooler areas. In more favourable districts grow early varieties in the open or on walls, and mid season varieties on walls.

White grapes are most successful, except in the hottest summers when black types can do well.

White
'Madeleine Angevine' – dessert and hock-type wine; good in cooler sites; heavy crop; prone to mildew.

'Madeleine Sylvaner' – light wine grape; early, consistent cropper; good for exposed sites.

'Müller Thurgau' – delicate flavour wine and dessert grape; heavy crops; needs sun for pollination.

'Seyval Blanc' – good for dessert and crisp dry wine; ripe mid autumn; heavy crops.

'Siegerrebe' – fine for dessert/ wine, full bouquet; early autumn.

Black
'Brandt' – sweet flavour for dessert and red/rosé wine; ripe mid autumn; crops well; red-gold autumn foliage; mildew resistant.

'Leon Millot' – intense black dessert and wine grape; suitable for unheated greenhouses in cold areas.

'Siebel' ('Cascade') – good wine variety; heavy cropper and early-ripening; ornamental foliage.

'Triomphe d'Alsace' – excellent wine grape; heavy crops in mid autumn; consistent; trouble free.

GREENHOUSE
The best varieties for a cold greenhouse are 'Black Hamburg' and 'Buckland Sweetwater'.

White
'Buckland Sweetwater' – sweet amber berries; heavy early crop.

'Chasselas d'Or' – good aromatic flavour for dessert and wine; ripe mid autumn.

'Foster's Seedling' – large, sweet, excellent for dessert; heavy crops late summer, early autumn.

Black
'Alicante' – good flavour; free-setting, heavy cropper; vigorous.

'Black Hamburg' – juicy, good for wine, dessert; ripe mid autumn; crops well; reliable, hardy.

instructions. Also wash glass and superstructure with disinfectant.

Mid winter – early spring Keep the ventilators open. Top-dress the rooting area in mid winter with a mixture of 100g per sq m (4oz per sq yd) of base fertilizer, plus an equal amount of dried blood. Then dress lightly with well-rotted manure or compost.

Early – mid spring Close the ventilators to raise the temperature and induce the buds to break. For an even break of buds, untie each rod and lay it on the ground. This encourages the buds nearest the soil to break at the same time as those at the top. Spray rods, soil and path with tepid water twice daily to increase humidity.

The buds will swell quickly. Select the strongest shoot from each spur and rub out the others.

Two weeks later, select the best shoots with the longest flowering trusses, stopping them at two leaves beyond the flower truss. Pinch out all others at the fourth or fifth leaf, and sub-laterals at the first leaf.

Late spring As the laterals reach 23cm (9in) in length, tie them to the supporting wires. When the flowers open, use a camel-hair brush to distribute pollen between them. Once the flowers have set, give a weekly potash-high liquid feed following instructions.

Keep the temperature high and the humidity fairly low until the flowers set, then open ventilators to lower the temperature. Keep damping down border and path.

Early summer – late summer Ventilate freely. A month after the fruit sets, gradually thin the berries over seven to ten days. With a free-setting variety, remove half the berries, evenly spaced, from the inside of the bunch, leaving the shoulders full.

When the grapes begin to colour, reduce watering to a mere dampening of the border. Stop applications of liquid feed.

Early autumn – mid autumn Use scissors to cut the bunches of grapes as they ripen. Close the ventilators to raise the temperature until the last bunches are cut.

Pests and diseases
The most common pests are glasshouse red spider mites, mealy bugs and scale insects. In the greenhouse, use biological controls.

Disease and disorders that may occur include grey mould, honey fungus, magnesium deficiency and powdery mildew.

LOGANBERRIES

A hybrid cross between raspberry and blackberry, loganberries produce good yields of large, sharp-tasting fruit.

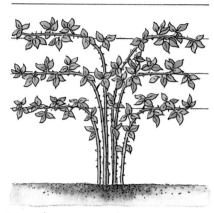

▲ **Loganberries** Similar in shape to raspberries but larger and claret red when ripe, loganberries have smaller thorns than their other parent, the blackberry, which makes them easier to handle.

1 Stretch strong wires between posts set about 2.4m (8ft) apart; allow 30cm (1ft) between each wire, and 60cm (2ft) from the ground to the first wire. Train the first year's growth upwards and then along the horizontals. Leave the top wire free.

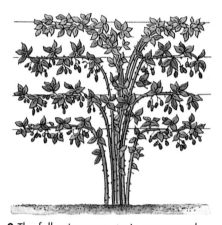

The loganberry – a cross between the blackberry and raspberry – was first bred in 1881. It is less vigorous than the blackberry and the canes are not so thorny. A further advantage is that the fruit is larger than either of its parents. The conical berries are claret red and very juicy with an excellent sharp flavour.

The loganberry's success has prompted the introduction of several other hybrid berries, such as the tayberry, wineberry and boysenberry – some of which deserve much more attention. They are similar to the loganberry, but each hybrid has its own characteristics – perhaps larger fruit size or tolerance of drought – to recommend it. They are all grown like the loganberry. Other berries, like Worcesterberry and jostaberry, are crosses between black currants and gooseberries; they are grown like other bush fruit.

Planning the crop

Loganberries give high yields in moisture-retentive, fertile soils, but dislike chalk. They prefer a sunny site – ideally a wall or fence with a southerly aspect.

Like most hybrids, they are heavy croppers, so one to three plants are sufficient for the aver-

age family. The plants are self-fertile, and each needs a space of about 2.5-3m (8-10ft).

Planting

Dig the ground thoroughly in late summer, and remove all weeds. On shallow or quick-draining soil, work in at least one bucketful of organic matter, such as strong manure, to each planting site.

Plant the canes in autumn. Immediately after planting, cut the canes back to a bud about 23cm (9in) above ground level, and mulch with well-rotted manure or garden compost.

Training

Loganberries and other similar cane fruits produce the finest fruit on canes developed during the previous season. They should be trained so that the fruiting shoots are kept well away from new replacement shoots. This makes management easier and reduces the spread of fungal diseases. They can be trained by the fan system or the one-way system; both methods require a support framework of posts and wires.

Use 10-12 gauge wire stretched horizontally between two posts or against a sunny wall or fence to a height of 1.5-1.8m (5-6ft); place

2 The following year, train new growth upwards through the middle of the fan. When the new canes reach the top wire train them horizontally along it. Leave last year's stems tied in – fruit will be produced on laterals from these canes.

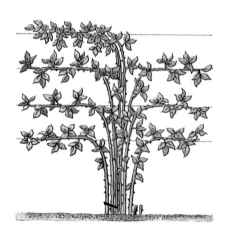

3 In autumn, when all the berries have been picked, cut the fruited canes down to ground level. Untie the current year's shoots from their temporary position along the top wire and tie them in to replace the fruited cut-down shoots. Repeat steps 2 and 3 annually.

Boysenberry

Japanese wineberry

the wires 30cm (1ft) apart, with the lowest 60cm (2ft) above the ground, and secure them to posts or to vine eyes set in the wall.

With the fan method, the fruiting canes are fanned out to the left and the right while replacement stems are trained vertically up the middle and tied to the top wire. With the one-way system, the fruiting canes are trained and tied in to one side of the centre of the plant, while the new stems are tied in to the other side (see also page 43).

In mid autumn when all the fruit has been picked, cut the fruited canes down to ground level. Untie the current year's shoots from their temporary positions and tie them in to replace the old cut-down shoots. Fruit grows on the laterals of the previous year's canes.

Watering and feeding
Water only during dry spells in summer. In late winter feed with 15g per sq m (½oz per sq yd) of sulphate of potash. Add 50g (2oz) of superphosphate every third year. In early spring every year feed with 15g per sq m (½oz per sq yd) of sulphate of ammonia and mulch afterwards with rotted manure or compost. Make sure all top dressings and mulches extend 90cm (3ft) each side of the row.

Harvesting
Pick loganberries when they turn claret red, starting around late summer and continuing for several weeks. Other hybrid berries turn different colours, such as black or purple, when ripe. Always pick loganberry fruit with its plug (unlike raspberries). Any surplus fruit is suitable for jam-making and freezing.

HYBRID BERRIES

Loganberry
The virus-free 'LY 59' is a good all-rounder, cropping well under most conditions. There is also a thornless variety, 'LY 654', which gives slightly smaller yields but is easier to manage. The New Zealand loganberry has near-black fruits.

Medana tayberry
A virus-free hybrid, raised by the Scottish Horticultural Research Institute, this berry has very large, bright purple fruits – twice the weight of raspberries – and a very high yield in mid to late summer. The flavour is sweeter and milder than the raspberry.

Boysenberry
This berry has thornless canes, making it easy to handle and pick. The purplish black fruits – large and sweet – are ready from mid to late summer. It will thrive in dry soils, but is not recommended for colder areas.

Japanese wineberry
Attractive crimson canes are covered with red hairs in autumn and winter. The plants are smallish and can be grown 1.8m (6ft) apart. The small, scarlet berries are best used for jam and wines as they have little flavour and consist of only a few drupelets.

Hildaberry
Named by an amateur gardener in honour of his wife when he crossed the tayberry with the boysenberry, this type has reddish-black berries the size of a fifty-pence piece. Crops in late summer.

Youngberry
Vigorous plants fruiting from mid summer to early autumn. Prolific cropper with black, square berries, similar in flavour to mulberries.

Pests and diseases
The most common pest is the raspberry beetle – small, soft patches on ripe fruits contain a yellow maggot. To prevent attacks, spray with derris or malathion at petal fall.

Plants may also suffer from cane spot, which shows as small purplish spots. Cut out and burn affected canes. Spray with benomyl or thiophanate-methyl at bud-burst and again at petal fall.

Spur blight (dark purple blotches on canes and buds) may attack loganberries. Treatment is the same as for cane spot.

MELONS

**Succulent cantaloupe melons are
not difficult to grow under cloches or frames
or in large greenhouses.**

Melons, which are related to cucumbers and marrows, are usually grown in the vegetable garden, under cloches and in frames in southern gardens. Greenhouse cultivation produces more reliable results, but while melons under glass are no more difficult to grow than cucumbers, they take up a lot more space.

Only two types of melon can be grown in the British climate – cantaloupes and casaba melons, also known as musk melons because of their distinctive scent. They are raised annually from seed.

Soil preparation
Choose the sunniest, most sheltered site available in the garden for cloches or frames. Melons do best in alkaline soil, so if a test shows the soil to be acid, lime it at least six weeks before preparing the site. In mid spring dig an area of approximately 30 x 60cm (1 x 2ft), 1 spit deep, for each plant. Spread a bucketful of well rotted organic matter liberally over the base, and return the top soil. On light soil, top-dress with a fertilizer which is high in potash.

Growing in frames and cloches
In mid spring sow single seeds of cantaloupe melons 20mm (¾in) deep in 7.5cm (3in) pots of seed compost. Raising the seedlings is the most critical stage in the development of melons, and any check to seedling growth is usually fatal. Ideally, raise the seedlings in a propagating unit, but failing that water each pot well and enclose it in a clear plastic bag. Leave in an airing cupboard or near a radiator, making sure that the compost remains damp and the temperature steady until the seeds germinate. Move the pots to a warm window-sill and

pot before the roots become cramped into 13cm (5in) pots.

A fortnight before planting out in late spring, place frames or cloches in position on the prepared site to warm the soil. Set the plants 60cm (2ft) apart under cloches or singly in the centre of average-sized frames and Dutch lights from the end of spring onwards. If low night temperatures are forecast, cover the glass

with newspapers, old carpet, or similar material.

Disturb the roots as little as possible when planting out, and water in the plants to ensure they don't suffer a growth check. Plant so that the top of the soil-ball is just above the surface. This lessens the chance of collar rot.

When a plant has developed four or five leaves, pinch out the growing point immediately above

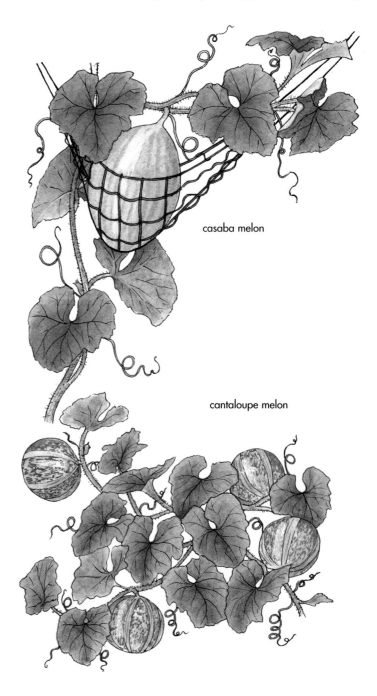

casaba melon

cantaloupe melon

▶ **Melons** Cantaloupes are the hardier type and can be grown in the open if protected with frames or cloches. The fruits are smaller than those of casaba melons, but have sweeter flesh. Casaba melons are only suitable for greenhouse cultivation.

MELONS IN COLD FRAMES AND CLOCHES

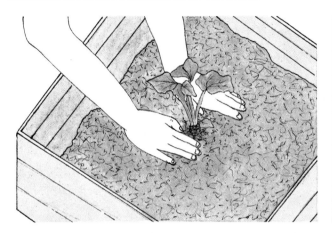

1 Place frames in the sunniest spot available. A fortnight later plant out one strong-growing seedling in the centre of each frame, with the soil-ball just above the surface, and water in.

2 When the plant has developed four or five additional leaves, pinch out the growing point immediately above the fifth leaf to encourage side-shoots to form.

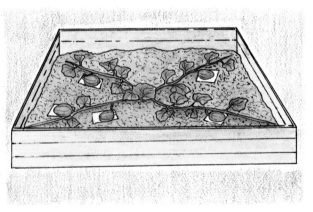

3 Allow only four side-shoots to develop – pinch out all the others. Direct them towards the corners of the frame; under cloches keep two shoots and train them in opposite directions.

4 In hot weather shade frames and cloches; water thoroughly every day. Pinch out shoot tips two leaves beyond the fruits. Rest fruits on ceramic or plastic tiles to keep them clean.

the fifth leaf to encourage lower side-shoots to form.

Only four side-shoots should be allowed to form on each plant in a cold frame – pinch out any others that grow. Direct these singly towards each corner; under cloches, retain only two side-shoots and train one lengthways in each direction.

To prevent the atmosphere from becoming too humid, increase ventilation when the plants become established, and again when flowers appear, to make it easy for insects to enter and pollinate the plants. Pollinate by hand when insects are scarce.

When the main shoots on each plant reach the limit of the frame

▶ **Melon props** Under cloches and in frames melons need protection from damp soil, slugs and snails. Set each fruit on a layer of straw or, for maximum protection, on an upturned plastic flower pot to avoid soiling.

GROWING GREENHOUSE MELONS

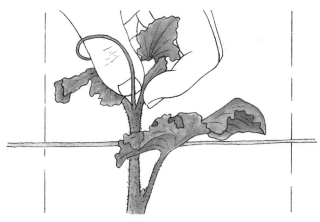

1 Remove the growing tip when the plants are 15cm (6in) high and pinch out all but the two strongest side-shoots. Tie them either side to eaves-height canes and train them up.

2 When plants reach the level of the crosswires, pinch out the growing point and train laterals horizontally. Slow down growth by lightly thinning laterals every few days.

3 Thin fruits when walnut-sized by removing any that are smaller or larger than the average size. Leave four fruits on each plant, more on small-fruited cantaloupe types.

4 Melons need supporting when they reach the size of tennis balls. Attach 5cm (2in) square netting to the horizontal wires and suspend the fruits in the nets.

or cloche, stop them by pinching out the growing point just above a leaf; do the same for side-shoots. If growth becomes very crowded, remove some side-shoots completely – but leave those bearing fruit.

Shade the cloches or frames with whitewash or proprietary shading, and water the plants heavily every day in hot weather. When the fruits are the size of a walnut, thin them out until there is only one on each shoot. Aim to leave similar-size fruits on each shoot, and remove any others that form too late to grow to maturity. Pinch out the tip of the shoot two leaves beyond the fruit.

Place a ceramic or plastic tile under the growing fruit to keep it clear of the soil, which can rot the fruit in damp weather, and to reduce the chances of slug damage.

Greenhouse melons
Different methods are needed for growing melons under glass,

ASSISTING POLLINATION

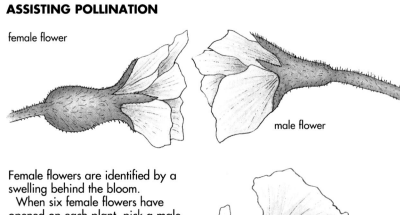

female flower

male flower

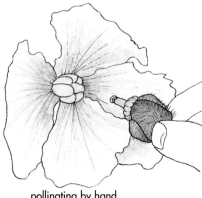

pollinating by hand

Female flowers are identified by a swelling behind the bloom.

When six female flowers have opened on each plant, pick a male flower – it needn't be taken from the same plant. Test the male flower for ripe pollen; it should leave yellow grains when stroked on the palm of the hand. Strip off the petals and gently press the centre to the centre of each of the female flowers. Or, transfer the pollen with a dry camel-hair brush or cotton wool.

Pollinate each female flower for two or three days in succession, using a new male each time.

VARIETIES TO CHOOSE

'Blenheim Orange' – casaba; medium-sized fruits; grey-green, finely netted skin; orange flesh; cold or heated greenhouse.

'Hero of Lockinge' – casaba; pale green skin; white flesh; large, oval fruits; cold or heated greenhouse.

'Ogen' – cantaloupe; dark green and yellow striped skin; round, small – 9-10cm (3½-4in) diameter – can be grown more densely; green flesh; early cropper; cold greenhouse, cloche or frame.

'Sweetheart' – F1 hybrid; cantaloupe; grey-green skin; firm, salmon-pink/scarlet flesh; medium-sized; very quick to mature; cloche, frame or cold greenhouse.

mainly because they require support. They are usually grown as double-stemmed cordons.

The greenhouse should be at least 1.8m (6ft) high because each melon is trained up the side wall and along the roof in order to receive maximum light and heat.

Sow in early spring in pots of seed compost at a steady minimum temperature of 16°C (61°F) before and after germination – this takes 10-14 days or seven at the ideal temperature of 21°C (70°F). A heated propagator guarantees the best germination conditions.

Make sure the young plants receive maximum light. The temperature during the day may rise sharply – ventilate the greenhouse if it reaches 27°C (80°F). Pot the seedlings on as they grow.

When the plants have developed four or five leaves, transplant them to their final growing positions in the greenhouse border, which should have been prepared in the same way as for frames and cloches – or to 23cm (9in) pots filled with a proprietary potting compost. Set the plants, or pots, 75cm (2½ft) apart.

Insert two canes 25cm (10in) apart along each plant to the height of the greenhouse eaves. Fasten horizontal wires, using vine eyes at least 15cm (6in) long, to the glazing bars on the side wall and to the underside of the roof at 30cm (1ft) intervals to allow air to circulate freely when the plants grow to full size.

If the greenhouse cannot accommodate permanent wires,

attach 15cm (6in) square mesh plastic netting to the gable ends and stretch it taut across the area.

Pinch out the growing points when the plants reach 15cm (6in) high. Pinch out all but the two strongest side-shoots that form and train them to the canes.

Continue tying the shoots to the canes and then the wires until they are 1.5-1.8m (5-6ft) long. Then pinch out their growing points.

Laterals develop from the two main stems. Tie these to the wires or plastic netting. Pinch out the tips of the laterals when they have developed four or five leaves, or remove entire laterals if growth becomes very crowded. Pinch out and thin every few days until growth slows down, but never too much at once.

To ensure that hand pollination works, check that male flowers are shedding pollen. Brush the tip of the centre with a finger or stroke it on the palm of the hand, and look for deposits of the fine pollen.

Pollinate when there are about six female flowers open on each plant. Female flowers are distinguished by a swelling of the embryo fruits behind the blooms. Pick male flowers, remove the petals and press the centre to the centre of each female plant.

When the young fruits begin to swell, remove the largest and the smallest, leaving only those of similar size on each plant. Any discrepancies in size encourage the large fruits to develop at the expense of smaller ones, creating an uneven crop. Allow four fruits to develop on each plant unless it is a small-fruited variety.

When the melons reach the size of tennis balls, they need to be supported in nets strung from the wires or plastic mesh. Use special melon nets or make your own slings from 5cm (2in) square netting.

Greenhouse management
During hot weather maintain a humid atmosphere by damping down and lightly misting the leaves daily. Ventilate when the temperature rises above 27°C (80°F) during the day, but try to ensure a minimum night temperature of 16°C (61°F) by closing the ventilators before dark.

From mid summer to early autumn, the greenhouse needs partial shade on the south side to prevent scald. Apply a wash on south-facing glass.

Harvesting
Cut melons from the stalks just before they are completely ripe. A change in colour indicates that maturity is imminent. Cut down or stop watering altogether at this stage. The fruit becomes slightly soft at the end farthest from the stalk, fine cracks appear around the stalk, and there is a delicious smell of ripening melon. Cut the stalk and put the fruit in a warm, dry place for a day or two.

Pests and diseases
In the greenhouse control red spider mites, scale insects and whiteflies biologically or with sprays of malathion.

Cucumber mosaic virus shows as a yellow mottling of leaves. There is no chemical cure; destroy affected plants.

Melon 'Ogen'

RASPBERRIES

**Raspberries are one of the most delicious
summer fruits and consistently produce large crops,
even in cool, wet summers.**

Raspberries are well worth growing in most gardens. Plot for plot, they provide a higher yield for the space they occupy than any other cane fruit; they freeze well, retaining their flavour better than strawberries; and they thrive under a variety of conditions. They are particularly suited to northern gardens where summer days are long and not too hot; commercially, Scotland is Britain's largest raspberry producer.

There are two types of raspberry plants: summer-fruiting varieties which produce fruit on the previous season's shoots between mid and late summer; and autumn-cropping varieties which fruit on the current season's growth from late summer onwards. Autumn varieties generally carry lighter crops than summer-cropping raspberries. Gourmets maintain that yellow-fruited autumn raspberries are superior in flavour to red summer berries.

Soil and site
Choose a sunny site if possible, although raspberry canes do tolerate some shade provided that the site is protected against strong winds. Raspberries need a moisture-retaining but well-drained soil. For the best results the soil should be slightly acid. Raspber-

PLANTING

Plant canes up to 38cm (15in) apart in trenches 23cm (9in) wide and 7.5cm (3in) deep. Ensure that the roots are well spread out. Use your heel to firm the soil.

ries can be grown in dry, sandy and alkaline soils as long as the plot is given plenty of water in dry weather and receives liberal amounts of good-quality manure.

Prepare the bed a few months before planting the canes. Dig a trench one spit deep, fork up the base and mix in a thick layer of well-rotted manure or compost with the top soil – this is particularly important if the soil is alkaline. Rake in a surface dressing of general-purpose fertilizer at a rate of 50g per sq m (2oz per sq yd). A plot measuring 3.6 x 2.7m (12 x 9ft) will support three rows of seven canes. Expect an annual yield of 10kg (20lb) from this.

A row of raspberry canes makes an attractive summer screen for the vegetable garden and does not cast too much shade.

Cultivation
Raspberries are extremely susceptible to virus diseases. Therefore always buy one-year-old canes, certified as disease-free, from a reputable nursery. Plant out the canes in mid autumn if possible, or any time during the winter until early spring.

Before planting, set stout 2.4m (8ft) high posts at the ends of each row, sinking them 60cm (2ft) into the ground. Make sure the posts

▲ **Raspberries** Vying in popularity with strawberries, raspberries have a much longer productive life. Well-managed canes will crop for up to 10 years, yielding deliciously juicy crops in summer or autumn.

are made of pre-treated timber to avoid rotting. Secure three 12-13 gauge galvanized wires to the posts, spacing them 75cm (2½ft), 1.1m (3½ft) and 1.7m (5½ft) from the ground for summer-fruiting varieties.

You can also attach short horizontal pieces of wood to the end posts and secure parallel wires to them. In this way, the canes grow up between the wires and do not need to be tied in.

Autumn-fruiting canes do not grow as tall as summer varieties. Space two parallel support wires 75cm (2½ft) and 1.5m (5ft) from the ground and set cross-ties every 30cm (1ft) so that the canes can be supported without being tied.

For each row dig a trench 23cm (9in) wide and 7.5cm (3in) deep. Plant the canes 38cm (15in) apart with their roots well spread out. Cover the roots with soil and firm it down with your heel. Space rows 1.8m (6ft) apart.

After planting out, cut down each cane to 30cm (1ft) above soil level. This will stop fruit being borne the following summer, but will make the plants more vigorous in the following years. Each year apply a mulch of coir, forest bark, well-rotted grass cuttings or garden compost in early spring to feed the canes and improve moisture retention. Apply 25g per sq m (1oz per sq yd) of sulphate of potash in mid winter and 15g per sq m (½oz per sq yd) of sulphate of ammonia in late spring.

Control weeds by shallow hoeing or by smothering the ground with rotted straw. Give the plants plenty of water in summer.

Protect the ripening fruit from attacks by birds by throwing plastic netting over the canes. Ideally, raspberries, like other soft fruit, should be grown in portable or permanent fruit cages. Such structures offer full protection from birds, in summer as well as winter when finches can completely destroy the immature flower and growth buds.

Raspberries throw out numerous underground suckers; unless these are needed for increasing the stock, pull them out as soon as they can be grasped – cutting them off merely encourages more suckers from below ground.

Training and pruning

In the first spring after planting, cut out the original stems at ground level and allow the new canes to grow on. Tie them to the wires with soft string, spacing them evenly, with about 10cm (4in) between them. These canes will carry the following season's crop. Rub out flower buds as they appear to prevent fruiting in the first year. After leaf fall, or in late winter, tip the canes to induce vigour in the lower buds; trim the tallest canes to just above the top wire (see also pages 42-43).

In subsequent years, after harvesting summer-fruiting varieties, remove the canes that have carried raspberries, severing them just above ground level. Select the strongest current-year canes (allow a maximum of eight per plant) and tie them to the wires, spacing them 7.5-10cm (3-4in) apart. Cut out the remaining new shoots.

In late winter, cut off the top of each cane to a healthy, strong-looking bud a little way above the top wire.

Autumn-fruiting raspberries fruit on canes of the current year. Cut the fruited canes down to the ground in late winter; new ones, which will carry that autumn's crop, begin to appear soon afterwards. Tie the canes in place as they grow.

Raising new plants

If the canes are healthy and free of any signs of disease, dig up suckers in late autumn and replant them to increase the stock and to extend the cropping area. Generally, raspberry canes begin to deteriorate after eight years when they should be replaced with new, virus-free stock. Plant the canes in a fresh site.

Harvesting and storing

Pick raspberries when they are a good colour all over. They will come away easily from their stalks, leaving the cores behind. Raspberries do not keep well, so eat or freeze them at once.

Pests and diseases

The most common raspberry pests are aphids, raspberry beetle and red spider mites; spray the canes with malathion or fenitrothion.

Diseases include cane spot, cane and spur blight, which show as discoloured and splitting canes; cut out badly affected canes and spray new ones with a copper fungicide. Grey mould rots the fruits; where the disease is known to occur, spray with benomyl as the flowers open and repeat several times. Virus diseases may show as yellow discoloration on the leaves; there is no cure and all affected plants should be dug up and destroyed. Replant, in a different site, with new canes which are certified as being virus-free.

Summer raspberry 'Malling Jewel'

Autumn raspberry 'Fallgold'

VARIETIES TO CHOOSE

Summer fruiting

'Glen Clova' – firm, bright red fruits; heavy cropper but susceptible to viruses; early.

'Leo' – slightly acid bright firm, orange-red fruits. Vigorous canes resistant to spur blight. Cane spot can be a problem; late-cropping.

'Malling Jewel' – large, firm fruit; popular variety; moderate cropper; resistant to aphids and virus diseases; early.

Autumn fruiting

'Autumn Bliss' – large, dark red fruits; heavy cropper; aphid resistant.

'Fallgold' – sweet, mild-flavoured yellow-fruited variety.

RED AND WHITE CURRANTS

**Easy to grow and long-lived, red and white
currants are grown as bushes or space-saving cordons.
They need different treatment to black currants.**

Red and white currants are closely related to black currants, but have a different growth habit and are therefore pruned in a different way. Red and white currants fruit on shoots of the current year, black currants on stems produced in the previous season. Both red and white currants can be grown as bushes or cordons; the latter are ideal for a small garden.

Site and soil preparation

Red and white currants grow well in any moisture-retaining soil, as long as it is not liable to become waterlogged. Ideally the soil should be neutral to slightly acid. They are not as greedy for nourishment as black currants, but like plenty of manure or garden compost dug into the soil.

Currants suffer from potash deficiency in the soil; before planting apply a potash-high fertilizer following the manufacturer's recommended rates, together with a dressing of well-rotted manure or good garden compost. An open site in full sun or semi-shade is best, though cordons can be trained against walls and fences of any aspect.

Cultivation

Mid autumn is the best time for planting, but any time from mid autumn to early spring is suitable,
as long as the soil is not frozen or wet. Space bushes 1.5m (5ft) apart each way and cordons 38cm (15in) apart. Plant double cordons 60cm (2ft) apart and allow 30cm (1ft) between each stem of a multiple cordon. After planting, cut the shoots of all bush forms back to outward-pointing buds, the fourth above the base of the shoot.

Cordons should be trained up vertical canes, for support and straight growth. Before planting, stretch wires between end posts or along a fence or wall, setting the first wire 45cm (1½ft) from the ground and the second wire 60cm (2ft) above the first. Set the canes at 38cm (15in) intervals.

After planting a cordon, choose the strongest shoot as the leader and eventual main stem – or choose two shoots for a double cordon. Cut off all other shoots to

PRUNING NEWLY PLANTED CURRANTS

1 Immediately after planting bushes, cut all shoots back to outward-pointing buds, the fourth or so from the base of each shoot.

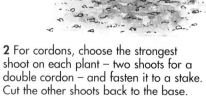

2 For cordons, choose the strongest shoot on each plant – two shoots for a double cordon – and fasten it to a stake. Cut the other shoots back to the base.

▲ **Red and white currants** Avoid planting in frost hollows. Currants flower early and hard spring frosts can ruin a crop. The long fruit trusses ripen from mid to late summer; late-ripening varieties are recommended for cold areas as the flowers usually escape spring frosts.

WINTER AND SUMMER PRUNING

1 Prune bushes severely in the second winter after planting, cutting the shoots back by about half their length, to just above outward-facing buds.

2 In succeeding winters, cut back the leading shoots to half their length and laterals to two buds. Aim for an open-centred goblet shape.

3 Prune cordons in winter by cutting back each leading shoot by one-third and reducing each of the lateral shoots to a single bud.

4 Both bushes and cordons should be pruned again by mid summer. Cut all lateral shoots back to three or five leaves from the base.

within 2.5cm (1in) of the base. Prune each of the lateral shoots that grow from the chosen stem to two buds (see also page 45).

Tie the cordons to their canes, and fasten the canes to the wires.

Mulch bushes and cordons in spring with a 5cm (2in) layer of well-rotted garden compost or manure and feed them with 25g per sq m (1oz per sq yd) of sulphate of potash in mid to late winter.

To promote strong growth, feed again in spring with 25g per sq m (1oz per sq yd) of sulphate of ammonia. Every third year, apply 50g per sq m (2oz per sq yd) of superphosphate.

Protect red and white currant plants on frosty nights by covering them with hessian or two layers of netting; net the bushes in winter as well, and when the berries are ripening.

Raising new plants
Propagate red and white currant plants in mid autumn, taking well-ripened shoots, 25-38cm (10-15in) long, as cuttings. Take out a V-shaped trench about 20cm (8in) deep. Sprinkle a layer of sand along the bottom and place the cuttings 15cm (6in) apart in the trench, with only two buds showing above soil level.

The rooted cuttings can be planted out in their final positions the following autumn. Plant them at the same depth as before and remove any low side-shoots so that the bush has a clean stem 10-15cm (4-6in) long. Cut upper branches back by half their length, to outward-facing buds.

Harvesting and storing
Pick red and white currants as soon as they are ripe and eat, cook or freeze them as soon as possible.

Pests and diseases
The main pests of red and white currants are aphids, sawfly caterpillars and capsid bugs; spray with a systemic insecticide just before flowering and repeat after flowering if necessary.

The diseases most likely to occur are coral spot and leaf spot. Cut out all diseased wood and improve growing conditions; healthy plants are less likely to be attacked by fungal diseases.

Red currant 'Laxton No 1'

White currant 'White Versailles'

RHUBARB

Rhubarb is a very reliable crop – its tender pink stems are ready for harvesting in late spring.

Rhubarb is a prolific crop and easy to grow: once established, it will keep growing well year after year, with little attention. It is usually grown in the vegetable garden, but it can also be fitted into a herbaceous border or the odd corner of the garden. In the vegetable garden, choose a spot that does not interfere with the annual rotation plan as rhubarb can occupy the same piece of ground for up to five years, or more.

Three or four plants should be enough for a family garden, but stalks should not be pulled for the first two years after planting while the crowns are built up.

Rhubarb which is three years old or more can be forced indoors or outdoors for use in late winter or early spring; the tender pink stalks of forced rhubarb have a more delicate, less acid flavour than maincrop stalks.

Planting

It is possible to raise rhubarb from seed sown in mid spring, but it is much easier – and quicker – to buy mature roots (crowns) from a nursery, or lift established plants and divide the roots. Each piece of root must have at least one strong new growth bud.

Plant while the buds are still dormant, in late winter or early spring, or in autumn. Rhubarb needs rich, fairly heavy soil which has been well manured and completely cleared of perennial weeds.

Allow 90cm (3ft) between plants. Before planting, dig holes deep enough to take the woody part of the rootstock – leave the buds just showing above the surface. Tread the soil in firmly round the roots and water well.

Sow rhubarb seed outdoors in mid spring, in drills 15mm (½in) deep and 30cm (1ft) apart, or in a frame in early spring. Thin seedlings to 15cm (6in) apart and transplant them to their permanent positions the following year.

forced stems

maincrop stems

▲ **Rhubarb** Occupying a permanent plot in the vegetable garden, rhubarb will crop for many years and established plants can be forced for a late-winter harvest.

Looking after the crop

Mulch the plants deeply in early spring with well-rotted manure or garden compost; fork in the mulch after cropping. Dress the soil in mid summer with a compound fertilizer at the rate of 100g per sq m (4oz per sq yd) and water it in.

Harvesting

Do not pull any stems in the two years after planting. Once the clumps are established, pull the stalks freely, but do not remove all the stalks from one plant at any one time. Harvest rhubarb from mid spring to early summer.

Rhubarb leaves are poisonous, so cut them off and leave them on the compost heap. Remove also at ground level any seed stalks which merely serve to deprive the roots of nourishment.

Forcing

Rhubarb can be forced indoors or

PLANTING AND HARVESTING RHUBARB

1 Plant the crowns (mature roots) so that the roots are covered but the growth buds protrude above ground.

2 To harvest, grasp the stalks firmly at the base and twist from the crown. Don't pull all the stems from one plant.

FORCING INDOORS

1 Lift one or two plants in late autumn and turn them over to expose the roots to frost. This will encourage early dormancy and faster growth during forcing. Use only plants approaching 'retirement age' – three years old.

2 In early winter set the crowns in boxes, the right way up, cover them lightly with moist soil or compost and water thoroughly. Place the boxes in a dark shed. Maintain a fairly warm temperature, about 7-18°C (45-64°F).

3 Cover the boxes with black polythene, to keep out the light. The stalks should be ready for pulling in five to six weeks. After all the stalks have been pulled, discard the crowns; they are too depleted to be replanted outdoors.

outside. Choose strong clumps of plants, at least three years old. For outdoor forcing, invert a large bucket or barrel over the crowns in mid or late winter, banking it round with plenty of straw. This should advance the crop by three weeks. For later forcing, cover the crowns in their beds with straw or strawy manure to advance the crop by a couple of weeks. Do not force crowns in successive years.

For indoor forcing, lift plants in mid or late autumn, after the leaves have died back, and turn them over, exposing the roots to frost. This produces a premature 'false winter', making the plants dormant, so they will grow faster when brought into warmth and darkness, as if it were spring.

FORCING OUTDOORS

1 In late winter, invert a bucket, barrel or dustbin over a mature crown and bank it round with straw or leaves, for insulation. You may have to weigh or rope the bin down and secure the insulation, to guard against winds.

In early winter, plant the roots in boxes, the right way up and cover them thinly with soil. Cover the boxes with black polythene and keep them in a dark shed, at a temperature of 7-18°C (45-64°F).

Pests and diseases
Rhubarb may suffer from crown rot – look out for spindly, pale leaves and stalks and cavities in the crowns. Dig the plants up immediately, and do not replant the infected area.

Yellow toadstools may indicate honey fungus. Dig up diseased roots and burn them.

Rhubarb is very rarely attacked by pests, but watch out for stem and bulb eelworms, and swift moth caterpillars.

2 The plants should not normally need watering and the crop should be ready for harvesting after about six weeks. The crowns can be forced again, but leave them to crop normally for at least two years before forcing again.

Rhubarb 'Timperley Early'

VARIETIES TO CHOOSE

Growing from seed
'Early Red' – long, bright scarlet stalks; plants crop early.

'Glaskin's Perpetual' – green stems; can be pulled in first year; least acid of varieties.

'Victoria' – green stalks shaded red; for harvesting in late spring.

Growing from crowns
'Strawberry Rhubarb' – deep red stalks retain their colour when cooked; late-maturing for harvesting into early autumn.

'Timperley Early' – early; thin stems; excellent for forcing in late winter and early spring.

STRAWBERRIES

Probably the most popular of all soft fruits, strawberries and cream are synonymous with summer. They are quick and easy to grow.

▲ **Strawberry pots** Frost-proof terracotta pots with holes in the sides are ideal where space is limited. They give maximum returns as well as making an attractive garden feature.

▼ **Strawberry 'Hapil'** This variety ripens in mid summer with conical-shaped bright red fruits.

There are three types of strawberry – summer-fruiting which crop once in early to mid summer; others, known as 'perpetual', ever-bearing or remontant strawberries, which produce several crops in succession between early summer and autumn; and alpine strawberries which bear small berries throughout the summer and are prized for their rich, sweet flavour.

In a large garden, strawberries can be picked from late spring to mid autumn if a number of different varieties are planted, and cloches can be used to extend the growing season. But even the smallest garden can accommodate strawberry plants, and if ground space is lacking, they can be grown in containers ranging from specially designed strawberry barrels and towerpots to hanging baskets and window boxes.

SUMMER-FRUITING AND PERPETUAL STRAWBERRIES

Usually grown from small plants called runners, strawberries will grow in most soils, although they prefer rich, well-drained, slightly acid soils.

Plant early varieties in a sheltered position and main crops in an open sunny bed, facing south.

Dig the bed thoroughly two or three weeks before planting. Work in one bucket of well-rotted manure or garden compost per sq

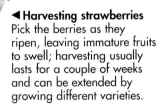

◀ **Harvesting strawberries** Pick the berries as they ripen, leaving immature fruits to swell; harvesting usually lasts for a couple of weeks and can be extended by growing different varieties.

▲ **Planting strawberries** Take out holes 5cm (2in) deeper than the roots. Make a mound in the bottom of the hole and spread the roots over it, so that the base of the plant is level with the surface. Fill in and firm the soil.

m/sq yd. Fork in a general fertilizer – about 75g per sq m (3oz per sq yd) – and rake to a tilth.

Change the site of the strawberry bed every three years to prevent the build-up of diseases and to give the soil a rest.

Planting

Strawberries give a quicker return than any other fruit – rooted runners set out in late summer will fruit early the following summer. Always buy young plants which are certified to be free of virus diseases.

Plant summer-fruiting varieties as early as possible – between mid to late summer, and no later than early autumn – to get a good first crop the following year. Space the plants 45cm (1½ft) apart, with 75cm (2½ft) between the rows.

If planting is delayed until late autumn or spring, the plants will not have time to become established in their first year. All flowers should therefore be pinched out the first summer to encourage sturdy plants for fruiting in the second season.

Summer-fruiting strawberries usually crop for three seasons. But some gardeners choose to grow them as annuals – setting

▶ **Block planting** Instead of planting in long rows, set young runners in blocks 75cm (2½ft) apart in all directions. This saves space in irregularly-sized plots.

out young plantlets each year. This produces higher-quality fruit and prevents virus diseases, but also reduces the yield.

Plant perpetual strawberries in late summer to produce fruit the following year, or plant in early spring to fruit the same year. Remove any flowers that appear before late spring.

Replace perpetuals each year as the size and weight of the crop deteriorate in the second year.

Care and maintenance

Water the plants thoroughly just after planting and during dry spells. As the fruits begin to ripen, water sparingly and only in the morning, to prevent mould.

Feed with sulphate of potash at the rate of 15g per sq m (½oz per sq yd) in mid winter. If the soil is light or growth is poor, feed again in mid spring.

Scatter slug pellets among the plants when the developing strawberries are heavy enough to weigh down the trusses.

Protect strawberry plants from birds and squirrels by covering them with nylon netting supported by canes.

Harvesting

Pick strawberries in the morning when they are still cool. Try to pick them by the stalk to avoid bruising them.

Clearing the bed

When the strawberries have finished cropping in autumn, clear up the strawberry bed.

On summer-fruiting varieties in the first and second years, cut off the old leaves and any unwanted runners. Rake off the old straw and leaves and burn them to kill pests and diseases. Fork lightly between the rows.

Perpetuals grown for one year only and summer-fruiting strawberries in their third year should be dug up and burnt. On perpetual plants grown on for a second crop, remove and burn old faded leaves. In early autumn, cover the plants with cloches to provide a late crop.

▲ **Fruit protection** To keep the berries clean and clear of the soil, use special strawberry mats. Once all danger of frost is definitely past, tuck the mats underneath the berries. Alternatively, you can spread black polythene or straw over the ground between plants – such mulches also smother weeds.

Propagation

Summer fruiters and most perpetuals are propagated by runners – new plants appearing on the mother plant. However, some perpetuals don't produce runners and these should be increased by division.

Runners appear near the mother plant in early and mid summer. The simplest method of propagation is to 'layer' the runners.

Look for the healthiest plants during summer, but avoid using more than two, or at most three, runners from the same plant. Peg them into the soil with pieces of bent wire. On dry and poor soils, it is preferable to peg the runners into small pots filled with compost and sunk into the soil. Pinch out the outer part of the runner extending from each pegged plant, but do not sever the runner from the parent until it is well-rooted. Remove all other runners not wanted for propagation.

Division Dig up mature perpetuals in late summer to early autumn, after fruiting. Break the crowns into pieces taken from the outside and with as much root as possible; plant the divisions in a fresh site and discard the old centre of the crowns.

Forcing strawberries

Strawberries grow well under cover – a protected crop is ready up to three weeks earlier than strawberries grown in the open.

Cloches and polythene tunnels Put the covers in place between mid winter and early spring. Cover perpetuals in early autumn for a late crop.

Cold frames Use pot-grown strawberries or alternatively, in

▲ **Taking runners** Peg the chosen runners into the soil with U-shaped wires and pinch off the outer part of each runner. After 4-6 weeks, when the runners have rooted, sever the plantlets from the parent plants and set them out.

mid to late summer, put newly rooted runners directly into the soil in the cold frame 30cm (12in) apart. Keep the lights closed from mid winter onwards, opening them during the day in mild spells and closing them before dark.

Greenhouses In mid winter put a batch of pot-grown strawberries into a cool greenhouse. The fruits should be ready in late spring.

If the greenhouse is heated, gradually increase the temperature as the flowers appear. The strawberries should be ready for picking in early spring.

Pests and diseases

Aphids, red spider mites and capsid bugs are the most common

▲ **Forcing strawberries** Set young plants at intervals of 30cm (1ft) in rows 45-60cm (1½-2ft) apart. Ventilate the cloches to avoid high temperatures during the day in spring and cover with sacking when frost is forecast.

pests, causing stunted growth and yellowing of leaves; spray with malathion or a systemic insecticide. Slugs, snails and beetles eat the fruits.

The most likely disorders are virus diseases, frost damage and leaf spot. Grey mould (botrytis) is a common disease which causes the fruits to rot; the fungus appears at flowering time when plants should be sprayed with benomyl, carbendazim or thiophanate-methyl.

▼ **Towerpot strawberries** Multi-storey containers can hold up to 12 plants. They save space and many have useful features such as self-watering devices.

▲ **Alpine strawberries**, with small flowers and fruit, are highly ornamental.

▲ **'Gento'**, a perpetual variety, produces large, crimson berries.

◄ **'Baron Solemacher'** is one of the most reliable alpine strawberries.

ALPINE STRAWBERRIES

The flowers and fruits of alpine strawberries are smaller than other kinds of strawberry, but they have several advantages. They are very decorative and can be grown as an edging to flower borders. They also seed themselves freely and are rarely troubled by pests and diseases. Finally, they survive in partial shade.

Alpine strawberries thrive in rich, well-drained and slightly acid soil. Raise them each year from seed (most varieties don't produce runners) or buy the young plants in spring.

Growing alpines

The soil and site preparation is much the same as for other types of strawberry. Sow seeds in early autumn in pots of seed compost. Alternatively, sow in early spring under glass at 20°C (68°F).

Germination is erratic, but the seedlings should be ready for pricking out by late autumn. Transplant into trays of potting compost at 2.5cm (1in) intervals.

Overwinter the plants in a cold frame or cold greenhouse before planting them out in mid to late spring. Plant every 30cm (12in) in rows the same distance apart.

Protect with cloches if there is frost about when they start flowering in late spring. Keep the soil moist and feed every two weeks.

Alpine strawberries fruit over a long period, producing small red berries continuously or in batches from summer to autumn. Late berries are often larger than early-summer fruits.

VARIETIES TO CHOOSE

Summer-fruiting varieties

'Pantagruella' – earliest cropper, in late spring.

'Elvira' – early, heavy cropper; large fruit; good for forcing.

'Cambridge Favourite' – fruits early summer; reliable heavy cropper.

'Grandee' – fruits early summer; large fruits; heavy cropper.

'Hapil' – fruits early summer; good cropper; suitable for light soils.

'Redgauntlet' – fruits mid summer; reliable heavy cropper.

'Tenira' – fruits mid summer; heavy cropper in first year, then deteriorates.

Perpetual varieties

'Aromel' – fruits late summer to mid autumn; moderate cropper.

'Calypso' – heavy crops from late summer to early frost.

'Ostara' – fruits late summer to first frosts; good cropper.

'Gento' – fruits late summer to mid autumn; produces runners.

Alpine varieties

'Alexandria' – fruits mid summer to late autumn; good-sized berries.

'Baron Solemacher' – heavy cropper.

'Fraise des Bois' – very heavy cropper with thimble-sized fruits.

▲ **'Tenira'** crops from mid summer onwards, with bright crimson fruits.

▲ **'Redgauntlet'** often crops twice in a season if protected with cloches.

Summer feast Crisp and succulent vegetables, from common cabbages to exotic artichokes, can be cropped from any garden.

Vegetables

Home-grown vegetables have a flavour and freshness far superior to those bought from a greengrocer or supermarket, and the choice of different varieties is much greater. They also have better texture, with a higher vitamin content, and the gardener controls which chemicals, if any, should be used as they grow.

In addition, home-produced vegetables can be a real money-saver, particularly if a greenhouse, cold frame and cloches are available for growing early and late crops. Harvested at their peak, any surplus vegetables will be in prime condition for freezing and other methods of preserving.

Tending a vegetable plot may be a little more time-consuming than looking after a flower garden, but it needs no special skills or aptitudes, the results of your labours are quickly visible, and at harvest time there is a satisfying sense of achievement. Essential factors, though, include properly prepared soil and a sunny and open site. It is almost impossible to fail given fertile soil, and provided seeds are sown at the proper time and seedlings are thinned out before they crowd each other.

In a garden large enough to set one area aside for a kitchen garden, it is sensible to grow vegetables in a rotation cycle where brassicas follow beans, peas and salad vegetables, and root crops take over from the cabbage family. Crop rotation makes the best use of manure, lime and fertilizers and also reduces the risk of soil-borne diseases. Root crops occupy the ground for longer than most other vegetables, but you can grow quick catch crops – lettuce, spinach and radishes – between the rows.

In a small garden, a sunny patio can be used for growing a number of vegetables in containers or grow bags. Tomatoes, leaf lettuces, peppers and aubergines are ideal for container-growing; cucumbers can be trained up a sunny wall, and radishes can occupy a kitchen window box.

PLANNING A KITCHEN GARDEN

**Fresh vegetables have a flavour rarely matched
by those bought from a shop – even a small kitchen garden
can yield good crops year after year.**

Many gardeners grow vegetables and fruit only if they have space to spare, yet they not only provide fresh, full-flavoured food, but can also be a money saver – if you have a greenhouse or cold frame you can grow early or late crops when they are out of season and usually expensive to buy. Good planning of crop rotation is the key to growing good crops of vegetables.

Siting a kitchen garden
Choose a light, airy spot for a vegetable plot – one that gets plenty of sun and is not shaded by trees or high fences. You may prefer to have only lawns and flower beds in view from the house, but don't, for this reason, relegate the vegetable plot to a corner of the garden with difficult access and where sun and wind directions are unsuitable.

You *can* grow vegetables on a plot that is in the shade for up to half the day, but they won't crop quite so well. Use cloches or a frame to provide a warm start in spring. If, however, the only available site is in shade for most of the day, it would be better to grow shade-tolerant plants such as raspberries and blackberries, although some sun is required even for these.

Do not plant fruit trees in the vegetable garden. They create shade and also rob the soil of water and nourishment needed by shallow-growing vegetable crops.

One good path made of solid

▼ **Vegetable plot** Every inch of space is utilized in this small plot. A brick-edged bed, surrounded by fruit bushes, is unobtrusive and still yields a good crop of summer vegetables.

A THREE-YEAR CROP ROTATION PLAN – FIRST YEAR

Row direction Except in exposed gardens, where east-west rows are best, the main requirement is to plant rows at right-angles to the path. If planting east-west, site tall crops where they will not shade low-growing crops planted next to them.

Greenhouse and cold frame Both need as much light as possible, especially during the spring. The greenhouse door should be alongside a path, and the frame placed nearby to save time when transferring plants. It is also helpful to have electricity and water nearby.

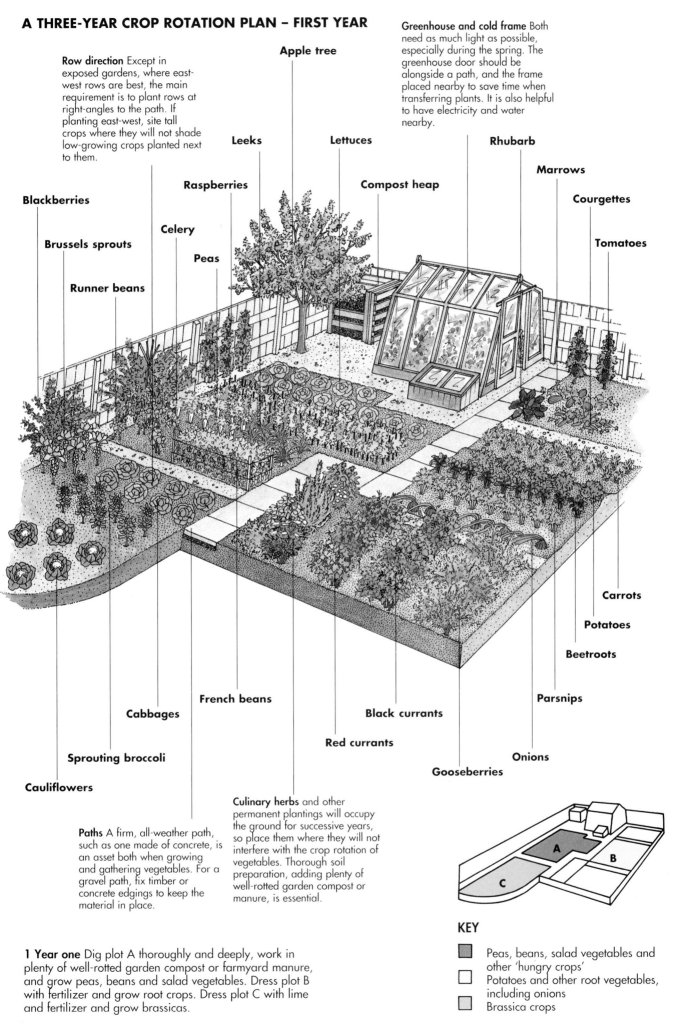

Apple tree

Leeks

Lettuces

Compost heap

Rhubarb

Marrows

Courgettes

Tomatoes

Raspberries

Blackberries

Celery

Brussels sprouts

Peas

Runner beans

Cauliflowers

Sprouting broccoli

Cabbages

French beans

Black currants

Red currants

Gooseberries

Onions

Parsnips

Beetroots

Potatoes

Carrots

Paths A firm, all-weather path, such as one made of concrete, is an asset both when growing and gathering vegetables. For a gravel path, fix timber or concrete edgings to keep the material in place.

Culinary herbs and other permanent plantings will occupy the ground for successive years, so place them where they will not interfere with the crop rotation of vegetables. Thorough soil preparation, adding plenty of well-rotted garden compost or manure, is essential.

1 Year one Dig plot A thoroughly and deeply, work in plenty of well-rotted garden compost or farmyard manure, and grow peas, beans and salad vegetables. Dress plot B with fertilizer and grow root crops. Dress plot C with lime and fertilizer and grow brassicas.

KEY

Peas, beans, salad vegetables and other 'hungry crops'
Potatoes and other root vegetables, including onions
Brassica crops

CROP ROTATION: SECOND AND THIRD YEARS

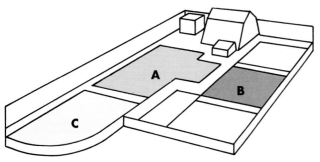

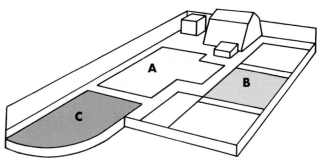

2 Year two Dig plot B thoroughly and deeply and work in plenty of compost or manure for peas, beans and salad crops, which follow the root vegetables. Dress plot C with fertilizer for root crops. Apply fertilizer and lime to plot A for brassica crops.

3 Year three Thoroughly and deeply dig and manure plot C in which peas, beans and salad crops will follow last year's root crops. Dress plot A with fertilizer for the root crops. Prepare plot B with fertilizer and lime for the brassicas. Start the cycle again in year four.

material, such as concrete or paving slabs, is useful for walking on and wheeling a barrow. Other paths can be narrower to maximize the cropping area – temporary ones are easily made by treading the soil down firmly so that they can be dug over when needed.

Beds can be of any convenient width, but it is worth remembering that the contents of seed packets are often based on the amount needed for a 9m (30ft) row. This length is enough to yield a worthwhile variety of crops.

Where a bed is much narrower at one end than the other – the lie of the land or the shape of the garden may demand such a shape – use the shorter rows for succession crops, such as lettuces and radishes, making small sowings at regular intervals.

For most crops, the direction of the row is not very important. Overwintered crops grown under cloches get the most sun when grown in east-west rows, and this direction is also slightly better for gardens exposed to strong westerly winds. In summer, however, vegetables – especially tall ones – get slightly more sunlight when grown in north-south rows.

A water supply is vital for growing vegetables and soft fruits, not only to increase the yield and prevent crop failure, but also to make seed sowing practicable. If the plot is some distance from the mains water supply, it is worth installing a standpipe.

A greenhouse or cold frame should be sited in the sunniest spot available – the axis running either east-west or north-south, with the door on the least exposed side. Permanent seed beds should

ideally face east. The compost heap should go in a shady corner.

Some form of windbreak may be needed around the vegetable plot if it is exposed to prevailing winds – a dwarf hedge about 60cm (2ft) high is generally adequate.

Crop rotation
Divide the vegetable garden into three plots – call them plots A, B and C – and grow different groups of vegetables in each plot each year in a three-year crop rotation cycle. This simple rotation system ensures the most effective use of composts, manures and fertilizers, and also helps to reduce attacks by soil-borne pests and diseases. As two years will always elapse before a particular vegetable is grown in the same soil again, pests are less likely to spread.

Plot A In the first year, use plot A for growing 'hungry' crops which need rich, freshly manured soil. These include peas, beans, celery, leeks, lettuces, endives, radishes, spinach, sweetcorn and chicory. Most are sown in spring and early summer and some will be harvested in time for a second crop later in the year.

Plot B Use plot B for root vegetables such as beetroots, carrots, onions, parsnips, potatoes, swedes and turnips. These prefer soil which was manured for a previous crop, but dressed with fertilizer. They are sown in spring and early summer and can be harvested in time for the plot to be manured in readiness for sowing peas and beans the next year.

Plot C Use plot C for cabbages, broccoli, Brussels sprouts, cauliflowers and kale – the brassicas –

which prefer soil manured for a previous crop and dressed with lime as well as fertilizer. Brassicas are chiefly sown in spring, in a seed bed, planted out in summer and harvested from autumn to the following spring.

Each year move the cropping plan to the next plot – the rotation in each plot is thus peas and beans, root crops and brassicas.

Onions and shallots will grow in any reasonably good soil, but there is probably more room in the root crop plot. For really large onions, grow them in rich soil in the pea and bean plot.

A fourth plot should remain permanent from year to year. This is used for long-term crops such as artichokes, asparagus, rhubarb and other special crops – including tomatoes, marrows and courgettes – which do not fit into the rotation system.

Fruit bushes and herbs should also be allocated permanent sites. Herbs should ideally be grown in a bed of their own which is easily accessible from the house.

Catch and succession crops
The main crops grown within a rotation plan don't make full use of the space available for the whole year, and so there is usually room for other crops to be fitted in. These are known as catch crops and succession crops.

Catch crops include quick-growing vegetables sown in the early part of the season before the main crop is sown or planted in the plot. A catch crop of salad onions, for instance, can be sown in the brassica plot in early spring before the winter cabbage is planted out in mid summer.

Catch crops can also be grown between rows of slower-growing vegetables, and lifted before the slower ones need more space. Lettuces and radishes, for example, can be grown between rows of parsnips or Brussels sprouts. Don't grow a catch crop that will cover the whole area with foliage, otherwise the main crop will be smothered.

Succession crops are those sown or planted after a main crop has been cleared. For example, a main crop of broad beans, sown in late winter and picked by early summer, can be followed by leeks.

Preparing a new plot

Clear and prepare the site for a new vegetable garden in autumn, or during a dry and frost-free period in winter. It will then be ready for sowing and planting the following spring. Work out a crop rotation plan.

Clear away all debris. If subsoil has been brought to the surface by builders, re-distribute it over the whole garden. Cut down all tall grass, weeds and brambles, and then skim off the remaining rough turf with a spade, cutting 2.5cm (1in) under the surface – it can be stacked for making into loam.

Dig the soil thoroughly and systematically. In the section that corresponds to plot A, add manure or well-rotted garden compost into the top spit at a rate of one bucketful per sq m/yd. Remove and burn the roots of all perennial weeds uncovered during digging – couch grass, docks, dandelions and nettles can be a problem if allowed to spread unchecked. Ashes from the bonfire can be returned to the soil.

Soils for vegetables

The ideal soil for growing vegetables is loam – a well-balanced mixture of sand, silt, clay and humus. It does not dry out quickly, does not get waterlogged and has an open, spongy texture.

Good loam is easily worked, and needs only the regular replacement of essential plant food in the form of manure and fertilizers.

Most vegetables grow best in neutral soils – neither acid nor alkaline – or slightly acid soils. Dress very acid soils with lime, using a proprietary soil-testing kit to check the amount required. Ideally, the reading should be between pH6.5 and pH7.0. Excessively alkaline soils are best improved with liberal amounts of organic matter.

Sandy soil is light and dry. It warms up quickly in spring in time for early crops, but also dries out quickly. Essential nutrients are easily washed out in drainage water and so need constant replacement. Feed with small amounts of fertilizer at regular intervals and dig in manure.

Clay soil is heavy, slow to warm up, and moisture-retentive. It may be rich in plant food but because it is poorly drained the roots are starved of oxygen. Dig in plenty of strawy manure, compost, sharp sand or weathered ashes to lighten clay soils and to improve drainage. Also add lime if the soil is acid.

Chalky soil is often shallow and drains very quickly – as with sandy soil, it loses essential plant foods. It may be sticky and hard to dig and is always strongly alkaline. Work in plenty of well-rotted garden compost or manure. Do not dress with lime but feed regularly with fertilizer.

Peaty soil is usually acid and may be poorly drained. Make drainage trenches around the vegetable beds to clear surplus water. Dress heavily with lime and regularly apply a good general-purpose fertilizer – peaty soil usually lacks phosphates and potash which are essential to plant health.

▶ **Vegetable rows** Grow vegetables in orderly rows or blocks of one kind to make hoeing and harvesting easier. Ensure steady growth with regular watering, applied in the evening.

ASPARAGUS

An asparagus bed takes three years to develop, but repays the long wait by cropping for at least twenty years.

Few vegetables can compare in flavour with tender home-grown asparagus. Its shoots, known as spears because of their shape, can be enjoyed on their own or in a variety of classic dishes.

Sadly, the asparagus cropping season lasts only six weeks, making it a brief seasonal treat to enjoy and relish. However, the asparagus plant, a perennial, also has a second phase. Only its first shoots are harvested in early summer. The rest are left to grow into attractive fern-like foliage which turns golden-yellow in autumn, and builds up food reserves in the crowns for the following year's crop.

Planning the crop
Asparagus does best in a fairly open position sheltered from wind. It needs rich, well-drained soil, so the initial preparation of the bed is vital for success in years to come.

The autumn before planting, dig a bed 1.2m (4ft) wide to accommodate two rows. Dig well-rotted manure or garden compost into the soil to one spade's depth at the rate of approximately a bucketful per sq m/yd.

Acid soil should be limed to make it neutral or slightly alkaline. Add lime in winter, after digging, at the rate suggested by a soil-testing kit.

If the soil tends to become sticky or waterlogged, make a raised bed enclosed by gravel boards, stones or breeze blocks.

The following spring, rake the bed level and work in 100-125g (3-4oz) per sq m/yd of a slow-acting general fertilizer such as Growmore.

Growing asparagus
Most asparagus are bought as one- or two-year-old plants. Don't transplant crowns older than this as they are difficult to establish

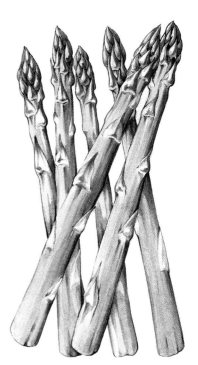

▲ **Asparagus tips** The fragile flower heads of asparagus spears need careful handling. They are the most succulent part of this delicacy.

and often die. One-year-old male crowns are best but will not yield spears large enough to eat for two years. Each mature plant – those more than three years old – should yield one average helping of spears a week.

Asparagus *can* be grown from seed, but this takes an additional year before cropping can start. In addition, some seedlings will be female and these crop less well than male plants. Female plants are identifiable by their attractive berries, but these take two years to show.

If you decide to grow from seed, choose 'Limbras Franklim', an F1 hybrid variety that produces only male plants (and is claimed to reach maturity in three years).

In mid spring soak seeds overnight in lukewarm water and sow in drills 12mm (½in) apart. When the seedlings are about 15cm (6in) high, thin them until 15cm (6in) apart. Water generously during summer and transplant to a permanent bed the following spring.

Asparagus crowns are dispatched from nurseries around mid spring and should be planted at once.

◄ **Asparagus fern** The top growth of culinary asparagus closely resembles the indoor asparagus fern. It turns a golden colour in autumn.

Dig trenches 20cm (8in) deep and 90cm (3ft) apart in prepared ground, and wide enough to allow the roots to spread out flat. Replace some of the soil to form a domed base.

Remove the crowns from their packaging and set them 45cm (1½ft) apart in the trenches. Spread out the roots over the domed base and cover with soil *immediately*. Never let the crowns dry out.

Partially fill the trenches with 7.5cm (3in) of fine soil, and firm the surface. Leave the remaining soil at the sides of the trenches.

For the first year, lightly hoe to keep down weeds. Water thoroughly in dry spells. When asparagus spears appear, leave them to

grow into ferns. In mid to late autumn, when their stems turn yellow, cut down the ferns to within 2.5cm (1in) of the soil and mulch with well-rotted manure or garden compost. Ridge up the soil left at the side of the trenches over the crowns.

The following spring, dress the rows with a general fertilizer at a rate of 50g (2oz) per sq m/yd. Again, leave the spears to grow into ferns before cutting them down when they turn yellow in autumn. Then add a mulch of compost and ridge up the soil.

In the third spring after planting and before the shoots appear, pile 20-30cm (8-12in) of fine soil on top of the plants and smooth it into ridges. The soil must not be too heavy or the asparagus spears will bend as they struggle upwards. Heavy soil can be lightened by mixing in organic matter or gritty sand.

The soil ridges will blanch the asparagus and produce long white

spears. The spears turn purple or green, depending on variety, where they appear above the soil. Harvest when about 10cm (4in) of the spears show above the surface – asparagus becomes stringy if it grows too far above the soil. In Britain it is uncommon to see completely blanched spears – and while colour doesn't affect taste, all-white asparagus looks very appetizing.

When the harvesting period is over (see below), clear any shoots that have already appeared. Always let later spears grow and develop their ferny foliage, and wait until the stems turn yellow in autumn before cutting them to 15cm (6in) from the ground.

Harvesting

The harvesting season usually starts towards the very end of spring. However, do *not* cut any spears grown from one-year-old crowns during the first two seasons. In the third year take only one or two spears from each plant and pick none later than the beginning of early summer.

In subsequent years harvest for about six weeks, slowly building up to eight, but always allowing later shoots to grow into ferns to feed the crown. Eventual heavy cropping depends entirely on this slow build-up of crown size.

Smooth the ridges to a fine tilth during mid to late spring, and the asparagus will appear by cracking the smooth surface. Scrape away some of the soil with your finger and check for the white tip of a shoot. You can harvest the spear by digging the soil away carefully with a small trowel and severing the spear at the bottom with a sharp knife. Alternatively, let the shoot grow up to 10cm (4in) above the ground.

▼ **Asparagus spears** Tall spears, like those on the left, are too woody and stringy to be edible; they should be left to develop foliage and help to build up the crown. The tender young spears on the right are ready for cutting.

Asparagus 'Connover's Colossal'

GROWING ASPARAGUS FROM CROWNS
FIRST YEAR

1 Dig trenches 20cm (8in) deep and 90cm (3ft) apart, and wide enough for the crowns. Replace part of the soil to form a domed ridge.

2 Spread out the roots over the ridge and quickly cover with 7.5cm (3in) of soil before they dry out. Leave the rest of the soil at the side of the trench.

3 Leave the first year's growth until the ferns start to turn yellow in autumn. Then cut them down to about 2.5cm (1in) from the ground.

SECOND YEAR

5 The following spring, dress the rows with a general fertilizer, such as Growmore, at the rate of 50g (2oz) per sq m/yd.

6 When spears appear at the end of late spring, do not harvest. Once again allow them to grow out as ferns to build up reserves in the crowns.

7 Cut ferns, as before, when they turn yellow in autumn. Clear the bed entirely of any weeds with a hoe and ridge up soil over the crowns.

THIRD YEAR

9 Spears growing within the ridge are blanched but colour when they surface. Cut only one or two spears from each plant during the first harvest.

10 Always cut spears at an angle and never pull them out. Use an asparagus knife or small trowel to cut below the surface of the soil, to the spear's base.

11 Stop harvesting at the beginning of early summer, and clear any shoots that remain. Add fertilizer to encourage later shoots to develop ferns.

4 After cutting down, mulch with well-rotted manure or garden compost. Ridge up the remaining trench soil 5-7.5cm (2-3in) deep over the crowns.

8 Add an extra dressing of compost in autumn. In spring, before shoots appear, mound 20-30cm (8-12in) of fine soil over the crowns and smooth.

12 Let the ferns grow up and treat as before. Future crops depend on this slow build-up of the crowns. The fourth year is the first real harvest.

Blanched asparagus

A special, serrated asparagus knife is available that cuts deep down to the base of the asparagus shoot without disturbing too much soil.

Cut spears should be around 20cm (8in) in length. Cut the spears as they are ready and be patient if you don't immediately have enough for a meal. Keep the amount you have harvested in iced water in the fridge until a sufficient number has been accumulated.

In their prime the small fat heads on the tips of the spears should be tightly compressed, above moist, glistening green, purple or white stems. The slightest trace of brown on the cut edge indicates that the asparagus is past its best.

Wash the asparagus very carefully so that you don't damage the fragile tips. Trim the woody parts from the bases of the stems. Green stems only need washing, but remove the hard exterior from white and purple stems by thinly peeling from the top downwards.

Pest and diseases

The most troublesome pest is the asparagus beetle. If it occurs during the harvesting season – usually from early summer onwards – spray several times with derris or pyrethrum. When the harvesting season is over dust liberally with HCH. Slugs and snails can be a problem and baits or pellets should be put down to deter them.

VARIETIES TO CHOOSE

'Accell' – an F1 hybrid; early cropping; dark green spears.

'Andreas' – all-male F1 hybrid; long straight spears; green and purple tinged.

'Boonlim' – early cropper; high yields of thick sturdy spears.

'Cito' – very early cropper; green tinged.

'Connover's Colossal' – early cropper; thick spears, plump tips; purple tinged; a long-established favourite.

'Limbras Franklim' – an all-male F1 hybrid; prolific cropper; fine quality, very tender spears; purple tinged.

'Martha Washington' – long thick spears; heavy crops; purple tinged; very reliable.

AUBERGINES

Tropical aubergines can be grown in the greenhouse or in pots on a sunny and sheltered patio.

The aubergine, which comes from tropical Asia, is sometimes referred to as the egg plant because of its ovoid shape and smooth skin. Most of the varieties available to gardeners are oblong and purple, but seeds of egg-sized, ivory-white types ('Ova') are also obtainable.

The aubergine needs warmth in order to bear its flowers and produce and ripen its fruits. In Britain it succeeds best when grown in a greenhouse.

It can also be grown outdoors in hot summers, provided the site is sheltered, but the young plants must be protected with cloches at night and in cool weather.

The bushy plants bear lilac flowers and large, broad leaves. The glossy fruits must be handled with care during harvesting, since the stalk and calyx around the fruit at the stalk end are prickly.

A plant grown in a greenhouse should produce about four good-sized fruits; one grown outdoors may have three. Four plants should provide a reasonable crop for the average family.

Site and soil preparation

Outdoors, aubergines will grow in fertile, well-drained soil, liberally dressed with well-rotted farm manure or similar material.

Before planting aubergines outdoors, first raise the seedlings indoors or in a greenhouse. Alternatively, buy seedlings from a nursery or garden centre. Plant them in a sunny, sheltered spot, ideally against a south-facing wall. A sunny patio also provides reasonable conditions for outdoor aubergines – either in pots or in grow bags.

Greenhouse cultivation

Sow seeds between late winter and early spring, distributing the seed finely in trays of moistened seed compost and covering them with a thin layer of compost. Place the seed tray in a propagator with a temperature of 18°C (64°F).

When large enough to handle, prick the seedlings out individually into 7.5cm (3in) pots containing a proprietary potting compost; provide a minimum temperature of about 16°C (61°F)

Pot on the seedlings any time from mid spring onwards, finishing in 17.5-25cm (7-10in) pots. Alternatively, transfer them into grow bags, with two plants in each

▲ **Purple aubergine** The most familiar aubergines are long and purple, although some varieties have egg-shaped white fruit. They are delicious when stuffed or served as an accompanying vegetable. Before cooking, sprinkle the sliced fruit with salt and let it stand for half an hour to remove any bitterness.

GROWING IN A GREENHOUSE

1 Sow the seeds in late winter or early spring – scatter them thinly and evenly in trays of moistened seed compost, covering with a fine layer of compost. For germination, the temperature should be 18-21°C (64-70°F), best maintained in a heated propagator unit.

2 Seedlings can be planted any time from mid spring onwards. Transfer them into pots or grow bags, with two plants in each standard sized bag. Water and liquid feed the seedlings before and after planting. Maintain the temperature at 15-18°C (59-64°F).

3 When a plant reaches about 23cm (9in), tie the main stem to a 1.2m (4ft) long bamboo cane. During summer, water thoroughly and give a liquid feed once a week. Spray the leaves regularly with water to keep down red spider mites.

PINCHING OUT AND HARVESTING

1 When the plants are 23cm (9in) tall, tie to canes and pinch out the growing point of each plant to encourage three or four strong side-shoots to develop. If the plants need support as the fruits swell, space out and tie the side-shoots to bamboo canes.

2 As soon as the young fruits start to swell, choose four that are about the same size, and spaced evenly apart on the plant. Nip off all the other fruit and any flowers or subsequent side-shoots. This ensures that each plant focuses its energy into fruit production.

3 Fruits are ripe when they have finished swelling and have a glossy skin. This is between mid summer and mid autumn for greenhouse crops, and late summer to mid autumn outdoors. Handle the fruits carefully and remove by snipping the stems with secateurs.

standard sized bag. Insert supporting stakes in pots and bags.

When the plants are about 23cm (9in) high, pinch out their growing points, and tie the main stem of each plant to the cane. When the young fruits begin to swell, nip off all but four fruits on each plant. Water regularly, and do not allow the soil to dry out.

Liquid feed once a week when the fruits become visible, and maintain a temperature of not less that 16°C (61°F).

Growing outdoors
Aubergines can be planted outside at the beginning of early summer, after hardening off in a cold frame in late spring.

First cover the soil with cloches. After a couple of weeks, plant the aubergines in the warmed, dry soil at 45cm (1½ft) intervals. Leave the cloches in place until the plants are well established, and all risk of frost has passed. Keep the plants well watered at all times. Continue as for greenhouse crops, but allow only fruit to develop on each plant.

Harvesting
An aubergine crop is generally ready for picking in late summer. Check for ripeness by pressing the fruit gently with a finger – if a dimple remains, swelling has stopped and the fruit is ripe. Harvest by carefully snipping the stems with garden secateurs. Aubergines can be kept for about a fortnight.

Pest and diseases
Grey mould can infect outdoor aubergines in both cool and rainy conditions. Aphids, red spider mites and whiteflies are very common greenhouse pests; spray liberally with permethrin or pirimiphos-methyl.

Aubergine 'Easter Egg'

VARIETIES TO CHOOSE

'Black Enorma' (F1 hybrid) – prolific cropper; large purple fruit weighing 450g (1lb) or more.

'Black Prince' (F1 hybrid) – long, slim purple fruit; matures early and will hang on plant for some weeks without deteriorating.

'Bonica' (F1 hybrid) – large, oval purple fruit; early maturing; compact plants.

'Easter Egg' – white, oval fruits; 7.5-10cm (3-4in) long.

'Ova' (F1 hybrid) – heavy cropper; small, egg-shaped white fruits.

'Slice-Rite No 23' (F1 hybrid) – large oblong purple fruits; up to 450g (1lb) in weight; excellent flavour.

BEANS, BROAD

Broad beans are especially rewarding to grow in the garden because they can be picked young, when they are at their most delicious.

Broad beans are one of the easiest vegetables to grow, and need very little care and attention. Aim to pick the pods when they are slim and the beans inside are no larger than a 1p piece and the flavour will be marvellous – a far cry from the large, leathery beans you buy in the shops.

Planning the crop

Broad beans need fertile, well-drained soil which has been given a dressing of manure.

Sowing can be done in late winter or early spring for main crop broad beans harvested in mid to late summer, or in autumn for a crop the following late spring. The large seeds rot easily in water-logged ground, so avoid cold, wet soils at all times, but particularly for autumn-sown crops. A double row 3m (10ft) long will provide about 9kg (20lb) of beans.

Spring-sown broad beans Dig the soil thoroughly in winter before sowing, incorporating one bucket of garden compost or well-rotted manure to every sq m/yd. Two weeks before sowing, rake in a general fertilizer such as Growmore at the rate of 50-75g (2-3oz) per sq m/yd. Because the seeds are so large there is no need to provide a very fine seed bed. Start sowing any time from late winter onwards, as soon as the soil is workable.

You can grow broad beans in either single or double rows – the yield is usually heavier from double-row plants. For single rows, make drills 7.5cm (3in) deep and 45cm (1½ft) apart and set the seeds singly at 15cm (6in) intervals. Cover and firm with the back of a rake.

For double rows, space the drills 23cm (9in) apart for dwarf varieties, and 45cm (1½ft) apart for taller varieties. Each pair of rows should be about 75cm (2½ ft) apart. It is a good idea to sow a few extra beans at the end of each row to replace any that fail to germinate or develop poorly.

Sow successive rows of broad beans at monthly intervals until late spring for crops right into the autumn.

Water the plants thoroughly during periods of drought, and hoe regularly around the plants to keep down weeds.

Dwarf broad beans do not need staking, except in very windy, exposed sites. For larger varieties, insert two stakes at both ends of each row and at 30cm (1ft) intervals along the rows. When the plants are large enough, run string around the stakes to provide support for the plants as they develop.

When the lowest bean pods are about 2.5cm (1in) long and there are still flowers at the top of the

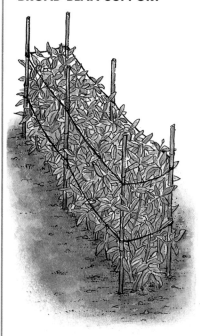

BROAD BEAN SUPPORT

Large varieties of broad beans need to be supported. When the plants are still small, insert two stakes at the end of each row of beans and at 30cm (1ft) intervals along the rows. As the plants grow, run string around the stakes to give support as they develop. Dwarf broad beans only need support on very windy, exposed sites.

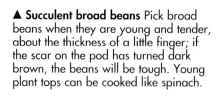

▲ **Succulent broad beans** Pick broad beans when they are young and tender, about the thickness of a little finger; if the scar on the pod has turned dark brown, the beans will be tough. Young plant tops can be cooked like spinach.

stems, pinch out the growing tip of each plant to encourage pod development. (These succulent young tips, cooked very lightly, are delicious.) Pinching out will also remove the part of the plant likely to harbour the greatest enemy of broad beans – black bean aphids. However, spraying is still likely to be necessary to control this pest. There is some evidence that growing summer savory nearby can discourage blackfly.

Longpod broad bean 'Aquadulce'

PEST CONTROL

To discourage black bean aphids, pinch out the growing tips when the lowest bean pods are about 2.5cm (1in) long and there are four sets of flower trusses at the top of the stems.

Autumn-sown broad beans
Early-cropping broad beans are sown at the beginning of late autumn, except in cold northern gardens. Use varieties recommended for winter growing – they are specially bred to be hardy enough to withstand very cold weather.

Do not apply fertilizer at sowing time – it will cause the plants to grow too tall too quickly, and they won't be hardy enough to survive winter. The aim is to produce strong plants about 10cm (4in) tall before winter. In severe weather protect with cloches.

In spring, when growth begins again, apply a top-dressing of a nitrogenous fertilizer such as nitro-chalk at the rate of 25-50g (1-2oz) per sq m/yd.

General cultivation is the same as for spring-sown broad beans.

If the garden is too cold or exposed to grow beans over winter, sow in mid or late winter in a cold greenhouse or cold frame and plant out the seedlings in early spring. Sow a main crop in mid or late spring outdoors.

Alternatively, if you want to save time and avoid sowing seed, buy small plants from a garden centre and plant them out in the prepared bed in mid or late spring.

Harvesting
The earliest crops are ready in early summer, but cropping from successive sowings can continue well into autumn.

Pick the first pods when they are no more than 5-7cm (2-3in) long and cook them whole. Keep picking as and when required – feel the pods gently with your fingers to gauge the size of the beans inside. Shell beans in pods larger than about 10cm (4in) long. Don't allow the pods to become tough and leathery. Broad beans freeze well; any surplus can be shelled and frozen, after blanching.

After harvesting, cut off the plant tops and dig the roots in well. They contain nitrogen-fixing bacteria which improve the fertility of the soil for the next crop. The roots can also be used for composting.

Pest and diseases
The worst enemy of broad beans is the black bean aphid – vast colonies of this pest gather to feed on the new growth at the top of each plant. They suck the juices of the plant and seriously weaken it; spray with pirimicarb or a similar insecticide. Slugs and snails can also be a problem.

Foot rot, which causes discoloration and the rotting of stem bases, can lead to the collapse of plants. Water young plants with Cheshunt compound.

VARIETIES TO CHOOSE

Two classes of broad beans – longpods and Windsors – subdivide into green and white types. Green-seeded beans are best for freezing. Longpods, with kidney-shaped beans, are hardier than the round-seeded, sweeter Windsors.

Longpod varieties
'Aquadulce' – white; good for autumn-sowing; early-cropping.

'Express' – greenish-white; fast maturing; heavy crops.

'Imperial Green Longpod' – high yields; excellent for exhibition.

'Jubilee Hysor' – white; closely packed pods make shelling easy.

'Red Epicure' – brown-red beans retain colour when steamed; superb flavour.

'Relon' – green; tall, vigorous; abundant pods; fine flavour; excellent for exhibition.

'Withien Vroma' – white; rapid grower; spring-sown pods mature at the same time as autumn-sown varieties.

Windsors
'Green Windsor' – heavy crops, freeze well; not autumn sowing.

'White Windsor' – heavy yields; flavoursome; not autumn sowing.

Dwarf varieties
'Bonny Lad' – white; bushy, 45cm (1½ft) high; small tasty beans.

'The Sutton' – white; up to 30cm (1ft) tall; ideal for small gardens; good flavour and yield; grow in single rows.

BEANS, FRENCH

**Crisp and succulent, French beans
are easy to grow and yield heavy crops
from mid summer onwards.**

Dwarf beans

Climbing beans
(purple-podded)

Haricot beans

Originally from South America, French beans are so called because of their long-standing popularity in France. They can be grown as a catch crop, the pods being ready for picking within 10 weeks of sowing. There are three types – dwarf, climbing and haricot – all of which need the same growing conditions and general cultivation.

Dwarf beans can be grown on the flat and in tubs and window-boxes. They do away with the effort and expense of staking since they reach a height of only 30-45cm (12-18in).

Climbing French beans need support from poles or netting like runner beans. They reach heights of 1.8-2.1m (6-7ft) and bear a heavier crop than dwarf beans.

Haricot beans are usually grown for their beans, which are used dried. Like the other types, however, the pods can also be picked to eat fresh while they are young and green.

French beans are either flat-podded or pencil-podded (round). Flat-podded beans tend to become stringy as they mature, while pencil-podded ones are generally stringless. There are green, yellow and purple-podded varieties.

Site and soil preparation

Most soils are suitable as long as they are not too heavy or too acid; a fertile and well-drained soil in a sunny and sheltered position is best.

The autumn before sowing, dig the plot deeply, adding a bucketful of well-rotted manure or compost per sq m/sq yd. Work in a dressing of lime at 75g per sq m (3oz per sq yd). A couple of weeks before sowing, apply a general fertilizer at the rate of 75g per sq m (3oz per sq yd) and rake the soil to a fine texture.

Sowing and planting

Cold, wet soils often prevent the seeds from germinating. If the soil is cold, or if the season is late, put cloches in position for a couple of weeks to warm it up; alternatively buy young strip-grown plants. Transplant them to the prepared bed at intervals of 23cm (9in) in rows 45cm (18in) apart, or 15cm (6in) apart in blocks. For climbing beans, put the supports in first.

French beans are half-hardy and should not be sown outdoors until a week or so after all risk of night frost has passed – usually in late spring.

Sow in drills 5cm (2in) deep and 45cm (18in) apart. Set the seeds in pairs every 23cm (9in), with 2.5cm (1in) between seeds and remove the weaker of the two after germination.

Sow another batch of seeds three weeks later to provide a succession of beans. If space allows,

◄ **Dwarf French beans** Ready for harvesting within 10 weeks of sowing, French beans should be picked when the pods are young and tender and about 10cm (4in) long.

successive sowings can be made until mid summer, for picking in mid autumn or before the first frosts. You can extend the picking period by a few weeks by covering the plants with cloches in early autumn.

An earlier crop can be grown if the beans are started off in a heated greenhouse or cold frame, or grown under cloches. Gradually harden the young plants off before transplanting them into the open in late spring.

When the young plants are 10cm (4in) high, thin those planted in pairs until 23cm (9in) apart, leaving the strongest. Support dwarf beans with short twigs or pea sticks or with string tied to canes around the rows.

In early summer, mulch around the stems. Water frequently during the flowering period to help the pods develop fully over a long period.

Harvesting

French beans start to crop within 8-10 weeks of sowing and many produce pods for up to eight weeks between early summer and mid autumn. The more they are picked, the more they produce.

Look over the plants every couple of days for young, tender beans. Pick when the pods are 10cm (4in) long – if they are left too long the pods become stringy, the beans floury and the plants stop producing.

When picking, hold the stem with one hand and pull the pods downwards with the other. Alternatively, use scissors.

Haricot beans

To dry haricot beans, leave the pods on the plants until they have ripened and turned white – in early to mid autumn. On a dry day, pull up the plants whole and hang them up in a dry, airy place.

When the pods are brittle, shell the beans and spread them out on sheets of paper to dry thoroughly. Store in airtight jars.

Pest and diseases

The main pests of French beans are bean seed flies; dust the seed drills with pirimiphos-methyl prior to sowing. Black bean aphids (see Broad beans, page 89) and slugs and snails may also be troublesome. Anthracnose, which shows as black sunken areas on leaves and pods, occurs in wet, cool summers; there is no treatment and diseased plants must be destroyed. Halo blight occurs under similar conditions, with similar results.

VARIETIES TO CHOOSE

Dwarf
'Early Wax' – straight, round, long yellow pods; succulent texture.

'Kinghorn Wax' – long, creamy-yellow, stringless round pods; excellent flavour.

'Masterpiece' – heavy cropper, with long flat pods; early maturing.

'Pros Gitana' – heavy cropper, with stringless, round white-seeded pods; good for freezing.

'Royal Burgundy' – heavy cropper, with straight, round purple pods; pods turn green when cooked.

'Tendergreen' – stringless round pods. Heavy cropper and early maturing; good for freezing.

'The Prince' – good cropper, with long, flat pods; excellent flavour.

Climbing
'Blue Lake' – consistent cropper, with white-seeded round pods; can be dried as haricots.

'Hunter' – flat, stringless, white-seeded pods; heavy cropper.

'Purple-podded Climbing' – heavy cropper with dark purple round pods which turn green when cooked.

Haricot
'Chevrier Vert' – good cropper, with round pods; can also be used fresh when green.

Purple-podded haricot bean

Dwarf French bean 'The Prince'

Climbing French bean 'Blue Lake'

BEANS, RUNNER

Runner beans are among the most popular of home-grown vegetables, especially prized for their heavy crops and their handsome flowering screens.

Runner beans are often called scarlet runners because many varieties have scarlet flowers. But many climbing and dwarf varieties also have white, pink or red and white flowers.

Some gardeners plant them specifically for their flowers – they can be used to form dense, attractive screens to separate functional areas from the ornamental garden. In the kitchen garden a wigwam of runner beans in full flower makes a particularly spectacular focal point.

Tall-growing runner beans normally reach a height of 2.4-3m (8-10ft), although they can be grown on the flat without support if the growing points are pinched out when the plants are about 30cm (1ft) high. Dwarf runner beans grow to about 45cm (18in) high.

Runner beans come into season just when most French beans are coming to an end. They have larger, coarser and more flavoursome pods than French beans, though they are slightly less hardy.

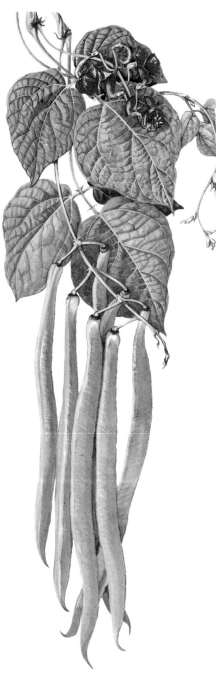

▲ **Runner beans** Standard varieties produce pods 25-40cm (10-16in) long and sometimes stringless. Dwarf varieties have pods 20cm (8in) long.

◄ **Bean support** Wigwams are an ideal and attractive way of supporting runner beans and particularly suitable for small vegetable plots. Use 2.5m (8ft) stakes – either hazel or ash poles or bamboo canes – pushing them into the ground at 60cm (2ft) intervals in the shape of a circle. Pull the tops together and tie them with string.

Site and soil preparation

Runner beans grow best in a sunny position, but they need as much shelter as possible to encourage pollinating insects.

Most garden soils, if properly prepared, are suitable for growing runner beans, although a deep rich soil is best. On heavy soil, dig the ground deeply the winter before sowing and work in plenty of compost or well-rotted manure; leave the soil rough so that frost can break down the clods.

A month or two before sowing, dig a trench, straight or circular, 45-60cm (18-24in) wide on the chosen site. Remove the top spit of soil (one spade's depth), then work a bucketful per sq m/yd of garden compost or well-rotted manure into the second spit of soil. Replace the topsoil and finish off the trench with a slight depression – this will help to retain water and prevent the roots from drying out in summer.

A couple of weeks before sowing rake in a general fertilizer at 25g per sq m (1oz per sq yd).

Staking and supporting

Both tall and dwarf runner beans need some form of support to keep the crop clear of the ground. Dwarf types need only 45cm (18in) stakes and can be tied to them as they grow. Taller varieties need longer supports – 2.5-3m (8-10ft) high – and a much firmer structure to withstand the wind.

Crossed poles Runner beans are often supported by stakes set on both sides of a double row. The stakes should be inserted before the seeds are sown. Hazel and ash poles are the least brittle, but sturdy bamboo canes are a suitable alternative.

Push the stakes into the ground in two rows about 45cm (18in) apart. Cross opposite pairs just above the half-way mark – this ensures that pods on the upper parts of the plants, where there is most growth, hang outwards and are clearly visible. Lash the poles together with wire or strong string. Set adjacent pairs 30cm (12in) apart. To strengthen the structure, secure a pole horizontally along the V-shaped intersections. Allow 1.5-1.8m (5-6ft) between each double row.

Wigwams Push a 2.5m (8ft) stake into the centre of a circle 1.5m (5ft) in diameter. Attach strings from the top of the stake

to pegs placed in the ground at 60cm (2ft) intervals around the edge of the circle.

Alternatively, use poles instead of strings – dispense with the central stake and tie the poles firmly together at the top.

Netting Set up a row of sturdy 2.5m (8ft) poles along the bean trench, placing them 1.5-1.8m (5-6ft) apart, with 75cm (2½ft) between rows. Staple plastic, string or wire netting to the poles. This forms a rigid, wind-resistant structure.

Alternatively, support beans against netting fixed to a permanent wall or fence.

Sowing and planting

Runner beans are half-hardy plants and should not be put outside until all danger of frost is past – in late spring or early summer. It is an advantage to get them off to an early start.

Strip-grown plants Hardened-off young plants can be purchased from garden centres and transplanted to the prepared bed. Position one plant at the base of each pole or at 15cm (6in) intervals

▲ **Net support** Push a row of strong 2.5m (8ft) stakes well into the ground – space them 1.5-1.8m (5-6ft) apart. Attach plastic, string or wire netting firmly to them.

PINCHING OUT

When the runner bean plants have reached the top of their supports, start pinching out the growing tips. This stops the climbing stems from growing any more, encourages side-shoots and bushiness and increases flowering (and therefore the number of pods as well).

Normally tall-growing runner bean varieties grown on the flat without supports should have the growing tips pinched out as soon as the plants reach a height of about 30cm (1ft).

against net supports. Set each one close to the support – about 7.5cm (3in) away – to allow the plants to develop. With poles, set the plants on the inner side of the supports.

Sowing outdoors The first outdoor sowing can be made in mid spring under cloches that have been in place for a couple of weeks to warm up the soil. Put the supports in place and take out drills 5cm (2in) deep. Sow two seeds at intervals of about 15cm (6in) with a few extra at each end to fill in any gaps. Leave the cloches on until early summer.

After germination, pull up the weaker of each pair of seedlings using these extra plants, if necessary, to fill in gaps where neither seed has germinated.

After sowing and transplanting, water the soil thoroughly and then scatter slug pellets.

Sowing under glass To produce the earliest crop, sow an early variety such as 'Kelvedon Marvel' in early to mid spring. Sow seeds 2.5cm (1in) deep in compost-filled pots or polystyrene moulds or in 12cm (5in) deep seed trays.

After germination, preferably in a propagator unit, transfer the small plants in their pots to an unheated greenhouse or cold frame. Harden the plants off gradually by increasing the ventilation in the greenhouse or by lifting the lid of the cold frame on warm days.

When the plants are sturdy, put them out in the open – in late spring or early summer, depending on prevailing conditions. Use a trowel to dig holes for each seedling and water them in well.

A sheet of clear plastic about 60-90cm (2-3ft) high fixed to the outside of the supports will protect the young plants in the early stages from the wind if necessary.

Looking after the crop
As the plants grow, spread a 2.5cm (1in) deep mulch of strawy manure, leaf-mould, grass clippings, garden compost or forest bark around the plants. This helps to prevent the soil from becoming too dry and also smothers weeds.

Twine the runners (climbing shoots) anti-clockwise around the supports – the natural way that the plants climb – and tie them in loosely with string if necessary. When the plants have reached the top of their stakes, begin to pinch out the growing tips.

You may choose to grow some of the normally tall-growing varieties as short and bushy plants. This means pinching out the growing tips when the plants are about 30cm (1ft) high, and then growing the beans as bushes without supports. Space the plants 60cm (2ft) apart. When flowering begins, assist fruit-setting by spraying the plants with water, daily during hot weather.

In general, it is better to grow runner beans on supports since more beans are produced and the pods grow longer and straighter. Beans raised off the ground are also less accessible to slugs.

Runner beans need frequent watering, so don't let the soil around them dry out.

Harvesting
Runner beans are ready to pick from mid summer onwards. Pick the beans every couple of days so that they don't have a chance to mature fully – even a small number allowed to mature will stop the flower-producing mechanism.

An ideal harvesting size is 15-20cm (6-8in) long: if you pick the pods at this stage a season of eight weeks should be guaranteed. The more you pick the beans, the more the plants will produce.

When the last beans have been picked, cut the foliage off at ground level. Burn the stems – they are too woody for compost. Leave the roots in the soil – they are a valuable source of nitrogen.

Pest and diseases
The major problem with runner beans is the failure of flowers to set. Dryness at the roots, a lack of pollinating insects or birds pecking off buds are the usual causes.

Chocolate spot occasionally attacks the plants; if serious, spray with a copper fungicide. Foot rot can usually be prevented by watering young plants with Cheshunt compound.

VARIETIES TO CHOOSE

Tall-growing varieties
'Achievement' – heavy cropper; long straight pods; good for freezing and exhibition.

'Enorma' – improved strain of 'Prizewinner'; long pods of fine flavour and shape; good for freezing and exhibition.

'Kelvedon Marvel' – semi-dwarf variety which can be grown as a bush; earliest of all croppers.

'Lady Di' – long slender, fleshy pods; slow seed development; heavy stringless crops.

'Prizewinner' – good cropper of large fleshy pods about 30-40cm (12-16in) long; excellent flavour.
'Scarlet Emperor' – popular all-round bean; heavy early cropper of high-quality pods; can be grown as a bush.

'Sunset' – very early cropper; good for freezing; can be grown as a bush; pink-flowered.

Dwarf varieties
'Gulliver' – heavy cropper; smooth, crisp and stringless pods on plants 38cm (15in) high.

'Pickwick' – bushy compact plant; early cropper; stringless; doesn't produce runners.

Runner bean 'Prizewinner'

Runner bean 'Achievement'

BEETROOT

A sweet-flavoured root vegetable ideal for salads and soups, beetroot is slow-growing but can be harvested and enjoyed throughout the year.

There are two main types of beet-root. Globe varieties are usually grown for eating freshly boiled in summer and autumn. Long-rooted varieties are harvested in autumn and stored for winter use. Inter-mediate varieties are similar to but generally shorter than longer types. Both have similar growing requirements. A 6m (20ft) row should yield 12kg (25lb) of globe beetroot or 21.5kg (45lb) of long-rooted types.

Beetroot thrive best in an open sunny site; although they produce generally higher yields on a light, sandy loam, they can be grown on heavier soils – if the ground is well prepared beforehand. Dig the plot in autumn or early winter before sowing. If the soil is heavy, fork in coir at the rate of one bucketful per sq m/yd.

Never grow beetroot on freshly manured ground – they are likely to separate into small, forked roots. Just before sowing, rake in a dressing of general fertilizer at a rate of 50g (2oz) per sq m/yd.

◄ **Types of beetroot** Round globe varieties are grown for a summer crop while the main crop of long-rooted beetroot is lifted in autumn for winter use. Both are easy to grow and thrive in light, well-drained loamy soil and an open, sunny site. Avoid freshly manured sites or the roots will fork.

globe beetroot

long-rooted beetroot

Growing beetroot

In sheltered sites in southern areas, sow bolt-resisting varieties of beetroot from early spring onwards. In colder areas, begin sowing in mid spring. For a succession of roots throughout summer and autumn, sow globe varieties from mid spring to mid summer. Sow long-rooted and intermediate varieties in late spring for winter storage.

A beetroot 'seed' is a fused cluster of between one and four separate seeds. They will germinate as a group, so sow seeds sparingly to make later thinning easier. Place seed clusters of globe varieties about 5cm (2in) apart. Sow long-rooted types in groups of two seeds every 20cm (8in) – thin out later.

For globe varieties sow seeds in drills 30cm (1ft) apart; for long-rooted types allow 45cm (18in) between rows. In both cases the drills should be about 2cm (^{3}/4in) deep. For early crops prepare the seed bed in a cold frame or under cloches. Harden off the seedlings gradually, finally removing the cloches after the danger of frost has receded.

When the seedlings of globe varieties are about 2.5cm (1in) high, remove the weakest from each group to leave a row of single seedlings spaced 5cm (2in) apart.

Once the roots reach the size of a golf ball, begin the next stage of thinning; the remaining, stronger roots should be 10cm (4in) apart. The discarded roots can be boiled as a summer vegetable.

The rows should be kept clear of weeds. Always use a hoe and avoid damaging the tender roots. Excessive dryness can produce

HARVESTING BEETROOT

1 Pull globe varieties by hand as needed. Long-rooted beetroot must be eased out using a fork – take care not to damage the roots.

2 Twist off the top foliage, leaving 5cm (2in) attached to the roots to prevent 'bleeding'. Store the roots in boxes of sand in a frost-free place.

woodiness and smaller yields – ensure that the plot is watered frequently, every two weeks in hot weather. Mulching will improve moisture retention. Alternatively, a return to very wet conditions can lead to splitting of the roots.

Harvest the rest of the crop as needed, but do not allow any to grow larger than the size of a cricket ball. Otherwise, they lose their sweet flavour.

Harvesting and storing

Harvest globe varieties by hand as required. Once out of the ground, shake off any soil and discard any damaged roots. To remove the leaves, hold the base of the leaves tightly in one hand and twist off the remainder with the other, leaving a 5cm (2in) crown of leaves. Cutting the leaf stems or twisting them off too close to the root will cause 'bleeding' – a process whereby the roots lose their juiciness and flavour.

Lift long-rooted varieties in mid autumn by placing a garden fork alongside the row and then gently breaking up the soil, so that the roots can be removed without damage. After twisting off the tops, store the roots in boxes of sand in a frost-proof place. However, if you are short of storage space, beetroot can be left in the ground and lifted as required.

Pests and diseases

Black bean aphid is the main pest. Diseases that can trouble beetroot include boron deficiency, damping off, leaf spot and violet root rot.

VARIETIES TO CHOOSE

Globe-rooted varieties

'Boltardy' – fine-textured, deep red root; resistant to bolting; can be sown early.

'Burpee's Golden' – golden-orange with yellow flesh that does not bleed; leaves can be cooked like spinach.

'Crimson King' – can be sown from mid spring to early summer for winter use; crisp, dark roots with fine texture.

'Detroit' – standard maincrop globe variety; sweet, crisp flesh; can be stored over winter.

'Detroit 2 Little Ball' – good for late sowing; baby beets ideal for pickling.

'Monogram' – rich red colour; smooth skin; each seed cluster produces one seedling only, no thinning necessary.

Intermediate varieties

'Cylindra' – oval-shaped root; deep red flesh with excellent storing qualities; good for even slicing.

Long-rooted varieties

'Cheltenham Green Top' – popular; very long roots; ideal for storage over winter and well into spring.

'Forono' – good flavour and texture; slow to become woody and stores well.

'Long Blood Red' – medium-length deep red root; exhibition quality.

Globe beetroot 'Burpee's Golden'

Globe beetroot 'Boltardy'

Long beetroot 'Forono'

BROCCOLI AND CALABRESE

Hardy and adaptable to poor soils, sprouting broccoli produces high yields early in the year. Autumn-maturing calabrese is less hardy.

The attractive purple and white heads of sprouting broccoli help to fill a gap in the garden vegetable plot between Brussels sprouts and spring cabbages. Calabrese (green-headed broccoli) is less hardy, but produces larger heads for autumn use and has a shorter growing season.

Sprouting broccoli produce many small leafy flower heads, 2.5-5cm (1-2in) across, on short stalks. If you pick the plants every few days, they should continue to produce young spears over a period of at least two months.

Sprouting broccoli is one of the most rewarding vegetables to grow because it crops at a time when there is a limited choice of vegetables in the shops.

Site and soil preparation

Broccoli can be grown on poor soils and in cold areas, though it does best in fertile, loamy soil and in a sunny position. Choose a site sheltered from winter winds, otherwise staking may be necessary.

Broccoli thrives in well-manured, alkaline soil dressed with fertilizer. Unless the soil was manured for a previous crop, dig in well-rotted manure or garden compost during the autumn or winter before planting, at the rate of half a bucketful per sq m/sq yd.

If a test shows the soil to be acid or neutral, give it a top-dressing of carbonate of lime at a rate of 100g per sq m (4oz per sq yd) in spring. A fortnight before setting out the plants, hoe in a dressing of general compound fertilizer at a rate of 75g per sq m (3oz per sq yd).

Sowing and planting

Sprouting broccoli takes up a lot of space for a considerable period of time – allow about 60cm (2ft) between plants. Ten plants in a row 6m (20ft) long should yield more than 7kg (15lb) of spears.

Like most other brassicas, broccoli is usually raised in an outdoor seed bed and transplanted. Level and rake the seed bed and cover it with sifted garden compost. Tread over the compost to firm it down, and then rake it lightly.

Sow the seeds in mid spring, in drills 12mm (½in) deep and 15cm (6in) apart. Scatter compost over them and firm the bed with the head of a rake. Keep the bed moist, using a watering can with a

▲ **Sprouting broccoli** Purple or white sprouting broccoli produce numerous small heads or spears 2.5-5cm (1-2in) across – which are cut with a length of stem and cooked in a bunch. Harvest regularly to prevent flowering and to stimulate further young growth.

fine rose. Thin the seedlings until they are 5cm (2in) apart.

When the young plants are about 10cm (4in) high, with four or five leaves, plant them out 60cm (2ft) apart, using a dibber to take out planting holes. For a succession of crops, sow again in early summer and plant out in late summer.

Check that the young plants

are firmly planted by tugging the upper leaves gently. Apply diazinon + chlorpyrifos or water in pirimiphos-methyl to protect the plants from cabbage root fly; water daily until they are fully established.

Water regularly during dry spells, and keep weeds down by hoeing. To save weeding time, put a mulch down between the rows. Use a strawy mulch in winter.

Gales may rock the plants and loosen their roots. If necessary tie them to stakes or strong canes.

Harvesting

Broccoli spears are ready to cut when the small flower heads are well formed, but before the flowers open. The main harvesting period is from early to late spring, although the earliest of the purple varieties may be ready in late winter. White varieties mature later.

Pick the central spear first, when it is 10-15cm (4-6in) long, cutting back to a point just above a pair of side-shoots. Side-shoots will produce fresh spears.

Pests and diseases

Broccoli may be attacked by aphids, cabbage root fly, whitefly, caterpillars and flea beetles. Like other brassicas, broccoli is prone to club root disease, most prevalent on poorly drained soils and those lacking in lime. Before transplanting seedlings, dip the roots in a solution of thiophanate-methyl or dust the planting holes with calomel.

Perennial broccoli

Perennial broccoli is a good option if you want to avoid the bother of sowing and transplanting every year. On good soils, a reliable variety will crop for several years, with heads of increasing size, provided that all the heads are used before they run to seed.

Perennial broccoli tends to grow very tall, so leave about 90cm (3ft) between the plants. Always stake them, or plant them against a fence.

Sow 2cm (³/₄in) deep in a prepared seed bed from mid spring onwards, and plant out from early summer. Apply a general-purpose fertilizer every spring and a mulch in early summer. Pick from mid spring onwards.

CALABRESE

◄ **Calabrese** is more solid than sprouting broccoli. Calabrese varieties bear flower heads that are excellent for freezing. They are prolific croppers from successional sowings.

Calabrese is a distinct type of broccoli and produces larger, dome-shaped heads of green or purple that open to reveal yellow flowers if they are left on the plants too long. It yields good crops of firm-textured heads, followed by smaller side-shoots, from late summer on.

Sowing and planting

Calabrese thrives in the same conditions as broccoli, but will not survive frosts. Seeds can be sown under glass for an early crop, but the most productive plants are from seedlings raised in open ground and left to grow on. Calabrese dislikes transplanting which often causes bolting.

Sow the seeds in mid to late spring, depending on soil and weather conditions, in drills 12mm (½in) deep and 30cm (1ft) apart. Cover them with sifted compost and firm the drills with the head of a rake. Thin the seedlings when they are large enough to handle, to 10-15cm (4-6in) apart, and later to final spacings of 15cm (6in).

Keep weeds down and water thoroughly during dry spells.

Harvesting

Cut calabrese heads with about 2.5cm (1in) of stalk in late summer and early autumn, when the flower buds are green and tightly closed. The side-shoots will produce further heads. Most varieties mature within 100 days after a spring sowing. Purple calabrese turns bright green during cooking, but retains its distinctive nutty flavour.

Pests and diseases

Calabrese is subject to the same pests and diseases as sprouting broccoli. Whiptail disease may be a problem where the soil is deficient in molybdenum.

VARIETIES TO CHOOSE

Purple sprouting

'Early Purple Sprouting' – spears ready for cutting in late winter or early spring.

'Purple Sprouting Red Arrow' – late-maturing, ready for cutting from mid spring; robust; produces numerous side-shoots.

White sprouting

'Early White Sprouting' – for cutting from early to mid spring; pronounced flavour.

'Late White Sprouting' – for cutting from mid to late spring; heavy cropper from compact plants.

Perennial broccoli

'Nine Star Perennial' – white, small, cauliflower-like heads; plants grow large and crop for several years on fertile soil.

Calabrese

'Corvet' (F1 hybrid) – ready about 90 days after sowing; large, round light green heads, uniform and of fine quality.

'Emperor' (F1 hybrid) – early-maturing and strong-growing; suitable for poor soils; thick, dark green domed heads.

'Express Corona' (F1 hybrid) – for cutting late summer to early autumn; side-shoots develop freely after the centre head is cut.

'Green Comet' (F1 hybrid) – early, from late summer; deep green heads, large and tight.

'Green Sprouting' – medium-sized central heads in late summer; numerous small side-shoots.

'Mercedes' (F1 hybrid) – heavy cropper; matures 75 days after spring sowing; tight, blue-green heads, turning dark green when cooked.

'Romanesco' – ready for cutting in late autumn; lime-green heads in 'pinnacles'.

'Shogun' (F1 hybrid) – tolerant of cold weather and crops into late autumn; dark green, dome-shaped heads.

'Topstar' (F1 hybrid) – mid-season variety; high yielding and very uniform; large heads, followed by side-shoots.

'Trixie' – purple-headed variety; domed heads and numerous side-shoots; resistant to club root.

Calabrese 'Corvet'

Broccoli 'Early White Sprouting'

Broccoli 'Purple Sprouting'

Calabrese 'Romanesco'

BRUSSELS SPROUTS

Rich in vitamin C, Brussels sprouts are an essential winter vegetable: plant both early and late varieties for a long cropping season.

Brussels sprouts may not be a wise choice for very small gardens, since they do best in open conditions. They also occupy a fair amount of space over a longer period than most crops (about eight months). However, they are well worth growing for green winter vegetables.

Modern F1 hybrids have largely superseded older varieties, as they are of compact growth and produce 'button' sprouts of uniform size, all at the same time.

By sowing early and late varieties, you can have Brussels sprouts ready for harvesting from early autumn to early or mid spring. If you have freezer space, it may be easier to make a single large sowing of one type and freeze the surplus.

Each 3m (10ft) row of plants should yield about 7.5kg (16lb) of sprouts.

Planning the crop

Sprouts grow well only in fertile soil with an adequate lime content, and in an open sunny site.

Dig the Brussels sprout bed during the winter before sowing, to give it plenty of time to settle. Ideally, it should have been well manured for a previous crop – if not, dig in well-rotted garden compost or manure.

◄ **Brussels sprouts** Said to have first originated in Belgium, Brussels sprouts may have a totally unprepossessing appearance, but they yield fresh green vegetables throughout winter. The modern F1 hybrids are reliable and compact, producing large numbers of uniform firm and tasty button sprouts. Sow early and main crop varieties for sprouts from autumn through to spring.

On acid soils, add hydrated lime in winter – spread the lime on the surface and leave it to be washed in by rain. Besides reducing the acidity, liming also improves soil structure, making for quicker drainage and firmer rooting.

Apply a dressing of hydrated or garden lime at the rate of 150g per sq m (6oz per sq yd) or ground chalk or ground limestone at 250g per sq m (8oz per sq yd), after digging, but be careful not to increase the pH value to unacceptable alkaline levels; a pH of 6.5 is the ideal.

Sowing and planting

By far the easiest way to grow Brussels sprouts is to buy young

HARVESTING BRUSSELS SPROUTS

1 Remove yellowing leaves and 'blown' sprouts from the lower part of the stem as the plants mature, to improve air circulation. Loose-leaved sprouts are tasteless and best discarded.

2 Harvest the lower sprouts first, while they are still small, not much larger than walnuts, and while their leaves are still tight. Harvest after a slight frost, for an improved flavour.

100

▲ **Straw mulch** Brussels sprouts need fertile soil that has been manured for a previous crop. A straw mulch protects roots from frost and the sprouts from mud splashes. At the end of the season the straw can be dug in to improve soil structure.

▲ **Spring greens** The cabbage-like top growths of Brussels sprout plants may be picked at the end of the cropping season when all the sprouts have been harvested. They can be cooked and served like cabbage and other spring greens.

plants from a garden centre and put them straight into a prepared bed. However, it is cheaper to sow from seed and transplant.

Make the first sowings of early varieties in the middle of early spring, in a sheltered seed bed. Sow the seeds 12mm (½in) deep in drills 15cm (6in) apart, and thin the seedlings to 5-7.5cm (2-3in) apart when they are 2.5cm (1in) high.

Sow maincrop (late) varieties in mid spring, using similar spacings. When plants of both early and maincrop sowings are about six weeks old and 10-15cm (4-6in) tall, transplant them to their final bed. Water the rows the day before moving the young plants, but do not fork the soil; it should be firm, otherwise the sprouts 'blow', becoming loose and open instead of tight and closed.

Select only strong, healthy-looking plants and set them firmly 60-75cm (2-2½ft) apart, in rows the same distance apart. Leave 45cm (1½ft) for dwarf varieties. Sprinkle diazinon + chlorpyrifos in the planting holes to deter cabbage root flies; or surround the plants with proprietary brassica collars.

Water the young plants daily in the evening during dry weather and stake large plants that are exposed to wind.

Harvesting
Early varieties will be ready for harvesting between early autumn and early winter; late varieties between late autumn and early spring.

Pick the sprouts while they are still small, not much larger than walnuts, and while their heads are still tight and firm.

Pick the lower sprouts first. You can cut off the cabbage-like top head, which can be cooked as a vegetable.

Pests and diseases
Brussels sprouts may be attacked by aphids, cabbage root fly, cabbage whitefly, caterpillars and flea beetles. They are vulnerable to club root, leaf spot and spray damage, especially if the soil is deficient in lime.

Brussels sprout 'Troika'

VARIETIES TO CHOOSE

'Citadel' (F1 hybrid) – heavy cropper; maincrop variety, maturing from early winter onwards.

'Fortress' (F1 hybrid) – dark green sprouts, for picking late, from mid winter to early spring; very hardy, good for northern areas.

'Mallard' (F1 hybrid) – medium-size, dark green sprouts; early to mid season variety; heavy cropping.

'Peer Gynt' (F1 hybrid) – matures early, from mid autumn onwards; small, compact, solid buttons on dwarf-growing plants; freezes well.

'Rampart' (F1 hybrid) – heavy, reliable cropper; firm dark green sprouts from mid winter.

'Roodnerf' – reliable maincrop; medium-size sprouts, ready from late autumn.

'Rubine' – medium size sprouts, flushed deep red; excellent flavour; moderate cropper, maturing late autumn onwards; can be eaten raw in salads.

'Troika' – good-quality, dark green oval to round sprouts in mid and late winter.

CABBAGES

In one form or another, cabbages are available throughout the year, providing a ready supply of crisp and nourishing greenery.

savoy cabbage

summer cabbage

winter cabbage

spring cabbage

red cabbage

Cabbages are fully hardy and easy to grow; they are harvested at the peak of freshness and many, especially the winter types, have excellent storage qualities.

Types of cabbage

Cabbage heads, or hearts, may be round, conical or drumhead (round with a flattened top). They range in colour from dark to light green and white, and from pink to purple.

Spring cabbages have bright green, loose-leaved, conical heads. They are ready for harvesting in mid to late spring, and they can also be used as spring greens.

Summer cabbages have larger, more compact and generally rounder heads. They are ready for harvesting in late summer and early autumn.

Autumn and winter cabbages are solid round-headed or drum-headed. They are ready from autumn to late winter.

Savoy cabbages are round-headed, with crisp, dark green, crinkled leaves. Sow them in succession for fresh crops from early autumn to late spring.

Red cabbages have solid heads of crisp leaves. They are another good autumn and winter crop.

Site and soil preparation

Cabbages of all types need a

BRASSICA COLLARS

After planting out young cabbages, carefully fit brassica collars around the stems. Available from most garden centres, they protect the plants against cabbage root fly.

sunny, open site in well-drained alkaline soil. They are raised in a seed bed and then transplanted to the position where they will grow and mature.

If you are growing vegetables in the plot for the first time, work in manure or compost at the rate of half a bucketful per sq m/sq yd during the winter before planting. If the cabbages are following pod-bearing crops or salads in a rotation plan, the plot doesn't need manuring.

Spread lime liberally on the surface after digging or just before planting. Tread the bed firmly and rake it to a fine tilth. Apply a general fertilizer at the rate of 50g per sq m (2oz per sq yd) to the main bed.

Sowing and planting

Strip-grown plants from nurseries or garden centres are treated as home-raised seedlings.

Summer cabbages Sow seeds in mid spring. Draw drills 5mm

TRANSPLANTING CABBAGES

1 When the young plants are ready for transplanting, prepare holes for them 30-60cm (1-2ft) apart, depending on type. Add calomel dust to each hole to discourage club root fungus.

2 Set the cabbage plants carefully in the holes and firm them in place before watering in thoroughly. Hoe regularly to remove weeds and water thoroughly to ensure the bed never dries out.

(¹/₄in) deep and 15cm (6in) apart in a seed bed and sow thinly.

Thin seedlings to 5cm (2in) apart and transplant them by early summer, setting them 45cm (18in) apart in rows the same distance apart. Plant firmly and water well.

Autumn and winter cabbages Sow seeds in mid to late spring as for summer cabbages. For a regular supply throughout the winter months, sow the seeds in two or more batches.

Transplant the seedlings to a permanent bed from late spring to mid summer. Set them 45cm (18in) apart in rows 60cm (2ft) apart.

Savoy cabbages Sow seeds as for summer cabbages. Seeds sown in mid spring will produce a crop from early autumn to early winter; those sown in late spring will provide cabbages from mid winter to early spring; a mid summer sowing will give a crop the following mid to late spring.

Transplant the seedlings to the permanent bed six weeks after sowing. Plant them 45cm (18in) apart in rows 60cm (2ft) apart.

Spring cabbages Sow seeds in a prepared bed during the first fortnight of August in the same way as for summer cabbages.

It is important to sow spring cabbages at the correct time – if sown too early, the plants may grow too large to withstand a hard winter, and if sown too late, they will not have enough time to develop beyond the seedling stage.

Thin seedlings to 5cm (2in) apart. Six weeks after sowing, transplant them to their permanent bed. Space spring green plants 30cm (1ft) apart. Allow 38cm (15in) between those that will be left to form hearts, and 45cm (18in) between rows.

Water them in with pirimiphosmethyl to guard against cabbage root fly. In early spring, hoe 15g per sq m (¹/₂oz per sq yd) of nitrate of soda into the soil surface.

Red cabbages Sow the seeds in late summer or early autumn. Leave the seedlings in the seed bed throughout autumn and winter, protecting them with cloches during severe weather.

Transplant the young cabbages in mid spring, setting them 60cm (2ft) apart in rows the same distance apart.

Harvesting
Cut cabbages when their heads are firm and fleshy. Savoy cabbages are at their best after a slight frost.

Pest and diseases
The main diseases of cabbages are club root and leaf spot. Cabbage root fly, whitefly and flea beetles are the most troublesome pests.

CHINESE CABBAGE

The Chinese cabbage is prized for its delicate flavour. Four plants should be adequate for average needs – the harvesting period occurs in autumn when other vegetables are plentiful.

At the end of spring, spread a light dressing of manure or compost on the site. If the soil is at all acid, sprinkle lime on the surface.

In early summer, sow seeds 12mm (½in) deep in rows 60cm (2ft) apart. As soon as the seedlings are large enough to handle, thin them out to 30-38cm (12-15in) apart.

Water the plants well during dry spells and hoe the bed regularly. Scatter slug pellets. If the hearts seem loose, bunch the outer leaves around them and tie in place with twine.

Chinese cabbages are ready for harvesting between seven to ten weeks

◄ **Chinese cabbage** Looking more like a large cos lettuce than a conventional cabbage, Chinese cabbages are raised from seed. Varieties include 'Mariko', 'Monument', 'Ruffles' and 'Tip Top'. They can be eaten either raw or cooked.

after sowing, when they should have firm hearts. They are prone to bolting if sown too early or watered insufficiently.

Chinese cabbages are used as a salad vegetable or cooked like cabbage.

Cabbage 'Wheeler's Imperial'

Cabbage 'Celtic'

VARIETIES TO CHOOSE

Spring cabbages
Durham Early' – early maturing; often used as spring greens.

'Pixie' – early maturing; small pointed heads; close planting.

'Spring Hero' – round-headed and compact; almost white heads.

'Wheeler's Imperial' – old favourite; dwarf; solid pointed heads.

Summer cabbages
'Greyhound' – medium size; compact, pointed heads; few outer leaves.

'Hispi' – large, solid, crisp, pointed heads; good flavour; very reliable cropper.

'Primo' – early maturing; dwarf; compact, round heads.

'Winnigstadt' – large, solid, pointed heads; few outside leaves.

Autumn and winter cabbages
'Celtic' – firm, round heads with leaves like a savoy cabbage.

'Christmas Drumhead' – dwarf and compact; very hardy.

'Holland Late Winter' – solid white ball heads; store well.

Savoy cabbages
'Best of All' – early maturing; extra large, solid drumheads.

'Ormskirk Late' – large heads; very hardy; good flavour.

'Savoy King' – large, green heads; excellent for year-round crops.

Red cabbages
'Red Drumhead' – firm, dark red heads; compact; good for pickling.

'Ruby Ball' – firm, round heads; few outer leaves; very early maturing; good flavour.

Cabbage 'Hispi'

Cabbage 'Ormskirk Late'

Cabbage 'Ruby Ball'

CARDOONS

**Resembling globe artichokes, the
handsome cardoon is grown for the delicacy
of its crisp stems and midribs.**

Related to globe artichokes, cardoons are grown for the stems and midribs of their young, inner leaves, which require blanching in order to be palatable.

They are large plants, up to 2m (7ft) tall, and can be planted as a decorative summer screen for the vegetable plot. They are normally pest and disease-free.

Cultivation

Cardoons need rich, moisture-retentive but well-drained soil. In mid spring, dig a trench 30cm (1ft) deep and leave the lifted soil on each side. Fork a generous layer of well-rotted manure, garden compost or similar organic matter into the soil at the bottom.

About a month later, sow the cardoon seeds in groups of three, 50cm (20in) apart and 12mm (½in) deep, using fine soil or pot

▼ **Supporting cardoons** Growing 2m (7ft) tall, cardoons need staking. Insert a stout 60cm (2ft) stake by each plant when about 38cm (15in) high. Tie the plant to the stake with string or raffia and add further ties as necessary.

ting compost to cover. Put cloches over the trench during the first month, and later remove the two weaker seedlings from each group.

Cardoons need generous watering throughout the summer, even to the extent of flooding the trench during a drought. Also apply weak liquid fertilizer every seven days in mid and late summer. When the plants are about 38cm (15in) tall, tie them to 60cm (2ft) stakes.

Growth is complete by early autumn, when blanching should begin (see right).

Harvesting

Lift whole plants with a fork and cut off the roots with a sharp knife. Then remove the wrappings and cut off stems, trimming off any foliage or pieces of damaged stem.

Alternatively, dig up a number of plants at the same time and store them, still wrapped in polythene, and with their roots well covered in moist soil. They should remain in good condition for several weeks.

Cook the blanched stems like celery or Florence fennel.

BLANCHING CARDOONS

1 In early autumn, tie the stems firmly together at the top and the bottom, using string or raffia. Make sure the plants are dry before they are blanched. Wrap black polythene around each plant, taking in the stake, and tie in place.

2 Earth up the base of each plant, using the soil piled near the trench. Earthing up is not vital, but gives extra protection from frost and strong winds and also assists blanching which makes the stems white and tender.

CARROTS

**Easy to grow and highly nutritious,
carrots can be enjoyed throughout the year if different
varieties are sown at regular intervals.**

Carrot varieties are grouped according to the length of their roots – stump, intermediate or long. Generally speaking, the longer and bigger the root of a particular variety, the later in the year the seeds should be sown and grown as a maincrop.

Stump-rooted varieties (also called short-rooted or round carrots) are sweet and succulent, and are a good choice for shallow soils. They take only 15 weeks to mature, so a crop sown in early spring should be ready for picking in early summer.

Intermediate-rooted carrots are good all-rounders. They taste sweet and mature early once the soil has warmed up. Pull them after 15 weeks and use as new carrots or leave them for 18 weeks to mature into a maincrop.

Long-rooted types taper to a point. They are a maincrop vegetable and require deep, rich soil.

Soil and site preparation

Carrots flourish in crumbly, soft, well-drained soil that was turned and dug the autumn before sowing. Lighten heavy clay soil with strawy manure.

A week before sowing, break up heavy lumps of soil and rake the topsoil until it is crumbly. Apply a general compound fertilizer, following the manufacturer's recommendations.

Carrots need plenty of sunlight. Avoid positioning rows on a site overshadowed by walls or trees. Use a site that was manured for a previous crop such as brassicas, but don't apply any more manure – it makes carrots hard skinned and can cause them to fork.

Sowing seeds

Carrot seeds are tiny and can be difficult to handle. Pelleted seeds make sowing easier but they don't increase the chances of germination, though thinning is quicker.

Avoid standing on the prepared soil as you sow seeds, since this compacts the ground.

Stump-rooted varieties The first outdoor sowing can be made at the beginning of early spring. Make shallow drills 12mm ($\frac{1}{2}$in) deep and 15cm (6in) apart. Sow seeds thinly, cover them lightly with soil and water well. Make other sowings in succession until late summer.

To get the seeds off to an early start, grow them under protection. Sow seeds in a cold frame or beneath cloches at the end of winter

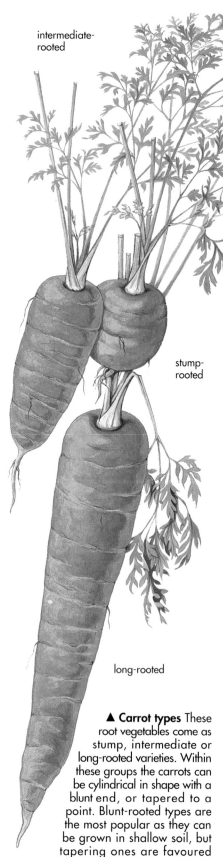

intermediate-rooted

stump-rooted

long-rooted

▲ **Carrot types** These root vegetables come as stump, intermediate or long-rooted varieties. Within these groups the carrots can be cylindrical in shape with a blunt end, or tapered to a point. Blunt-rooted types are the most popular as they can be grown in shallow soil, but tapering ones are favoured for exhibition.

1 When the plants are large enough to handle, thin them out in two stages, first to 2.5cm (1in) and later to 5cm (2in) apart for stump-rooted types and to a final spacing of 10cm (4in) for intermediate and long-rooted carrots. Work in the evening or on a dull day to avoid attracting carrot fly.

2 When pulling carrots, hold the foliage with one hand and, using a fork with the other hand, ease the carrots out of the ground. If you intend to store the carrots in boxes of sand, clean the soil away and trim off the foliage about 12mm (½in) above the top of the carrot. Don't store damaged roots.

(put the cloches in place a fortnight before sowing to warm up the soil). Leave the cloches in place until the plants are growing strongly and danger of heavy frost has passed.

For tender carrots in late autumn and early winter, sow a stump-rooted variety in late summer; cover them with cloches after thinning in early autumn.

Intermediate and long-rooted

Sow in the open any time from the middle of spring to mid summer. Make drills 12mm (½in) deep and 15cm (6in) apart. Sow seeds thinly, cover lightly with soil and water well.

Looking after the crop

Tend carrot plants on dull days or in the evenings – the combination of sun and the smell of bruised foliage attracts carrot fly.

As soon as the plants are large enough to handle, thin out the weaker specimens. Stump-rooted varieties should be spaced about 5cm (2in) apart, and intermediate and long-rooted types about 10cm (4in) apart.

After thinning, firm remaining plants, water well and treat the roots with diazinon + chlorpyrifos to deter carrot flies, wireworms and cutworms. Pull up any weeds.

Harvesting and storing

Pull stump-rooted and early intermediate-rooted varieties in early and mid summer, easing them out with a fork if the ground is hard.

Harvest maincrop carrots (both intermediate and long-rooted types) in early and mid autumn, about 18 weeks after sowing.

Surplus maincrop carrots can be stored in the freezer or in wooden boxes of sand. Before storing in sand, cut the foliage off close to the top of the carrots and remove any clinging soil (but don't wash them). Lay the carrots in the box, and pack dry sand between them. Store the boxes in a cool, dry place such as a shed or garage – check stored carrots regularly and remove any that show signs of rotting.

Pests and diseases

The main carrot pests are cutworm, carrot fly and aphids.

The diseases and disorders likely to affect carrots are sclerotinia rot and bacterial soft rot of stored carrots. Splitting and violet root rot are usually caused by unsuitable growing conditions.

VARIETIES TO CHOOSE

Stump-rooted varieties

'Amsterdam Forcing' – matures early and can be grown under glass; juicy roots with little core.

'Early French Frame' – crops early; round roots which are good for shallow soils.

'Parmex' – recommended for shallow soils; globe-like roots; good colour and flavour.

Intermediate-rooted varieties

'Autumn King' – a hardy carrot that can be left in the soil over winter; slightly resistant to carrot fly.

'Chantenay Red Cored' – plump carrots with smooth skins; good for early and late sowings.

'James Scarlet Intermediate' – a favourite maincrop carrot with tapering roots.

'Nantes Tip Top' – uniformly cylindrical, blunt-ended coreless carrots about 15cm (6in) long.

Long-rooted varieties

'New Red Intermediate' – despite its name it has very long roots; good flavour; stores well.

'St Valery' – long tapering roots; little core; stores well.

Stump-rooted 'Amsterdam Forcing'

Intermediate 'Chantenay Red Cored'

Long 'St Valery'

CAULIFLOWERS

**Delicate-flavoured and versatile,
cauliflower is a popular year-round vegetable, but it
demands perfect growing conditions.**

Cauliflowers are the most difficult of all brassicas to grow successfully – any setback, such as a period of drought or a check to growth, can result in failure of the crop.

In spite of this, they have always been popular with gardeners. Given the right conditions, and by selecting varieties that mature at different times, you can harvest cauliflowers all year round. They also freeze well.

Cauliflowers are divided into three main groups – summer, autumn and winter-maturing. Winter cauliflowers can be harvested from early winter to late spring, depending on variety. They are also known as broccoli, but should not be confused with sprouting broccoli – like summer cauliflowers, they have large white heads or 'curds' of tightly packed immature flowers. The most popular varieties of winter cauliflowers are less delicately flavoured than summer and autumn types, but are generally easier to grow.

Summer varieties are compact plants and mature from early to late summer, depending on the individual variety. They overlap with autumn cauliflowers, which are usually larger and more vigorous and demand rich, moisture-retentive soil.

▼ **Cauliflower curds** The crisp, creamy-white head of a cauliflower is protected by a nest of green-blue leaves.

Planning the crop

Cauliflowers need rich, loamy, deep soil. Grow them on land manured the previous year for pod-bearing crops. Dig thoroughly in autumn, working in plenty of well-rotted manure or garden compost on a new vegetable plot, and leave the ground rough for several months between digging and planting or sowing the seeds.

Choose a sunny site, open but not exposed, avoiding possible frost pockets – this is especially important for winter varieties. The soil pH should be neutral – between 6.5 and 7.5. At planting time, apply a general compound fertilizer at 75g per sq m (3oz per sq yd). If the soil is acid, top-dress

CULTIVATION

1 Select young plants with four or five leaves and a good ball of soil on the roots. To check the plants are set firmly, tug a leaf – it should tear.

2 Water the plants well and keep watering through the growing season. If the plants dry out, they produce undersized heads lacking in flavour.

3 When the curds begin to form, break two or three of the large outside leaves over them, to prevent sunlight from turning the curds yellow.

GROWING MINI-CAULIFLOWERS

Mini-varieties of cauliflower are easy to grow, ideal for a small plot and handy for freezer storage – one mini-cauliflower makes a single helping. Sow them directly in well-prepared ground, 15 x 15cm (6 x 6in) apart, and harvest when 4-9cm (1½-3½in) across.

By sowing in succession from mid to late spring, mini-cauliflowers can be successfully harvested from mid summer to mid autumn. Choose a suitable early maturing summer variety such as 'Garant' or 'Idol', followed by a late maturing variety such as 'Dominant'.

with lime in winter, several weeks after manuring.

About 14 cauliflowers can be grown in a 6m (20ft) row. Plant a mixture of varieties, maturing at different times, for a succession.

Sowing under glass
Sow the earliest summer-heading varieties in a cold frame in early autumn, or in a heated greenhouse in mid to late winter – for cauliflowers ready for cutting in late spring and early summer.

Cold frame sowing Prepare the soil as for an outdoor seed bed (see opposite). Scatter the seeds lightly and cover them with seed compost or sifted soil to a depth of 5mm (¼in). Keep the frame light closed until germination takes place, then allow a little ventilation during mild weather.

Thin the seedlings to about 5cm (2in) apart when they are large enough to handle. Cover the frame with sacking during hard night frosts. Keep the plants in the frame, continuing to ventilate in mild weather, until they are planted out around mid spring.

Greenhouse sowing Sow in late winter in a pan of seed compost, at a temperature of 10°C (50°F). When the seedlings are large enough to handle, prick them out 5cm (2in) apart in each direction into a tray of potting compost.

In early spring, put the tray into a cold frame, to harden off the plants before transplanting.

Planting out Use a trowel to make holes 45cm (1½ft) apart in a prepared bed, spacing the rows 45cm (1½ft) apart.

Make sure that seedlings for transplanting each have four or five leaves and a good ball of soil on the roots. Check that each plant has a growing point – a small half-folded leaf at the tip of the stem. Plant carefully without disturbing the root-ball, so that the stem is covered up to the lowest leaf. Firm the soil down well by pressing with your heel close to the stem.

Water well and keep watering as necessary. Never allow the plants to dry out, or they will produce undersized heads.

Sowing outdoors
For a later crop of summer-heading cauliflowers, sow outdoors from early to mid spring. Prepare the seed bed in a sunny, sheltered spot by raking it to a fine tilth and giving it a top dressing of a general fertilizer.

Sow the seeds in drills 5mm (¼in) deep, spacing the drills 15cm (6in) apart if you are sowing more than one variety. Take care to label the rows after sowing, then cover the drills with soil and firm.

Keep the seed bed moist. Thin to 5cm (2in) apart when the seedlings are large enough to handle. Plant out when the plants are 10-15cm (4-6in) high, following the method already described, but spacing these larger-growing plants 60cm (2ft) apart, and the rows also 60cm (2ft) apart. Do not fork the soil beforehand, or the plants will not form good heads.

Keep the plants well watered and give a dressing of nitrate of soda or nitro-chalk once or twice during the growing season, to improve the quality of the curds.

When the curds begin to form, break two or three of the large outside leaves over them, to prevent sunlight from turning the curds yellow, or frost from turning them brown.

Covering can be left until the curds are nearly mature, or omitted altogether in the case of some varieties with in-curving leaves.

The same methods of sowing, thinning and planting out are used for autumn-heading and winter-heading cauliflowers.

Harvesting and storing
Cut the heads while they are still firm – left too long, the florets will begin to separate. Cut cauliflowers in the morning, when the heads still have dew on them. In frosty weather, wait until midday.

If too many of the cauliflowers mature at the same time, pull up the plants and hang them upside-down in a cool shed. They should keep for up to three weeks.

Pests and diseases
Like other brassicas, cauliflowers are subject to attack by aphids, cabbage root fly, cabbage whitefly, caterpillars and flea beetles. Brassica collars (see page 102) can reduce their incidence.

They are also vulnerable to club root, damping off, downy mildew, leaf spot, spray damage, whiptail and wire stem. Chemical treatment is available for most of these, but healthy, strongly growing plants are less likely to succumb to disease.

CELERY

Grow your own celery for a fresh supply of crisp, juicy stalks from late summer to late winter.

There are two types of celery – trench-grown and self-blanching. **Trench-grown** celery must be earthed up or covered as it grows to blanch the stems – the aim of blanching is not to whiten the stems (celery can be white, pink, red, yellow or green) but to make them crisper, longer, more tender and less fibrous, and with a less bitter flavour. Trench varieties can be lifted from the open ground any time between mid autumn and late winter.

Self-blanching celery is grown on level ground and needs no earthing up – plants are set in blocks instead of in rows so that they shield each other from the light. Only those on the outside are shaded with straw. Self-blanching varieties are less hardy than trench-grown types, and should be lifted between late summer and mid autumn.

There are several variations on these two growing methods. Trench celery is usually enclosed

▲ **Celery stalks** Eaten raw in salads or cooked as a vegetable, celery should be crisp and juicy. Harvest self-blanching varieties before the first frosts; trench types, whose flavour is improved by frost, can be left in the ground and lifted as required from mid autumn to late winter.

within collars of cardboard or black polythene to discourage pests and to keep the hearts free from soil. The same type of collar can be used to improve the flavour of self-blanching varieties. You can even put loose collars round the growing plants and pack them with earth to exclude light. Such options are labour saving where only a dozen or so plants are grown – they cut down on the amount of trenching needed or cut it out altogether.

Soil and site preparation
Celery grows best in an open position in rich soil.

For self-blanching varieties, work in a bucketful of well-rotted farmyard manure or garden compost per sq m/yd during the winter before planting.

◄ **Blanching celery** Tie cardboard or black polythene collars round the stems to blanch them. Self-blanching celery is grown on the flat, but the hardier trench-grown types should also be earthed up to improve the flavour.

For trench-grown varieties, dig the trench in mid spring in readiness for planting out in late spring or early summer. The trench should be 30cm (1ft) wide for a single row of celery and 60cm (2ft) wide for a double row.

Dig the trench 30cm (1ft) deep and place the excavated soil on each side of it. Fork over the bottom of the trench and work in well-rotted garden compost or manure at the rate of a bucketful per sq m/sq yd. Replace some of the soil so that the base of the trench is about 15cm (6in) below true ground level. The rest of the soil will be used for earthing up the plants later.

The space on each side of the trench can be used for an early catch crop. Plant out a row of lettuce seedlings 30cm (1ft) apart or sow lettuces or stringless dwarf French beans.

GROWING SELF-BLANCHING CELERY

1 Use a trowel to loosen and lift the young plants with the soil ball intact; set them in a block so that they are 23cm (9in) apart in all directions. Water them in well.

2 Self-blanching celery plants do not need earthing up. The inner plants in a block are completely shielded from the light by the outer ones, but those on the outside should be packed with straw in mid summer.

▲ **Harvesting self-blanching celery** Push the protective straw to one side and lift the required number of plants with a garden fork. Afterwards, pile the straw around the newly exposed plants to continue the blanching.

Just before planting out the celery, rake in 50-75g (2-3oz) of a general fertilizer per sq m/sq yd.

Sowing and planting

Young strip-grown plants can be bought from nurseries and garden centres. If they are a self-blanching variety, plant them out by the beginning of early summer. Set the young plants 23cm (9in) apart in each direction so that a block is formed. Water in well.

Plant out trench-grown varieties at the same time. Space the plants 23cm (9in) apart along the centre of the prepared trench. If planting double rows, allow 45cm (18in) between them. Water the plants in well.

Alternatively, sow seeds of either type in early spring in a pan of seed compost – cover them thinly with sifted compost. Place the pan in a plastic bag and put it in an airing cupboard until the

seeds have germinated. Or leave the seed pan in a greenhouse with a temperature of 10-13°C (50-55°F).

When the seedlings are large enough to handle, prick them out 5cm (2in) apart in trays of potting compost. Grow on in the greenhouse or on a window-sill until the beginning of late spring. Harden them off in a cold frame before planting out in late spring or early summer when all danger of frost is passed. Space as for strip-grown plants.

For a later crop, sow a second batch of seeds in the same way in a greenhouse or cold frame in mid spring. Plant out at the end of early summer.

Self-blanching celery

Remove any side-shoots from the base of the plants as they appear, to encourage the main shoots to grow vigorously.

Pack straw around the outside plants in mid summer to blanch the outer rows. (The shade from the leaves will help blanch plants growing in the centre of a block.) If the plants are grown in a cold frame (with the lights removed), there is no need to pack straw around them for blanching.

Water generously every week if the weather is dry.

Trench-grown celery

Begin earthing up when the plants are 30-38cm (12-15in) high – this will be in late summer for those planted out in late spring, and in early autumn for those planted out in early summer.

Before earthing up, cut off any suckers that are growing from the base of the plants, then loosely tie black polythene, newspaper or corrugated cardboard (with the smooth side facing inwards) around each clump of stems. Water thoroughly, then with a spade draw soil from the ridges at the sides of the trench to form a slight slope reaching about halfway up the stems of each plant. Avoid getting soil into the heart of the plants.

Three weeks later, draw more soil around the plants to the base of the leaves – be careful not to earth up higher than the base of the green leaves.

Make the final earthing up three weeks after the second – you will probably have to excavate from each side of the row. Slope the soil to form a ridge.

GROWING TRENCH CELERY

1 Dig a trench, piling the excavated soil on either side of it. Fork the bottom and work in compost or manure. Replace some of the soil until the bottom is 15cm (6in) below true ground level.

2 Plant out young seedlings in late spring and those from a second sowing in early summer. Set the plants 23cm (9in) apart along the centre of the trench. Water in well.

3 When the celery plants are 30-38cm (12-15in) high, trim off any suckers from the base and loosely tie newspaper, corrugated cardboard or black polythene around the stems.

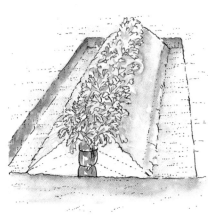

4 With a spade draw soil about halfway up the stems of the plants and form a slight slope. Three weeks later, earth up again. Repeat this once more after another three weeks.

DOING WITHOUT TRENCHES

As an alternative to digging out trenches for just a few plants, grow celery on level ground. When the plants are 30-38cm (12-15in) high, trim off any suckers, then tie corrugated cardboard (with the smooth side innermost), newspaper or black polythene around the stems. Pack earth down inside this collar to exclude light still further.

If there is any likelihood of snow or hard frost, lay straw along the ridge tops of late celery to give it some protection.

Water freely, especially during dry spells in autumn, to maintain steady growth.

Harvesting

Start lifting self-blanching celery with a fork at the end of late summer. Pile up the straw against newly exposed plants. All self-blanching varieties should be lifted before the onset of severe autumn frosts.

It takes from six to eight weeks from the first earthing up to blanch trench-grown celery properly. Early varieties are ready by mid autumn. After this, lift plants as needed. Open the ridge from one end, remove the plants with a fork, then earth up again as a protection against frost.

Pests and diseases

The most common pests of celery are the carrot and celery fly (spray with dimethoate) and slugs and snails.

The most common disorders and diseases include leaf spot (blight), celery heart rot after a wet season, and splitting if the crop has suffered from drought.

'Lathom Self-blanching'

Trench-grown 'Giant White'

VARIETIES TO CHOOSE

Self-blanching

'Celebrity' – long creamy-white stalks; crisp; early maturing; resistant to bolting.

'Golden Self-blanching' – creamy stalks; nutty flavour; stringless; early maturing.

'Greensleeves' – long green, smooth stalks; heavy cropper.

'Lathom Self-blanching' – yellow stalks; vigorous; early maturing; resistant to bolting.

'Utah' – long, light green stalks; crisp and succulent.

Trench-grown

'Giant Pink' – very long, solid, pink stalks.

'Giant Red' – dark red, solid stalks; robust growth.

'Giant White' – large and solid, white stalks; crisp.

'Hopkins Fenlander' – pale green, stringless stalks; trench or self-blanching.

'White Pascal' – large, pure white stalks; very hardy.

CELERIAC

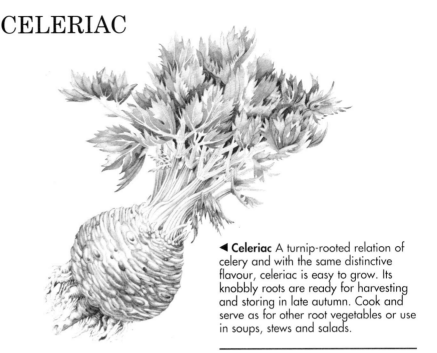

◀ **Celeriac** A turnip-rooted relation of celery and with the same distinctive flavour, celeriac is easy to grow. Its knobbly roots are ready for harvesting and storing in late autumn. Cook and serve as for other root vegetables or use in soups, stews and salads.

Celeriac is a turnip-rooted form of celery. Its swollen roots, with creamy-white flesh, have a very similar flavour and are particularly good for using in soups, stews and salads. Comparatively rare in shops and therefore expensive, it is an easily grown crop for home gardeners.

Soil and site preparation

Celeriac needs a long growing season and prefers well-drained soil in a sunny position. The winter before planting, enrich the site with rotted manure or garden compost at the rate of one bucketful per sq m/sq yd.

Sowing and planting

Sow seeds in a seed pan in early spring. Before sowing, press down the seed compost to make it level and firm, then sprinkle the seeds thinly over the top and cover with a shallow layer of compost. Keep the seed pan in an airing cupboard or in a greenhouse at a temperature of 10-13°C (50-55°F).

When the seedlings are about 12mm (½in) high, prick them out into trays of potting compost – spaced 4cm (1½in) apart in all directions. Keep the trays indoors or in a greenhouse for three or four weeks, then harden them off in a cold frame.

Set the plants out at 30-38cm (12-15in) intervals in rows the same distance apart. Plant the seedlings so that the roots are completely buried and the leaves are just resting on the surface of the soil.

Looking after the crop

Water the plants well in the early stages. Hoe frequently to kill weed seedlings which can seriously check growth.

Feed fortnightly with liquid manure, following the manufacturer's instructions and applying it either just before or just after watering.

To ensure that roots develop properly, remove any side-shoots above ground, from late summer to mid autumn.

Harvesting

Lift the roots as they are needed during the autumn months, leaving them in the ground as long as possible so that they reach an optimum size of about 450g (1lb), when the sweet celery flavour is most pronounced – there is no advantage in using celeriac roots when they are still young, and older roots tend to become woody and hollow.

In late autumn, lift all those that remain, cut off the foliage and store in damp sand in a cool shed or cellar.

Varieties to choose

There isn't much difference between varieties, but some to look out for are 'Alabaster', 'Balder', Brilliant', 'Iram', 'Monarch' and 'Tellus'.

Pests and diseases

The principal pests of celeriac are carrot fly, celery fly, slugs and snails. Leaf spot is the most common disease.

CHICORY

Chicory is a useful, dual-purpose, winter vegetable. Green, red and white-leaved varieties are available.

Chicory is a hardy perennial plant, native to Europe and related to dandelion. There are two types, forcing and non-forcing.

The forcing varieties are grown outdoors, then forced to produce the slender, pale leafy heads known as chicons. They are usually blanched indoors, in complete darkness though they may also be forced outdoors. Non-forcing types are grown outdoors, for harvesting in autumn and winter – they produce large crisp heads that closely resemble cos lettuce.

Radicchio is a red-leaved form of non-forcing chicory, ideal for growing outdoors as it is usually reliably hardy.

Planning the crop
Chicory is deep-rooted and prefers a medium to light, moderately rich soil. If possible, choose a patch of soil already manured for a previous crop. Alternatively, dig in well-rotted garden compost or manure before sowing, although such rich soil may encourage forked roots, which are less suitable for forcing. Chicory does best in a sunny, open site.

Rake in a general fertilizer a few days before sowing, at 25g per sq m (1oz per sq yd).

Cultivation
Sow forcing varieties outdoors in late spring and early summer, and non-forcing varieties from early to mid summer. Sow thinly in rows 12mm (½in) deep, allowing 45cm (1½ft) between rows.

Hoe to keep down weeds and water the soil thoroughly in dry weather. When the seedlings are

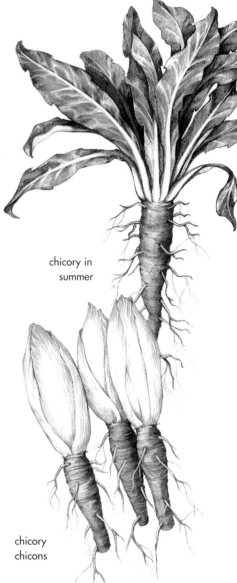

chicory in summer

chicory chicons

▲ **Winter chicory** After forcing and blanching, chicory produces pale, tightly packed crisp heads known as chicons.

large enough to handle, thin them until they are about 15cm (6in) apart (for forcing varieties) or until 30cm (1ft) apart (for non-forcing varieties). Keep hoeing regularly and water thoroughly during prolonged dry spells.

Forcing indoors Lift forcing varieties in mid to late autumn, when the leaves have died down. The roots should by then be at least 30cm (1ft) long, about 5cm (2in) across the top and shaped like parsnips. Discard any that are fanged, or less than 5cm (2in) wide at the top.

Shorten the roots to 15-23cm (6-9in), removing side-shoots and cutting off any remaining leaves to 2.5cm (1in) above the crown. Store the roots until needed for forcing in a cool, frost-proof shed, packed horizontally in a box of

STAGES IN FORCING CHICORY

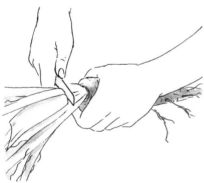

1 Lift forcing varieties in mid or late autumn, when the leaves have died down. Cut off remaining foliage 2.5cm (1in) above the crown of the roots.

2 Shorten the roots to 15-23cm (6-9in) by trimming off the lower end. Rub off any side-shoots at the top, leaving the main crown.

3 Force the roots a few at a time. Put four or five roots in a 23cm (9in) pot, in soil or compost, leaving the crowns exposed. Cover with an inverted pot.

4 The chicons should be ready for harvesting about four weeks later, when they are 15cm (6in) high. Cut or snap them off at the base.

Chicory 'Crystal Head'

Radicchio 'Rossa di Treviso'

sand, or in a shallow outdoor trench beneath a layer of soil.

If the weather is mild, stack the roots outdoors to wait for a sharp frost, which will break their dormancy and make them easier to force later.

Force the roots a few at a time, between late autumn and early spring. Put four or five roots in a 23cm (9in) plastic pot, packing moist soil or potting compost around them, but leaving the crowns exposed.

Water them lightly, then cover the pots completely with black polythene, boxes or inverted pots. Make sure that light is completely shut out, as it will cause the young chicons to turn green and to develop a bitter taste.

Place the pots in a greenhouse, shed or kitchen, at a temperature of 7-16°C (45-61°F). Pale chicons will sprout from the crowns.

Forcing outdoors Chicons forced outdoors *in situ* are said to have a better flavour, but they take longer to mature. Make sure there is no danger of the soil becoming waterlogged. Cut off the foliage at the beginning of late autumn and ridge up the soil to a depth of 17-20cm (7-8in) over each row, firming the top and sides. Cover the soil with cloches.

The chicons should be ready from late winter to early spring, when they start to break through the soil surface.

Harvesting and storing

Chicons of forcing varieties will be ready within four weeks from the start of forcing, when they are about 15cm (6in) high. Cut or snap off at crown level. They are best eaten or cooked immediately after harvesting. Smaller secondary chicons may follow, if the compost is watered after the first harvesting and the cover replaced. Discard the roots after the second crop of chicons has been harvested.

Cut non-forcing leaf chicory in late autumn and early winter. Ideal for winter salads, they can be stored for several weeks in a cool, frost-free shed.

Radicchio

Radicchio or red chicory varieties should be sown in mid summer – the crisp, white ribbed heads will be ready for cutting in late autumn.

Red varieties are hardy and can often be left outdoors throughout winter, with or without the protection of cloches or frames.

Pests and diseases

Chicory is seldom troubled by diseases, but may fall victim to cutworms, slugs, snails and swift moth caterpillars.

VARIETIES TO CHOOSE

Chicory
'Crystal Head' – non-forcing variety; easy to grow; crisp, bright green, cos lettuce-like heads, produced from mid autumn to early spring; slightly bitter taste.

'Flash' – forcing variety; crisp creamy-white chicons; sown in late winter, they can be harvested in early autumn.

'Sugar Loaf' – looks like a well-grown cos lettuce; firm heart; crisp leaves with broad, white central vein.

'Witloof' – good for forcing outdoors; cone-shaped, golden chicons; the green leaves can be picked for summer salads.

Radicchio
'Alouette' – round, tight heads of crunchy deep red and white leaves.

'Palla Rossa Bella' – round hearts of deep red with fine white veins; not frost-hardy.

'Rossa di Treviso' – green in summer, turns red in cold weather.

'Rossa di Verona' – salad variety; round-hearted; deep red in winter; may be forced for maroon and white chicons; sharp and tangy flavour.

CUCUMBERS

Crisp and juicy, cucumbers are an essential ingredient of cool summer salads; gherkin varieties are ideal for pickling.

There are two main types of cucumbers – outdoor varieties and greenhouse or frame cucumbers. Outdoor types, formerly known as ridge cucumbers from the custom of growing them on ridges of compost, are easier to cultivate than greenhouse types and grow rapidly in rich moist soil. They are suitable for grow bags, containers and tubs.

Also suitable for outdoors are the all-female Japanese varieties, apple-shaped cucumbers and pickling gherkins.

Greenhouse cucumbers can reach 30cm (1ft) in length, and well-grown specimens are straight and smooth-skinned. Most varieties are all-female types, which are more resistant to disease and more prolific than males – a single plant may yield as many as 20 fruits.

OUTDOOR CUCUMBERS

Choose a warm, sunny site and take out planting pockets on level ground a couple of weeks before planting. Dig out square holes, 30 x 30cm (1 x 1ft), with 60-90cm (2-3ft) between holes, and fill them with a mixture of well-rotted manure or compost and good, fine soil. Rake a general fertilizer into the soil surface.

Cultivation

In mid spring, sow two or three seeds 12mm (1½in) deep in 7.5cm (3in) pots of seed compost and germinate in the greenhouse at a temperature of 21°C (70°F). After germination, remove the two weakest seedlings. Pot the seedlings on if necessary and harden them off in late spring. Plant out in the prepared sites by late spring or early summer when danger of night frost has passed.

Alternatively, sow directly in the planting pockets – late spring in the south and early summer in the north. Sow three or four seeds 2.5cm (1in) deep and 7.5cm (3in) apart in the centre of each pocket. Remove all but the strongest seedling from each group. and protect with cloches at night.

Looking after the crop

Unlike greenhouse cucumbers, the female flowers of some outdoor types require pollination by the male; do not remove male flowers. Insects usually carry out pollination, but if few are about, transfer pollen from male flowers

---

▶ **Cucumber types** Modern greenhouse cucumbers are cylindrical and smooth-skinned; outdoor types are shorter, but old-fashioned knobbly cucumbers have been superseded by smooth-skinned types. Apple cucumbers are exceptionally crisp and juicy.

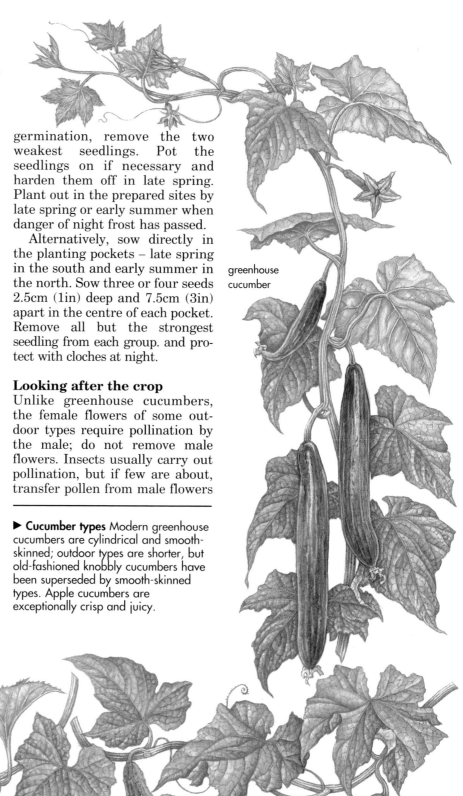

greenhouse cucumber

apple-shaped cucumber

outdoor cucumber

to the females with a paintbrush. Keep the plants moist by watering, give regular liquid feeds and scatter slug pellets. When the fruits begin to swell, keep them off the soil with pieces of board or glass.

Harvesting

Cucumbers have the best flavour if harvested before they reach their maximum size. Depending on variety they can be picked from mid summer until early autumn.

Pest and diseases

Outdoor cucumbers may be attacked by aphids. They are also vulnerable to cucumber mosaic virus, grey mould, powdery mildew and soil-borne diseases.

Gherkins

Gherkin varieties can be grown outdoors in exactly the same way as cucumbers. Alternatively, grow them in 23cm (9in) pots and train the plants upwards on a cane and wire support.

GREENHOUSE CUCUMBERS

Modern varieties are all-female and require a constant temperature of 21°C (70°F). Sow seeds between late winter and early spring in 7.5cm (3in) pots of seed compost, setting a single seed edgeways and 12mm (½in) deep in each pot.

Prepare planting pockets in the greenhouse bed as for outdoor cucumbers. Alternatively, fill 25cm (10in) pots with a proprietary potting compost or put grow bags in place. Fix horizontal wires, on which to train the cucumbers, from one strut to another, and shade from late spring onwards.

When the seedlings have developed two true leaves, transplant them to their growing positions and fix a stake beside each plant.

Shade the plants from strong sunlight, water them well and keep the air moist and well ventilated, by spraying the greenhouse floor twice a day. Once the fruits begin to swell, feed the plants with fertilizer every fortnight.

COLD FRAME CUCUMBERS

Prepare planting stations by late spring, and set the plants out a few weeks later, using varieties recommended for cold frame or cold greenhouse cultivation. Sow seeds by late spring, in the same way as for greenhouse cultivation, and leave them to germinate in the cold frame.

Transplant the seedlings, one underneath each frame light at the highest point. Then replace the frame lid and cover the glass with shading. Open the lid 5cm (2in) on the sheltered side during warm days, but close it to just a crack at night.

Water the plants frequently and spray the inside of the frame twice a day during hot weather.

Harvesting

Greenhouse cucumbers have a longer cropping season than outdoor types, from mid summer to mid autumn. They should be harvested before they reach their maximum size, and they are best used immediately after cutting.

Pests and diseases

Cucumbers are susceptible to glasshouse red spider mites and glasshouse whitefly.

GREENHOUSE CUCUMBERS

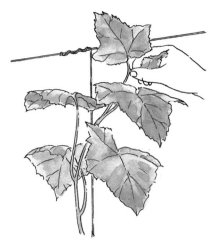

1 When the plants have grown to a height of about 2.4m (8ft), or up to the greenhouse roof, pinch out the tips of the leading shoots. This will encourage growth of lateral shoots, which should be attached to the wires.

2 If no cucumbers have appeared on the laterals by the time these are 60cm (2ft) long, pinch out the growing tips. When laterals start to produce fruit, pinch them out just at the second leaf after the first cucumber.

3 Laterals often put out fruit-bearing side-shoots. Pinch these out in the same way as the laterals – at the second leaf after the first fruit.

GROWING OUTDOOR CUCUMBERS

1 Pinch out the growing tip of each plant after six or seven leaves have appeared, to encourage fruit-bearing lateral shoots to develop.

2 If a lateral shoot shows no sign of fruiting by the time the sixth or seventh leaf appears, pinch out the tip. Do not remove male flowers.

Outdoor cucumber 'Long Green Ridge'

Greenhouse cucumber 'Telegraph'

VARIETIES TO CHOOSE

Outdoor varieties
'Burpless Tasty Green' (F1 hybrid) – fruits 25-30cm (10-12in) long; tender skin, mildew-resistant.

'Bush Champion' – heavy cropper; compact plants; suitable for grow bags and tubs; dark green, slightly ribbed fruits 25cm (10in) long.

'Crispy Salad' (F1 hybrid) – early and heavy cropper; chunky, thin-skinned, dark green fruits 12.5cm (5in) long; outdoors, cold greenhouses and frames.

'Crystal Apple' – round, pale green fruits, pale yellow when mature; prolific.

'Long Green Ridge' – well-flavoured deep green fruits up to 30cm (12in) long; good all-rounder.

'Tokyo Slicer' (F1 hybrid) – smooth, dark green fruit, often 20cm (8in) long; vigorous; heavy cropper; suitable for training up poles.

Gherkins
'Conda' (F1 hybrid) – early; heavy cropper; uniform; fine colour, shape and quality.

'Hokus' – early, heavy cropper; uniform dark green fruits.

'Venlo Pickling' – good for pickling, best as small fruits.

Greenhouse varieties
'Conqueror' – good cropper; dark green fruits; cold frames and unheated greenhouses.

'Danimas' (F1 hybrid) – all-female mini type; disease-resistant; heated and cold greenhouses; indoor pot culture.

'Diana' (F1 hybrid) – all-female type; good for cold greenhouses.

'Femspot' (F1 hybrid) – all-female type; minimum temperature 15°C (59°F); long fruits; fine flavour and colour; early maturing; disease-resistant.

'Kyoto' – Japanese giant variety; vigorous; slim fruits up to 64cm (25in) long; heated greenhouses, cold frames and outdoors.

'Mistral' (F1 hybrid) – all-female type; heavy cropper; resistant to powdery mildew; heated and cold greenhouses.

'Pepinex' (F1 hybrid) – all-female; dark green, smooth fruits to 50cm (20in) long; heavy cropper.

'Pepita' (F1 hybrid) – dark green fruits, about 20-23cm (8-9in) long; heated or cool greenhouses.

'Sigmadew' – thin, very pale green, almost white skin.

'Telegraph' – good for both greenhouses and cold frames; straight smooth, dark green fruit.

ENDIVES

Crisp and tender endives make a pleasant change from lettuce in autumn and winter salads.

Endive has been grown as a winter salad vegetable in Britain since the sixteenth century, but has never achieved the popularity of lettuce. This is possibly because the bitter leaves are inedible until they have been blanched, which is relatively easy to do.

Planning the crop

Two kinds of endive are grown. Curly varieties, such as 'Green Curled' and the darker 'Moss Curled', are sown in mid summer to provide salads in late summer and autumn. Sowings made earlier than this often result in bolting during hot weather. The hardier, wavy-leaved types, such as 'Batarian Broad Leaved', are sown in late summer for cropping in autumn and winter.

Endive thrives in light, well-drained soil that has been matured for a previous crop. Late crops should be sown under the protection of cloches.

Nine or ten plants can be grown in a 3m (10ft) row. Two such rows, one containing early and one late endive, should be sufficient for most families.

Sow the seeds thinly in drills 12mm (½in) deep and 38cm (15in) apart. Water seedlings thoroughly and thin in stages to stand 30-38cm (12-15in) apart.

Blanching the crop

Endive must be blanched to make it palatable. The first plants are usually ready 12 weeks after sowing, or when they are about 30cm (1ft) in diameter. Choose a day when the leaves are completely dry, draw them together and upwards and bind them with loose string about half-way up the leaves. This excludes light from the heart and inner leaves of the endives but does not blanch the whole head.

It is preferable to exclude light altogether. Cover each endive with an upturned flower pot to block out light. There should be a small gap at the bottom to allow air to circulate, but cover the drainage hole with a stone or a

endive 'Green Curled'

small piece from a broken terracotta flower pot.

After two to three weeks in early autumn, and up to five weeks in winter for wavy-leaved types, the centres of the plants turn creamy white and are then ready for cutting and eating.

Harvesting

Use endive as soon as possible after cutting, as the leaves toughen quickly in storage and soon regain their bitter taste once they are exposed to light. Any surplus can be kept in a black plastic bag in the fridge for up to three days.

Pests and diseases

Slugs and snails may attack the plants during blanching. Encircle them with bands of coarse sand.

BLANCHING ENDIVES

1 Choose a sunny or windy day when the leaves of mature plants are dry; pull the leaves upwards and bunch them, then tie loosely with string.

2 Alternatively, blanch the endives under upturned flower pots. Leave a small gap at the bottom to let plants breathe, but cover the drainage hole.

FLORENCE FENNEL

**Florence fennel is grown for its firm
and crisp bulbous stem base, which has a delicious
aniseed flavour and smell.**

An annual plant, Florence fennel – also called finocchio or sweet fennel – has ferny leaves which make a decorative backdrop in a herb or vegetable garden.

The root, which is really a swollen stem base, is used raw in salads or cooked as a vegetable in stock. The leaves and seeds can be used for flavouring in the same way as those of common fennel. As they are slightly more pungent, use them with discretion.

Site and soil preparation
Florence fennel prefers rich, well-drained but moisture-retentive soil in a sunny position. Heavy clay soil is not suitable.

Dig well-rotted manure or garden compost into the ground the winter before planting, and rake in a dressing of a general fertilizer at 50g per sq m (2oz per sq yd) shortly before sowing seeds in mid to late spring.

As Florence fennel is quick to mature, it can also be grown as a catch crop if sown in early or mid summer, but no later because it is unlikely to mature before cold autumn weather sets in. A 3m (10ft) row, yielding 10-12 plants, is about the right amount for most families.

Cultivation
Florence fennel should not be

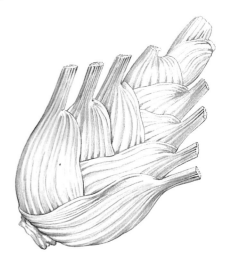

▲ **Florence fennel** The plump bulbs of Florence fennel are prized for their sweet aniseed flavour. Varieties include 'Herald', 'Sirio', 'Sweet Florence' and 'Zefa Fino'.

sown until the danger of night frost has passed. Delay sowing until the soil has warmed up in spring, or put cloches in position for a couple of weeks before sowing and replace them until the seeds have germinated.

Sow the seeds thinly in 12mm (½in) deep drills with 50 cm (20 in) between the rows in late spring. Thin the seedlings twice, first to 23cm (9in), then to 30cm (1ft) apart. Keep the plants well watered otherwise the stem bases will not swell. When they begin to develop, apply a general fertilizer at 50g per sq m (2oz per sq yd) and water them in well. Draw earth over the stem bases in the same way as for potatoes, covering the stems to approximately three-quarters their height.

Harvesting
Use a sharp knife to cut the swollen stem bases when they are the size of tennis balls or larger, from late summer onwards. Continue to harvest as required. Cut off the leaves to use for flavouring or as garnish.

Pests and diseases
Florence fennel is generally trouble-free, but look out for aphids, cutworms and root fly.

Florence fennel

GLOBE ARTICHOKES

Though primarily grown as a delicious vegetable, the artichoke's silver-grey leaves make them popular plants in herbaceous borders.

Globe artichokes are the flowers of a herbaceous perennial plant. Their thistle-shaped heads contain pockets of edible, fine-flavoured flesh. They are large plants but needn't take up much space in a vegetable plot: their attractive foliage provides the perfect foil for summer flowers in a mixed border.

Growing artichokes

To produce a good crop, artichokes need rich, well-drained soil, adequate shelter and plenty of sun.

The winter before planting dig in well-rotted garden compost or manure and leave the ground rough. In spring, rake the soil and fork a fertilizer such as Growmore into the topsoil at the rate of 75g per sq m (3oz per sq yd).

Globe artichokes can be raised from seed, which will begin cropping in the second year, but it is easier to buy young plants and set them out in mid spring, 1m (3ft) apart to the same depth as they were in the nursery bed. In late spring apply a liberal mulch of manure or garden compost. This helps to retain soil moisture. Water well in dry weather.

Each year cut the harvested stems back to ground level in autumn, and protect the crowns of the plants from frost with a mulch of straw or bracken. Plants crop best for the first three or four years of their life, but new stock can be raised from cuttings.

◄ **Globe artichokes** The edible part of this handsome plant is the immature flower head. It can grow more than 1.5m (5ft) in height and is a valuable border plant whose silver-grey foliage contrasts well with more colourful flowers. It grows best in a sheltered, sunny part of the garden. Culinary varieties, much prized by gourmets, include 'Green Globe' and 'Purple Globe'.

Harvesting

In their first year, plants produce flower buds, but they are best removed to allow strong plants to develop. In subsequent years allow four to six flower stems to develop on each plant and harvest the heads from summer to early autumn.

Pick the heads, starting with the central, highest globe – the king head – while still green and tightly wrapped. Harvest lateral heads when no bigger than an egg. Use secateurs to cut the tough stalks. Heads that have opened or are purple on the *inside* of the scales have passed their best and should be discarded.

Pests and diseases

In damp weather slugs and snails may attack the leaves. The major disease is petal blight, which causes the heads to rot.

RAISING NEW PLANTS FROM OLD STOCK

1 Use a knife to remove strong shoots, about 23cm (9in) tall, from older plants in spring. Cut vertically through the crown and include some rootstock.

2 Transplant the cuttings to their permanent growing sites. Cuttings taken in autumn should be potted up and overwintered in a cold frame.

JERUSALEM ARTICHOKES

Attractive as a kitchen garden screen, Jerusalem artichokes produce sweet-flavoured tubers which are treated like potatoes.

Jerusalem artichokes look nothing like globe artichokes yet share the name because the tubers have a slightly similar flavour. They are not from Jerusalem either; the name is a corruption of the Italian for sunflower, 'girasole'. The plants, related to the sunflower, reach 2-3m (7-10ft) high and make effective screens in the vegetable garden.

Cultivation
Plants are grown from seed tubers. Each seed tuber yields about 1.5kg (3lb) of artichokes. Plant tubers 30cm (1ft) apart to produce about 5kg (11lb) per m/yd. A warm position in well-drained soil is best.

Prepare the soil in late autumn by digging and adding manure. Rake to a smooth tilth before planting.

In late winter to early spring, use a draw hoe to take out a furrow 15cm (6in) deep. Plant the tubers at 30cm (1ft) intervals at the bottom of the furrow. Allow 90cm (3ft) between rows.

When covering the tubers, leave a ridge about 5cm (2in) high over the top. Add a dressing of general fertilizer along the ridge at the rate of 50g per sq m (2oz per sq yd) and hoe it into the surface.

When the plants are 15cm (6in) high, draw up another 2.5cm (1in) of soil. Repeat this every two weeks until the ridge is 15cm (6in) high – tubers will form close to the surface.

Support the plants on wires and canes, and keep them well watered. Nip off any flowers.

Harvesting
Tubers are ready for lifting from mid autumn. Cut the stems back to 30cm (1ft) of the ground.

Leave the tubers in the ground until they are needed during winter. When harvesting, make sure to dig up even the smallest tubers. Any left in the ground will sprout and grow again the following year.

Pests and diseases
The tubers may be attacked by cutworms and the caterpillars of swift moth. Apply diazinon + chlorpyrifos granules at planting time.

▶ **Jerusalem artichokes** Easy to grow and cropping prolifically, the potato-like tubers contain no starch.

GROWING JERUSALEM ARTICHOKES

1 Plant good-sized tubers at 30cm (1ft) intervals in 15cm (6in) deep furrows in rows that are 90cm (3ft) apart. The tubers grow best in a warm site and well-cultivated soil, but will tolerate a wide range of soil conditions.

2 Use a hoe to start forming a shallow ridge along the row of plants when they are about 15cm (6in) high. Continue drawing soil around the plants every two weeks or so until the ridge is about 15cm (6in) high.

3 In early summer, support the plants by inserting stakes at each end of the row. Secure two wires between them, spaced about 30cm (1ft) apart, and tie the plants to these with soft garden string or raffia.

KALE AND BORECOLE

Kale – one of the hardiest winter vegetables – survives frost and poor soils. For the best flavour, pick the leaves when they are young.

Kale (also known as borecole) is often regarded as the poor relation of the brassica family. This is a pity since it has a number of strong points in its favour.

It is ultra-hardy, often surviving prolonged frost that will harm broccoli and Brussels sprouts – a touch of frost even improves the flavour of kale. It tolerates poor soils and is rarely troubled by the normal cabbage pests and diseases; even birds leave it alone.

Kale is a valuable winter vegetable, providing greens from mid winter to mid spring when other green vegetables are scarce. It is a good source of iron and vitamins A, C and E. Curly and plain-leaved varieties are available; they are grown in the same way and have identical flavour. Some varieties, such as 'Pentland Brig', produce crown leaves, for harvesting during winter, as well as numerous leafy side-shoots and young flower spears, like sprouting broccoli, for gathering in spring.

A 4.5m (15ft) row of either curly or plain varieties should give about 4kg (9lb) of leaves – harvest them while young and tender, after the first frost.

Cultivation

Kale grows best on well-drained, medium or heavy soil which has been manured for a previous crop. Dig the plot thoroughly during winter and apply a lime dressing before planting if necessary to make the soil alkaline.

About two weeks before transplanting kale, dress the soil with a general fertilizer at a rate of 50g per sq m (2oz per sq yd).

Sow seeds in a 12mm (½in) drill in mid spring, and mix diazinon + chlorpyrifos into the soil as a precaution against cabbage root fly.

Thin to 5cm (2in) apart when the seedlings are large enough to handle, giving them enough space to form sturdy plants.

Transplant to the prepared bed in mid summer, spacing the young plants 60cm (2ft) apart in each direction, dwarf varieties 45cm (18in) apart. Dip the roots

plain-leaved kale

curled-leaved kale

◄ ▼ Winter kale
Rich in both iron and vitamin C, the leaves of kale can be used for soups, in purées and as a vegetable – cook in a minimum amount of boiling water. Raw young kale sprigs make tasty winter salads: toss freshly chopped leaves in a lemon dressing.

in a solution of thiophanate-methyl to guard against club root disease. Firm in the plants with your feet and keep them watered until they are well established. Hoe to keep weeds down. On exposed sites, tall plants may need staking.

Harvesting

Kale is ready for cutting from late autumn onwards, and tastes better after a frost. Cut the centre of each plant first to encourage side-shoots. Pick the leaves when they are young and tender. Discard yellowing and very large leaves. When the plants start to flower, pull them up, chop the tough stems into small pieces to speed rotting, and put them on the compost heap.

Pests and diseases

Generally trouble free, though cabbage root fly, cabbage whitefly and flea beetles can be a problem. Club root is the most common disease.

VARIETIES TO CHOOSE

Kale – curly
'Dwarf Green Curled' – compact; tightly curled, dark green leaves.

'Fribor' (F1 hybrid) – mid green leaves; ready autumn to winter.

'Pentland Brigg' – crown leaves in winter; flower spears in spring.

'Westland Autumn' – neat, compact plants; tight curly leaves.

Kale – plain
'Thousand Head' – hardiest plain variety; prolific.

KOHL-RABI

This versatile vegetable has a pleasant nutty flavour. Resembling a turnip in appearance, it's quick and easy to grow and is well worth a place in the vegetable garden.

Kohl-rabi resembles a root vegetable but the edible part is actually a swollen stem base or globe. Kohl-rabi is a member of the brassica family, and so succeeds in shallow soils where root crops like turnips or swedes would fail.

It is not a particularly large plant, being about 30cm (1ft) tall when fully grown.

Kohl-rabi is highly regarded on the Continent and deserves to be more popular in Britain, because it matures in only 8-12 weeks from sowing and withstands autumn frosts; some varieties can be left in the ground throughout winter. It is an unusual, delicious and easy-to-grow vegetable, provided it is planted in rich soil and never runs short of water. It can even be grown as a catch-crop after the ground has been cleared of other, earlier crops.

Although the flesh is white in all varieties, some have pale green or purple skins. All have a delicate nutty flavour, best described as a cross between a turnip and a cabbage, and are ideal for people who prefer vegetables that are mild tasting rather than full flavoured.

The young globes can be boiled or braised and served as an accompanying vegetable, or used raw – coarse-grated or cut into strips – in salads. The young leaves can be boiled like spinach.

Planning the crop

Kohl-rabi grows best in fertile, well-drained soil. If the ground is poor, fork in a quantity of well-rotted compost and hoe in a general compound fertilizer at the rate of 50g per sq m (2oz per sq yd).

Acid soils should be given sufficient lime to bring them up to a slightly alkaline level – about pH 7.5. Allow several weeks to elapse between the applications of fertilizer and lime.

Growing kohl-rabi

Generally the green varieties have a slightly better flavour than purple types. Green-skinned kohl-rabi is usually grown for summer crops whereas those with purple

skins, which are hardier, are better for autumn and winter.

Sow the seeds in drills about 12mm (½in) deep where the plants are to grow, spacing the rows about 30cm (1ft) apart. Thin the seedlings to 23cm (9in) when they are large enough to handle. Keep the plants well watered, especially during very dry spells; kohl-rabi needs generous amounts of water throughout the growing season for the stems to swell.

For a steady succession of crops, sow rows about 3m (10ft) long at four-week intervals from early spring to late summer. Those which are to be left in the ground through autumn should not be sown after mid summer, otherwise they will continue to grow and become too large and unpleasantly tasteless. Late sowings can be left in the ground all winter for maturing and harvesting in the spring.

Harvesting

Pull the plants out of the soil when the bulbous stems approach

▲ **Kohl-rabi** Green and purple-skinned varieties all have white flesh. Quick growing, kohl-rabi is easily cooked and has a mild, nutty flavour.

Purple-skinned kohl-rabi 'Purple Vienna'

VARIETIES TO CHOOSE

White- or green-skinned

'Green Vienna' – pale green skin; crisp white flesh slow to become fibrous.

'Lanro' – white-skinned, good flavour; stands longer without deteriorating than most of the other varieties; pull at golf-ball size.

'Rowel' (F1 hybrid) – exceptionally sweet flesh; slow to bolt; early maturing; good variety for eating raw in mixed salads.

'White Danube' (F1 hybrid) – early maturing; bright green skin; crisp white flesh; exceptionally large globes; non-fibrous and slow to bolt.

'White Vienna' – early maturing; pale green skin; especially delicate flavour and crisp texture; it is particularly resistant to bolting.

Purple-skinned

'Purple Vienna' – purple skin; purple-marbled foliage; crisp white flesh; for later cropping; with its purple skin it looks decorative grated raw in salads if picked when quite young and tender.

the size of a tennis ball. A diameter of about 4cm (1½in) is ideal, as they are then at their most tender and have the best flavour. Larger bulbs are often tough and woody.

The young leaves of kohl-rabi can be cooked like spinach, but the leaves and stalks of older plants should be completely removed and disposed of on the compost heap.

Kohl-rabi will keep for two weeks if put into a polythene bag and stored in the fridge.

Pests and diseases

As kohl-rabi is quick to mature it is less likely to be affected by pests that attack at a particular time or diseases that develop slowly. Aphids can be troublesome, and netting may be necessary to protect the crop from birds.

Cabbage root fly and cabbage whitefly, caterpillars and flea beetle may strike occasionally. They can usually be prevented with appropriate seed dressings.

Diseases to watch for – though they are rarely severe – are club root, damping off, downy mildew, leaf spot, spray damage, whiptail and wire stem. Limy soil and good cultural practices are very sensible remedies.

HARVESTING AND STORING

Sown at intervals from mid spring to late summer, thinned to allow for the development of each globe and kept well watered, kohl-rabi should be ready for harvesting in 8-12 weeks from sowing. Pull from the soil when they are about the size of a tennis ball. In dry weather, use a fork carefully. Trim off the leaves and roots, and prepare for cooking (unlike beetroot, kohl-rabi does not 'bleed'). The globes can be stored in a dry, cool place for about a fortnight.

LEEKS

Easy to grow and able to survive the hardest winters, leeks are one of the most popular and worthwhile vegetables for a small garden.

Leeks are not difficult to grow. They can stand up to the harshest winter, are generally pest and disease free and will tolerate a variety of growing conditions. To grow the very best crop, however, they need careful tending and they occupy the land for a long time. A 3m (10ft) row will yield an average of 5kg (10lb) of leeks. It is a popular vegetable for exhibitions and competitions.

Site and soil preparation

Leeks grow in most soil types, as long as the earth is neither compacted nor badly drained. Choose a sunny position. The site does need to be well manured – dig thoroughly in winter and add compost or well-rotted manure, at the rate of a bucketful of manure or compost per sq m/yd. The soil should be left rough after winter digging, but level the surface in spring. Rake in a general fertilizer one week before planting.

Sow seeds 12mm (½in) deep in an outdoor seed bed during early spring. When the seedlings are large enough to handle, thin to 4cm (1½in) apart. In early or mid summer the seedlings should be about 20cm (8in) high and about as thick as a pencil; they are then ready for transplanting. Always water the seed bed thoroughly the day before lifting if the weather is particularly dry.

Before planting the seedlings, trim off the root ends and leaf tips with scissors and then set out in 15cm (6in) deep holes, leaving at least 23cm (9in) between each young leek and its neighbour. Use a dibber to make the holes, drop in the plants and then gently fill the holes with water. Avoid filling the holes directly with soil as grit is difficult to remove from between the leaves.

The amount of soil carried into the holes by the water will hold

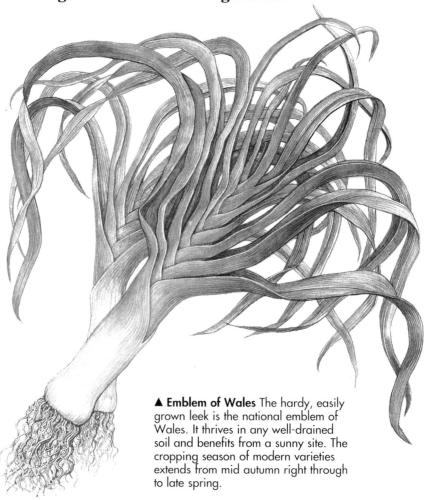

▲ **Emblem of Wales** The hardy, easily grown leek is the national emblem of Wales. It thrives in any well-drained soil and benefits from a sunny site. The cropping season of modern varieties extends from mid autumn right through to late spring.

▶ **Lifting leeks** To prevent the stems from breaking, leeks should be lifted out of the ground with a spade or fork – never wrench plants out by hand. Remove root ends and trim the leaves before cleaning.

126

the leeks in place without the need to firm them in by hand. Subsequent watering and hoeing will complete the job. Rows should be 38cm (15in) apart.

Caring for the crop
Hoe the bed regularly to keep down weeds and water well during dry spells. To increase the height and quality of the white stems, blanch by gently drawing earth up around the stems in autumn. Take care not to let loose soil settle between the leaves. Complete the earthing-up process by late autumn.

Regular feeding increases the thickness of the stems, but do not feed after late summer. Sprinkle a general fertilizer along the rows.

Harvesting and storing
Begin lifting the leeks when they are about 20mm (¾in) thick. Ease them out of the soil with a fork, otherwise they may break. Cut off the roots and trim back the leaves. Wash thoroughly.

Continue lifting during winter as needed. Leeks can remain in the ground throughout winter and will continue to grow, though only slowly during the coldest months.

Pests and diseases
Onion fly is a common pest; water with pirimiphos-methyl during the growing season. Rust and white rot are the main diseases; dust the seed drills with calomel.

CULTIVATING LEEKS

1 Use a dibber to make planting holes 15cm (6in) deep and 23cm (9in) apart. Water the seedlings in gently to prevent loose soil from washing into the leaves and stems.

2 To blanch and lengthen the stems, draw earth around the plants at regular intervals throughout the season. Begin harvesting leeks when the stems are 20mm (¾in) thick.

VARIETIES TO CHOOSE

Early varieties
'Autumn Mammoth' – matures rapidly; extremely thick, long, crisp white stems. Recommended for exhibition use.

'Lyon Prizetaker' – long, thick stems with dark green leaves; blanches pure white; mild flavour; good for exhibition.

Mid-season varieties
'King Richard' – long, uniform white stems; can be pulled early, like salad onions.

'Musselburgh' – the most popular variety, very reliable and easy to grow; thick, short stems with dark green leaves.

Late varieties
'Giant Winter-Catalina' – heavy, thick, long-stemmed; non-bulbous root end; continues until late spring.

'Winter Crop' – extra hardy with large white stems and dark leaves; harvest until mid spring.

'Yates Empire' – similar to 'Musselburgh' with thick, pure white stems; can be left in the ground until mid spring.

Leek 'Autumn Mammoth'

Leek 'Musselburgh'

LETTUCES

Cool, crisp lettuce is the essence of a salad – by growing different varieties you can pick fresh greenery throughout the year.

There is room for lettuces in almost every garden. They are one of the easiest vegetables to grow, and do well in almost any soil. With just a little know-how you can ensure a regular supply and a wide choice of taste and texture throughout the year.

Types of lettuce

There are several different types of lettuce – with slightly different growing requirements.

Butterhead is round – like a cabbage – with smooth, spreading leaves. Quick to mature, it is exceptionally easy to grow.

Crisphead resembles the butterhead. It has large hearts of crisp, curled leaves.

Cos lettuces grow upright, with oblong leaves and are usually crisp in texture. They take a little longer to mature than the other types, and need more watering.

Loose-leaf has a profusion of leaves but no heart. The leaves, which are curly and indented, are picked a few at a time.

Greenhouse lettuce has been specially bred for growing in unheated greenhouses to mature from autumn to spring.

Other salad vegetables include corn salad and oriental leaf vegetables, such as Chinese cabbages and leaves.

Site and soil preparation

Lettuces do best on fertile, well-drained soil, in a sunny, sheltered site. During the winter dig the site thoroughly, incorporating well-rotted manure or compost. Before sowing or planting in spring, rake the soil to a fine tilth and apply a general fertilizer at the rate of 50g per sq m (2oz per sq yd).

Sowing and planting

Avoid a summer surplus followed by shortages by sowing at two to three-week intervals from early spring to mid summer. Sow thinly in drills 5mm ($\frac{1}{4}$in) deep and 30cm (1ft) apart.

Thin the seedlings to 7.5cm (3in) when they are large enough to handle. Thin again when plants touch and transplant to another bed; spacing depends on variety.

Alternatively, sow seeds under glass, setting two seeds in small

crisphead

cos

miniature butterhead

loose-leaf

bronze-tinted butterhead

butterhead

pots of seed compost; remove the weakest seedling from each pot and gradually harden off in a cold frame before planting out 30cm (1ft) apart.

If you have room for only a few lettuces, buy strips or trays of young plants and transplant them 30cm (1ft) apart into a prepared bed. Set the plants carefully in holes deep enough to take the roots without overcrowding and handle the lettuces by the base of the stalk, not by the delicate leaves.

Other space-saving methods include the leaf lettuce technique. Cos varieties are the most suitable for this. Sow seeds at 2.5cm (1in) intervals in rows 10cm (4in) apart. Begin in mid spring and sow every two weeks until late spring. Do not thin – this method is meant to produce a block of closely grown lettuces. Cut the leaves for the first time four to six weeks after sowing, but leave the stumps in the ground to produce a second crop about six weeks later.

Intercropping In a small garden, lettuces need not occupy a special bed. Plant them between slower-maturing vegetables such as parsnips. The lettuces will be out of the ground before the other crop needs the space.

Autumn lettuces Sow a forcing variety, such as 'Kwiek', in a prepared seed bed in the open not later than early August. Move the seedlings to a cold frame in early autumn, when growth is well established.

Alternatively, leave the seedlings where they are, but thin to 30cm (12in) apart and cover with cloches in early autumn, remembering to close the ends of the cloches overnight and when the weather becomes cold. These lettuces should be ready to pick in late autumn and early winter.

Greenhouse lettuces Butterhead and crisphead varieties can be sown from early autumn on, and grown under glass for harvesting in winter and spring.

Overwintered lettuces In milder parts of the country grow hardy varieties such as 'Arctic King' or 'Winter Density', without the protection of cloches or frames. Sow seeds in late summer or early autumn, and thin in mid autumn to 7.5cm (3in) apart. If you lose some because of severe weather, there should still be enough left for a good crop. Thin again in early spring to 30cm (12in) apart. They will be ready to cut in mid or late spring.

Harvesting

Lettuces are ready to eat as soon as a firm heart has formed. Pick leaves of loose-leaf varieties as and when required.

Pests and diseases

Lettuces bolt easily due to late transplanting, overcrowding or shortage of water.

Slugs and birds can be very troublesome. The main diseases are damping off, downy mildew and grey mould.

▼ **Autumn lettuces** Cloches extend the growing season for lettuces. Sown in late summer, butterhead types can be ready for cutting in autumn and winter.

CORN SALAD

Corn salad 'Large Leaved'

Corn salad is sometimes called lamb's lettuce – a reminder that it crops as late as the lambing season. This late harvest is corn salad's chief advantage as it provides tender dark green lettuce-like leaves when most salad vegetables are in short supply.

The plant is completely hardy but receives less of a check in severe weather if covered with cloches. This maintains a steady supply of succulent young leaves. Alternatively pot young plants and shelter them from severe weather.

Cultivation

Corn salad likes a sunny, well-drained site with plenty of well-rotted manure or compost. By sowing seeds from early spring to early autumn, fresh plants may be picked all year round. For a winter crop, sow in succession from late summer to early autumn.

A 3m (10ft) row supplies 20 plants – enough for most families. 'Large Leaved' is the most common variety.

Sow the seeds in drills 12mm (½in) deep, with 23cm (9in) between rows, and thin the seedlings to 15cm (6in) apart. Keep the ground well watered after sowing and hoe to keep down weeds.

Harvesting

The plants are ready for use after producing a fourth pair of leaves. Cut off the roots and use the whole plant, or pick a few larger leaves from each mature plant, like spinach.

Pests and diseases

Slugs and snails may attack the leaves. Protect them with pellets.

CHINESE CABBAGES

Though grown in the Far East for centuries, Chinese cabbages are fairly new to European gardeners in spite of being versatile vegetables. There is a certain amount of confusion about their names, especially with the introduction of so-called Chinese greens and Pak Choi.

Chinese cabbages, also known as Chinese leaves or Petsai, come in a wide range of shapes, but they mostly resemble conventional cabbages, having a compact head of leaves. They can be easily-distinguished by their broad white leaf veins, and by the succulent inner leaves, which are paler than the coarse outer ones. The long, slim types – which look rather like cos lettuces – can either be cooked or used as a salad vegetable.

Pak Choi, also known as celery cabbage, is open-leaved and the white leaf stalks are invariably bare and fleshy. The tender stalks can be eaten with the leaves.

The outer leaves of Pak Choi are cooked or stir-fried. The inner leaves can be used raw in salads.

Chinese greens, also known as mustard spinach, usually have fairly open heads. The mature leaves can be boiled like spinach or spring greens, or stir-fried; the young, tender, mild-flavoured leaves can be plucked and eaten raw.

BLANCHING

In mid summer, after the hearts have begun to swell, tie the outer leaves of Chinese cabbages together with raffia around the base and top. Water plants regularly if the weather is hot.

▲ **Chinese cabbages** Resembling cos lettuces, Chinese cabbages or leaves are fast-growing. Sown in summer, they are ready for use in autumn.

Site and soil preparation

The basic cultivation requirements for all types of Chinese cabbage are the same as for ordinary cabbages or any other brassicas. The bed should be in an open, sunny spot with well-drained slightly alkaline soil.

On a new plot, dig in a light dressing of well-rotted manure or garden compost. In a crop rotation system, where they follow legume or salad crops, no extra manure or compost is needed. But lime the bed well and apply a general-purpose fertilizer at the rate of 50g per sq m (2oz per sq yd) before sowing.

Sowing and growing

Chinese cabbages resent transplanting and should be sown where they are to grow. They may succumb to autumn frost unless given cloche protection, and they bolt easily if sown too early in the summer.

Sow most varieties from June to early July for a late summer and autumn crop, setting seeds 12mm (½in) deep in rows spaced 60cm (2ft) apart. As soon as the seedlings are large enough to handle, thin them to 30-38cm (12-15in) spacings.

Water Chinese cabbages well during dry spells and hoe the bed regularly to eliminate weeds. Protect plants from slug and snail damage by sprinkling proprietary slug bait regularly during summer. If the hearts become loose, raise the outer leaves round them and tie them gently in place with raffia or soft garden string. This will prevent the heart becoming dark green and tough.

Harvest the crop when the hearts are firm and before they show signs of bolting.

Pak Choi Sowings can be made in mid spring to produce a mass of tender young leaves in summer. Alternatively, sow like Chinese cabbage, harvesting throughout autumn.

Chinese greens Sowing times vary from variety to variety, and good seed merchants usually give full instructions on the packet. Some are resistant to bolting and are ideal for both spring or summer sowing; others are resistant to cold weather and can be sown in late summer or early autumn for a winter harvest.

VARIETIES TO CHOOSE

Chinese cabbages
'Ruffles' (F1 hybrid) – British- bred variety; strong upright, loose-hearted creamy-white plants.

'Tip Top' (F1 hybrid) – large pale green, crisp heads; cylindrical shape; good resistance to bolting.

Pak Choi
'Joi Choi' (F1 hybrid) – multi-purpose; loose-headed; dark green leaves; white stalks.

'Mei Quing Choi' (F1 hybrid) – large plants; green stalks.

Chinese Greens
'Mitzuna Green Youzen' – glossy, dark green, deeply cut leaves; sweet mild flavour; bolt resistant; tolerant of cold weather.

Cos 'Lobjoit's Green'

Crisphead 'Windermere'

Cos 'Winter Density'

LETTUCE VARIETIES				
	BUTTERHEAD	**CRISPHEAD**	**COS**	**LOOSE-LEAF**
SPRING CROP	**Cynthia** forcing variety for growing under glass, large hearts **May King** red-tinged leaves, for sowing early under cloches	**Kelly's** Iceberg-type, for growing in cold frames		
LATE SPRING/ EARLY SUMMER CROP	**Arctic King** compact, small heads, extremely winter-hardy **Imperial Winter** large, winter-hardy **Valdor** solid, dark green hearts, winter hardy		**Winter Density** dark green heads, sweet flavour; also crops in winter	
EARLY SUMMER CROP	**Fortune** large heads, quick maturing **Musette** uniform large mid green heads **Sangria** red-tinged leaves **Suzan** large, pale green hearts; sow under glass for an early crop **Tom Thumb** small, quick-maturing	**Windermere** quick-maturing, fine flavour, sow in cold frame	**Little Gem** quick-maturing, sweet flavour **Lobjoit's Green** large, deep green, very crisp	
SUMMER CROP	**All-the-Year-Round** suitable for spring, summer, autumn sowing, slow to bolt **Buttercrunch** compact, crunchy heart **Continuity** red-tinged leaves, long-standing, good for sandy soils **Fortune** large heads, quick maturing **Tom Thumb** quick-maturing, small heads	**Great Lakes** large, spreading **Iceberg** super-crisp, white-hearted **Lakeland** reliable, solid **Webbs Wonderful** large-hearted, slow to bolt **Windermere** quick-maturing	**Little Leprechaun** red-leaved, slow to bolt **Lobjoit's Green** large, deep green, very crisp	**Salad Bowl** intricately cut, curled **Red Salad Bowl** as above, red-brown
LATE AUTUMN/ EARLY WINTER CROP	**Avondefiance** mildew-resistant, slow to bolt, dark green heads **Kwiek** large hearts, forced under glass	**Avoncrisp** resistant to mildew and root aphids, slow to bolt **Dynasty** disease-resistant	**Jewel** similar to 'Little Gem' but larger	
EARLY/MID WINTER CROP	**Diamant** force under heated glass **Kloek** large, solid hearts, for growing under heated glass			

Butterhead 'Valdor'

Crisphead 'Iceberg'

Loose-leaf 'Salad Bowl'/'Red Salad Bowl'

131

MARROWS AND SQUASHES

**Marrows, courgettes, squashes and pumpkins
all belong to the cucumber family – bush and trailing
varieties are available.**

Marrows and their smaller relatives, courgettes (sometimes known as zucchini), produce a large yield in a modest area. Although any immature marrow may be called a courgette, certain varieties have been specifically selected for producing a large crop of baby marrows.

Other common relatives of the vegetable marrow include pumpkins, squashes and edible gourds. They are plants from tropical regions, but are suitable for growing outdoors in Britain from early summer onwards.

MARROWS AND COURGETTES

There are two types of marrow plant – bushy and trailing – but both have similar growing characteristics. Both types are half-hardy – seeds can be sown under glass, or outdoors when danger of frost is past. Of the two types, bushy varieties are the best choice for smaller vegetable plots as they require less growing space.

Marrows and courgettes need a sunny position and deep, rich soil. They can be sown in a cold frame, in peat pots under glass or directly in a prepared bed outdoors. Alternatively, sow on an old heap of thoroughly rotted manure or compost – if this is not needed in the garden. In general, two or three marrow plants and four to six courgette plants should be sufficient for most needs.

Prepare the bed by taking out planting holes, at one spade's depth, for each seedling and work in a bucketful of manure or well-rotted compost. Return the topsoil and heap it into a ridge about 5cm (2in) high for each plant. This will help to retain moisture around the young plants.

If you are using a compost heap, mix a little soil around each planting position. Do not allow the site to dry out in spells of hot weather. Bush marrows are more suited to growing in this way than trailing varieties.

Bush marrows should be spaced 60cm (2ft) apart and occupy much less space than trailing

plants which, under ideal conditions, require 1-1.2m (3-4ft).

Courgettes need much the same growing space as bush marrow varieties.

Cultivation

Marrows and courgettes are grown in much the same way. Prepare the beds for sowing or

planting outdoors in mid spring, as already described. Sow seeds in a greenhouse or cold frame at the same time.

Ideally, sow two seeds to a depth of 2.5cm (1in) in each of a number of proprietary grow pots with seed compost. Grow pots are ideal as the seedlings can be planted out without removing the

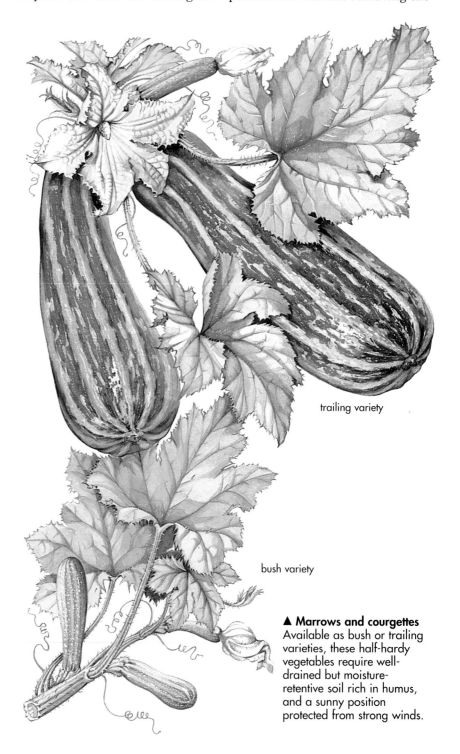

trailing variety

bush variety

▲ **Marrows and courgettes**
Available as bush or trailing varieties, these half-hardy vegetables require well-drained but moisture-retentive soil rich in humus, and a sunny position protected from strong winds.

pots, thus causing minimum disturbance to the roots. The pots disintegrate in the soil.

Place the pots in a cold frame and keep it covered; place sacking over the lights if frost is forecast. Alternatively, germinate the seeds indoors on a shaded window-sill where a minimum temperature of 18°C (64°F) can be maintained.

When the seed leaves begin to develop strongly remove the weaker of the two seedlings from each pot. By late spring, when all danger of frost has passed, plant out the hardened-off seedlings in their pots. The rim of each pot should be below the soil ridge so that the roots will not be exposed to dry conditions on top of the earth mounds.

If the seedlings have been raised in clay or plastic pots, knock them gently out of their containers before planting.

Marrow and courgette seeds can also be sown directly in the prepared planting sites in late spring, or earlier if cloches have been placed in position to warm up the soil in sheltered gardens. Sow bush marrow and courgette seeds at a depth of 2.5cm (1in) in groups of four or five; each seed should be 15cm (6in) apart from its neighbour with a minimum of 1m (3ft) between each group. Thin out to one seedling at each station once the plants have taken hold. Space trailing varieties 1-1.2m (3-4ft) apart.

Before the fruits begin to appear, surround the plants with a mulch or black polythene to discourage weeds. Once the marrows and courgettes start to grow, feed every two weeks with a liquid fertilizer. However, if the plants are treated with fertilizer that is high in nitrogen,they develop too much leafy growth at the expense of flowers. If this happens, cut back some of the leaves to permit air to circulate freely around the flowers and young fruits.

Keep the soil moist but do not pour water over the young plants; instead water around them. To prevent damage from slugs and snails use slug pellets, and as the marrow fruits increase in size place them on glass or tiles to prevent rot and severe slug attack.

▼ **Trailing marrows** Support is necessary for trailing varieties. Train them up tripods made of strong canes lashed together at the top and tie in the shoots as the heavy fruits develop.

▲ **Pumpkins and squashes** Available in a range of varieties and shapes, these vegetables need lots of space.

Cultivation

Sow one or two seeds in 7.5cm (3in) pots of seed compost in mid to late spring. Germinate in a propagator unit where a temperature of 18-20°C (64-70°F) can be maintained; harden off the seedlings in a cold frame. Transplant them to their final growing positions in late spring or early summer, setting the plants a minimum of 1m (3ft) apart. Pinch out the growing point of each plant when it has about five leaves. Water heavily and regularly during dry spells.

For exceptionally large fruits, heap soil over the axils of fruit-bearing laterals at the point where they emerge from the main stem. Roots will then be forced out in the search for more food and moisture.

Both marrows and courgettes produce male and female flowers. The female flower is distinguished by an embryo fruit behind the bloom; the male has no swelling. Pollination is normally carried out by insects, which transport pollen between the male and female flowers. In dull, cold or wet weather, however, there may be fewer insects about and it becomes necessary to pollinate the flowers by hand to ensure the development of fruits. Each male flower will pollinate up to three female flowers.

Harvesting and storing

Marrows are at their peak during the summer months. Harvest when the fruits are 23-30cm (9-12in) long and when their skins yield to gently applied pressure. Always cut the marrows free first and then lift them away.

A few late marrows can be left on their stalks to ripen in early autumn. Harvest them just before the first expected frost and suspend them in netting in an airy, frost-free place at a temperature of 16°C (61°F) – stored in such a way, they will last for several weeks.

Courgettes should be harvested in summer when the fruits are 10cm (4in) long.

Pests and diseases

Marrows and courgettes are mainly pest-free, though slugs and snails can be a problem in wet summers. Cucumber mosaic virus, grey mould and powdery mildew may be troublesome dur-ing the growing season; spray the plants with benomyl, carbendazim or thiophanate-methyl.

SQUASHES AND PUMPKINS

Squashes and pumpkins come in a range of shapes, and as bushy or trailing varieties. They have the same cultural requirements as marrows, but need a great deal of space. Two or three plants should be adequate for most needs.

Planning the crop

Squashes and pumpkins thrive in full sun and in a position sheltered from winds. They need rich, well-drained soil – the top of an old compost heap is ideal. Alternatively, dig planting holes about 38cm (15in) square and fill with well-rotted compost – leave a shallow, water-retaining depression at the surface. It is a good idea to sprinkle slug pellets to prevent damage.

POLLINATING MARROWS

In cold or dull weather, marrows must be pollinated by hand. Detach a male flower (with no embryo fruit), pick off the petals (or fold them back) and brush it gently against the open centre of several female flowers.

Harvesting and storing

Small-fruited varieties should be cut as they mature during summer. Large-fruited varieties should be left on their stems until late autumn, but harvested before the first frost. Store them in a frost-free shed for winter use.

Winter-harvested squashes have considerably more nutrient value than marrows and courgettes and, as an added bonus, they are often highly decorative, in both their trailing and bushy varieties.

Pests and diseases

Like marrows and courgettes, the most troublesome pests of squashes and pumpkins are glasshouse red spider mites, glasshouse whitefly and aphids at seedling stage. Spray with malathion or pirim-iphos-methyl. Possible diseases include cucumber mosaic virus and powdery mildew.

HARVESTING MARROWS

To harvest marrows, cut the fruits from the plants when they are about 25cm (10in) long. Pick courgette fruits when they are 10cm (4in) long. Do not pull the fruits from the stems.

VARIETIES TO CHOOSE

Marrows and courgettes

'All Green Bush' – bush variety; giving a large crop of courgettes if cut regularly.

'Burpee Golden Zucchini' – courgette bush variety; excellent cropper; golden-yellow fruits.

'Early Gem' – early bush courgette; heavy cropper; dark green fruits for early harvesting.

'Gold Rush' – bush courgette variety; heavy early cropper with shiny golden fruits.

'Long Green Bush' – compact bush marrow; dark green fruits with pale green stripes.

'Long Green Trailing' – produces cylindrical dark green marrows with pale green stripes.

'Zucchini' – early cropper; profuse, slim dark green courgettes.

Squashes and pumpkins

'Atlantic Giant' – huge orange-fleshed pumpkin; suitable for exhibitions.

'Butternut' – winter squash with firm flesh and sweet flavour.

'Custard White' – scalloped-edged, flat fruits on compact plants; summer variety.

'Sweet Dumpling' – small, rounded summer squash; green-striped fruits, orange-yellow, sweet flesh.

'Tivoli' – bush type squash; creamy-white oblong fruits; spaghetti-like flesh.

Marrow 'Long Green Bush'

Marrow 'Opal'

Courgette 'Zucchini'

Courgette 'Burpee Golden Zucchini'

Squash 'Custard White'

Pumpkin 'Atlantic Giant'

MUSHROOMS

Freshly picked, home-grown mushrooms have superb flavour. They are easy to grow from prepared kits and take up little space.

button mushroom

cup mushroom

flat mushroom

In the wild, the common mushroom proliferates in fields in which horses or cows have been kept so that the soil is greatly enriched by manure. A similar soil is required when growing them under less natural conditions, whether in a shady corner of a lawn, in boxes at the back of a shady shed or in a cellar. They need a compost that is well rotted

and has been treated with neither fungicide nor weedkiller.

You can make your own mushroom compost, but it tends to crop erratically. The most successful crops are on ready-made mushroom compost obtained from a garden centre. Prepared mushroom kits are even simpler and consist of a container, chemical-free compost and mushroom-spawn.

Mushroom compost

Use fresh, damp, strawy (wheat not barley) manure from a stable. Buy manure by the hundredweight for home-made compost – any spare can go on the garden. Mix it up thoroughly, lightly hose with water, and pile it in a heap outside to generate heat.

After about a week, turn the heap over, dampen it again and repeat the process every two or three days until the manure becomes crumbly and has lost its smell of ammonia. Check the temperature – 24°C (75°F) means it is ready. Pack it firmly into open boxes or tubs to a depth of 25-30cm (10-12in).

Compost is merely the growing medium for a mushroom crop. It is necessary to buy spawn to obtain mushrooms. This can be bought from most garden centres and nurseries. You need at least 50g (2oz) of spawn for every 10 kg (22lb) of soil.

Planting

Decide where the crop will grow. Ideally the spot should be dimly lit, humid and at a steady 10-13°C (50-55°F). Potting sheds are ideal, but during the winter months choose a greenhouse with controlled heating.

Break the spawn into walnut-sized pieces and gently insert them in the compost, 2.5cm (1in) deep and 25cm (10in) apart. Water the compost lightly.

◄ **Home-grown mushrooms** Firm-textured and fine-flavoured, home-grown mushrooms are often superior to shop-bought types. Two or three crops can be expected from one set of spawn.

GROWING MUSHROOMS

1 Insert pieces of spawn, about the size of a walnut, 2.5cm (1in) deep and 25cm (10in) apart in boxes of compost at a temperature of 24°C (75°F). Water the compost lightly and put the box in a dimly lit position.

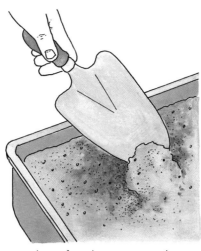

2 Ten days after planting, cover the compost with a 2.5cm (1in) layer of chalk and peat substitute to help maintain temperature and minimize moisture loss. Sprinkle regularly with water to keep the compost moist.

3 Harvest the mushrooms by gently twisting them free of the bed; cut any debris free with a sharp knife. Refill the holes with loose bedding material. Repeat until successive crops of mushrooms stop appearing.

Within a few days the spawn will start to spread fine threads – the mycelium or mushroom tissue – throughout the box.

Ten days after planting, cover the compost with a 2.5cm (1in) layer of mixed chalk and peat substitute (1 part chalk to 3 parts peat) to help maintain the temperature and level of moisture in the bed. Water regularly using a fine watering-can rose, maintaining dampness rather than soaking the compost.

For outdoor mushroom cultivation, choose a warm, damp day between late spring and autumn and lift small squares of lawn turf about 5cm (2in) thick and 30cm (1ft) apart. Insert a walnut-sized piece of spawn into each hole and replace the turf.

If the weather becomes dry, keep watering the spawn area. Do not mow the lawn.

To grow from prepared mushroom kits, simply follow the manufacturer's instructions.

VARIETIES TO CHOOSE

Most mushroom spawn is of the common field mushroom variety. This may be creamy, off-white or brown in colour, but with no difference in flavour.

Larger, flat, oyster mushrooms are also available, in grey, brown, pink or white.

Harvesting
Mushrooms first appear as tiny pinheads about three or four weeks after planting. This period can be longer if conditions are variable, so be patient. Indoor crops are more reliable.

It takes another seven to ten days before they reach a good size for picking. Although 'button' mushrooms are ready first and look appetizing, cup and flat mushrooms have more flavour. A second and third flush, perhaps more, will follow over six to eight weeks.

When the mushrooms stop sprouting, use the compost as a garden mulch; it cannot be used again for mushroom growing.

Mushrooms are at their finest when eaten as soon as possible after picking. They are not suitable for freezing. Washing mushrooms ruins their taste so wipe them clean with a damp cloth.

Pests and diseases
The larvae of various species of mushroom fly may tunnel into the stalks and caps, making the plants inedible.

▼ **Mushroom culture** A regular, light supply of moisture is essential for a successful crop. A capillary watering system is highly practical, with absorbent material that allows the mushrooms to take up water from a reservoir as required.

ONIONS

**The most versatile of all vegetables,
onions come in so many varieties that fresh supplies
are at hand throughout the year.**

In order to have home-grown onions all year round, they should be allowed reasonable growing space and quite a lot of time to grow to a useful size. Nevertheless, the superior flavour of home-grown onions – and their good long-term storage qualities – make them well worth the effort.

The main choice facing anyone wanting to grow maincrop onions is whether to grow them from seed – which takes anything from six or seven months to a full year – or to grow them from sets (immature bulbs), which takes about five months.

Maincrop onions from seed
These can be grown in four different ways.
Japanese varieties are sown in their cropping bed in late summer and left over winter. They are thinned the following mid spring and harvested in early summer.
Late summer varieties are sown in late summer, thinned in autumn, and the young plants transplanted to their permanent bed in spring. The bulbs are pulled and stored in late summer.
Winter varieties are germinated under glass in mid winter, transplanted in early spring to their permanent bed and harvested as an autumn crop.
Spring varieties are sown in their permanent bed in early or mid spring for harvesting in early autumn, though they will keep in storage until the following spring.

Maincrop onions from sets
These are planted in mid spring and harvested in late summer. Onion sets are immature bulbs which have been stored at high temperatures to induce dormancy and prevent the formation of a flower embryo. They have distinct advantages over seeds: they are easier to handle, less likely to be attacked by mildew or aphids, and much quicker to grow. They have a greater chance than seed-grown onions of succeeding in colder areas. While they are more expensive than seeds, the time and

effort saved is well worth it. Seedsmen list onion sets by the pack, and usually indicate how much footage of a row a pack will plant with 10cm (4in) spacing. It is best to buy onion sets that are not too large – roughly 1.8cm (¾in) across – as larger sets are more likely to bolt.

Plant sets in early to mid spring to produce a late summer crop. They mature earlier than winter-sown varieties.

Red-skinned onions are becoming increasingly popular. They are grown for their flavour and colour. Some varieties have a blood-red skin and white flesh, while others are pink-fleshed all the way through.

In addition to large maincrop varieties, several other onion types are available. They include shallots, pickling onions, which are small and quick maturing, salad or spring onions to be used raw, and Welsh onions, which grow in tufts of pencil-thick stalks and look like salad onions.

Planning the crop
Onions need a site in full sun on well-drained deep loam which – for maincrop varieties – has been well manured. Neither peas nor beans should be grown close

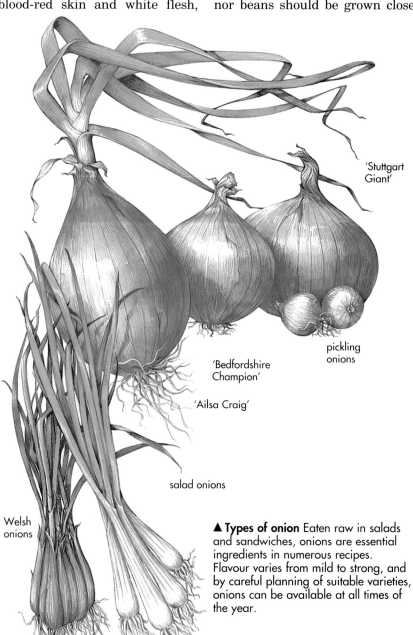

'Stuttgart Giant'

'Bedfordshire Champion'

'Ailsa Craig'

pickling onions

salad onions

Welsh onions

▲ **Types of onion** Eaten raw in salads and sandwiches, onions are essential ingredients in numerous recipes. Flavour varies from mild to strong, and by careful planning of suitable varieties, onions can be available at all times of the year.

GROWING ONION SETS

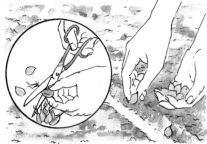
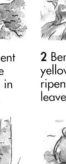

1 Plant the sets in prepared permanent beds in early to mid spring. Snip the small roots off before planting. Firm in well and cover the bed with netting.

2 Bend the leaves down when they turn yellow. This will encourage early ripening. Don't, however, snap the leaves off.

3 Loosen the onions two weeks later by pushing a garden fork underneath the bulbs. Ease them out slightly, but leave them still in the ground.

4 After another two weeks, lift out the bulbs and spread them out in a shed or greenhouse to ripen fully, handling them carefully.

---

to onions because they repel each other. Dig the plot deeply in the autumn, as early as possible, and work in two buckets of well-rotted manure or compost per sq m/yd.

Pickling, salad and Welsh onions will grow in any fertile well-drained soil. Welsh onions are a good substitute for salad onions. They are smaller and can be grown from sets.

All onions grown from sets require less finely textured soil than seed-grown ones.

All onion types grow best in firm ground, so prepare the bed well in advance to give the soil a chance to settle. In late winter add a dressing of 100g (4oz) of bonemeal and 50g (2oz) of sulphate of potash per sq m/yd. Alternatively, rake in 75g per sq m (3oz per sq yd) of a general fertilizer such as Growmore before sowing or planting.

A bed measuring 4.5m x 1m (15ft x 3ft) should produce about 6kg (12lb) of onions, but the yield can be increased with good feeding. The size of the crop on this plot applies to both onion seeds and sets. A 3m (10ft) row of pickling onions will yield up to 150 onions.

Growing onions

It is important to choose a plant-ing or sowing date and method of cultivation suited to the particular type of onion.

Onion sets are planted in their permanent beds in early to mid spring, when they are dispatched from nurseries.

Never plant onion sets in cold or wet soil; if you have to delay planting, take the bulbs out of their packaging and spread them out in a cool, light place to avoid premature sprouting. Make drills about 2-5cm (1-2in) deep and 23-25cm (9-10in) apart. Space the bulbs in the drills 10cm (4in) apart and cover with soil so that only the tips are showing.

Firm in well and cover the bed with netting to prevent birds from lifting out the bulbs. Check the bed daily and replace any sets that have been lifted out of the soil as the roots grow. Hoe between the rows regularly, and hand weed between the young onions to prevent damage. Make sure that they have enough water: in dry conditions, sets may bolt (flower prematurely). Remove any flower heads.

Japanese varieties are sown 2.5cm (1in) apart in their permanent bed during late summer, in 12mm (½in) drills with the rows 23cm (9in) apart.

In spring, thin the seedlings to 10cm (4in) apart. Water well in dry spells, and hoe frequently to keep down weeds. Use Japanese varieties in summer before main-crop varieties ripen.

Late summer varieties sown in late summer, need a seed bed on well-drained soil which has been raked to a fine tilth. Sow the seeds thinly in 12mm (½in) deep drills 23cm (9in) apart, and thin in autumn to 2.5cm (1in) apart.

The following early spring, as soon as the soil can be worked easily, transplant the seedlings to the prepared permanent bed.

Use a trowel to plant the seedlings, covering about 12mm (½in) of white stem with soil. Space the seedlings 15cm (6in) apart in rows 30cm (1ft) apart.

Winter varieties are sown in pans or pots of seed compost in mid winter. Firm the compost level 12mm (½in) from the top of the container and dust the surface with lime to make the seeds easier to spot. Sow them 25mm (1in) apart.

Press each seed just under the surface with the point of a pencil. Sift a little compost over them and water through a fine rose or with a spray. Cover the pots or pans with clear plastic sheets or glass and a sheet of newspaper, and place in an unheated greenhouse, or cold frame or under cloches. Germination will be quicker if a temperature of 16°C (61°F) can be maintained. Remove the covering as soon as the seeds germinate and harden off the seedlings ready for planting out in early spring, in the same way as summer-sown seedlings.

Spring varieties are sown directly in a prepared permanent bed in early spring, or as soon as the soil can be raked to a fine tilth. Sow seeds 12mm (½in) deep in drills 23-30cm (9-12in) apart. When the seedlings are 5cm (2in) high, thin them to 2.5cm (1in) apart. When they are 10-15cm (4-6in) high, thin them to 10cm (4in) apart for medium-sized bulbs. Use the seedlings in salads. Lift the bulbs in autumn.

Pickling onions do best on light soil that has not been manured recently, as it is important to keep them small. Sow from late winter to early spring in a bed raked to a fine tilth. Either scatter the seeds or sow them to a depth of 12mm (½in) in drills a minimum of 15cm (6in) apart.

Little thinning is necessary, provided the plants have sufficient space to form small bulbs. Harvest from mid summer onwards.

Harvesting and storing

When the outer leaves begin to turn yellow, bend the tops over to assist ripening. About two weeks later, push a fork gently under the bulbs to loosen the roots and, after another fortnight, lift them right out. Spread them out in a sunny place to dry thoroughly. In wet weather, dry indoors in a warm place such as an airing cupboard. Complete the process in a cool, dry place.

Always handle the bulbs carefully to avoid the risk of bruising. Do not trim off the withered tops completely, as they will be needed for stringing. Tie them to a length of rope or store the onions in netting hung up in a cool, dry place.

Pests and diseases

Pest include onion eelworm and onion fly. Common diseases are neck rot and white rot. Plants grown from seed are more likely to be attacked by onion fly than onions grown from sets.

SHALLOTS

Shallots are smaller than onions. They are used for flavouring or pickling rather than as a vegetable. Shallots grow in bunches or clusters of about ten small bulbs.

Since they are often expensive to buy and difficult to find in shops and supermarkets, shallots are an obvious choice for growing yourself. Properly stored, they will last all year.

Like onion sets, shallots are grown from bulbs. They are sold by pack or weight, roughly 40-60 to the kilo (2lb). Thirty shallots planted in a 4.5m (15ft) row will produce a crop of about 2-2.5kg (4-5lb).

Plant shallots from late winter until early spring, or as soon as the ground can be worked, in a sunny position on land manured for a previous crop.

If the soil is light, push the bulbs firmly into the soil so that they are three-quarters buried. On firmer soils, make a hole with the tip of a trowel or draw a drill with a hoe. In each case leave only the tip of the bulb protruding. Allow 15cm (6in) between the bulbs and 23cm (9in) between rows.

After a few days, replant any

bulbs that have become dislodged. Hoe and water regularly

Harvesting and storing

When the foliage dies back in mid summer, lift the shallot clusters and lay them out in single layers to dry for a few days.

Once the foliage has withered completely, split the clumps into single bulbs and leave them to ripen for a few days longer. Store them in a cool, dry place, reserving some for planting the following season.

SALAD ONIONS

Salad or spring onions are among the easiest vegetables to grow. The stems can be used as a substitute for chives. Being extremely quick-growing, they are usually out of the ground before onion fly strikes. They take up little room and need no special care.

Salad onions do well in any fertile, well-drained soil. Choose a sunny site and dig the soil over in the autumn before sowing.

Just before sowing, rake in 75g (3oz) of a general fertilizer. Sow the seeds thinly in drills 12mm (½in) deep and about 20cm (8in) apart, starting in early spring and repeating at four-weekly intervals until mid summer.

Cover the drills gently with soil after sowing, taking care not to disturb the seeds. Water lightly.

For early spring crops make a first sowing in early autumn, with a second sowing in late winter in a cold frame or under cloches for pulling in early summer.

GROWING ONIONS FROM SEED

1 Sow the seeds thinly in 12mm (½in) drills 23cm (9in) apart. Winter varieties should be sown in pots or pans and germinated under glass.

2 Onions sown outdoors in spring and late summer, and Japanese varieties, must be thinned when they are approximately 5cm (2in) high.

3 In spring transplant late summer varieties as well as onions sown in pots under glass during winter to permanent beds.

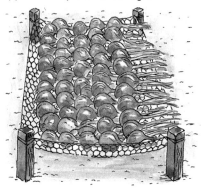

4 If the weather is settled, spread the lifted onions to dry out on a raised wire netting frame in the garden.

ONION VARIETIES TO CHOOSE

Sets
'Red Delicious' – globe-shaped bulbs; red-skinned, white flesh; keeps well.

'Stuttgart Giant' – bolt-resistant; long-keeping; flattish bulbs.

'Turbo' – deep amber skin; early maturer; globe-shaped; bolt-resistant; long keeper.

Japanese varieties
'Express Yellow' – dark yellow skin; earliest of Japanese varieties.

'Senshyn Yellow Globe' – heavy cropper; may be sown in autumn and overwintered in the ground.

Late-summer varieties
'Buffalo' – classic globe shape; hard; straw-coloured; thin-necked.

'Hygro' – high yielding; globe-shaped; good keeper.

'Rijnsburger' – large with white flesh and straw coloured skin; heavy cropper.

Winter varieties
'Ailsa Craig' – large, globe-shaped, yellow; popular all-rounder; mild-flavoured.

'Red Baron' – red-skinned; good flavour; stores well.

Spring varieties
'Bedfordshire Champion' – large; globe-shaped; heavy cropper; good keeper, susceptible to mildew.

'North Holland Blood Red' – large, semi-flat, red-skinned; good keeper.

Pickling onions
'Paris Silverskin' – very quick growing; early ripening.

Shallots
'Atlantic', 'Hative de Niort' and 'Pikant' are the usual varieties on offer.

Maincrop onion 'Red Baron'

Maincrop onion 'Hygro'

Maincrop onion 'Bedfordshire Champion'

If space is at a premium, sow salad onions between rows of slower-growing vegetables, such as carrots: the onions will help to fend off carrot fly.

Salad onions should need no thinning. Water the plants well in dry weather and weed carefully.

Harvest salad onions onions when they are about 15cm (6in) high and the stems are pencil-thick.

WELSH ONIONS
Otherwise known as cibouls or green onions, Welsh onions look like multi-stemmed salad onions. The pencil-thick shoots grow together in close tufts, up to 30cm (1ft) high. Use the shoots as salad onions and the leaves as chives.

Welsh onions do best on well-manured, well-drained deep loam. Dig over the plot the previous autumn. Sow from late winter to late spring, where the plants are to grow, and thin until 25cm (10in) apart. Lift and divide every three years.

Salad onion 'White Lisbon'

VARIETIES OF SALAD ONIONS

'Hikari Bunching' – multi-stemmed; winter-hardy.

'Ishikura' – white and straight; long harvesting period.

'White Lisbon'– mild flavour; quick-growing. 'White Lisbon Winter Hardy' is similar; sow in autumn for harvesting in spring.

PARSNIPS

**Parsnips are a staple winter vegetable which is easy
to cultivate. Other root crops, such as the lesser-known Hamburg
parsley, salsify and scorzonera, make a pleasant change.**

Parsnips are excellent vegetables for roasting, baking or boiling and are available when other root vegetables, such as carrots, have already been harvested.

They are the earliest vegetable seed to be sown outdoors – often in early spring if the weather is favourable – but are not harvested until winter. Therefore they occupy the ground for almost a year, taking up valuable space in the vegetable garden.

One way to get a little extra out of the parsnip bed is to sow a catch crop of lettuces between the rows; or to grow radishes alongside the parsnips. The lettuces and radishes will grow quickly and be ready for harvesting before the parsnips need all the available growing space.

Growing parsnips

Parsnips will grow in any soil, but do best in deep, rich, fairly light ground. Choose an open sunny position and a bed that has been well manured for a previous crop. Do not grow them on freshly manured soil – it will cause the parsnips to fork or split. A 4.5m (15ft) row will provide about 30 parsnips.

Sow seeds in early spring as soon as the soil is dry enough and the weather not too severe. First rake in a general fertilizer such as Growmore at the rate of 50-75g per sq m (2-3oz per sq yd), preferably a few days before sowing. Make drills 12mm (½in) deep and 30cm (1ft) apart and sow thickly – germination can sometimes be unreliable.

Thin the seedlings for the first time when they are about 2.5cm (1in) high, then continue thinning until they are 15cm (6in) apart. Alternatively, sow in groups of three or four seeds 15cm (6in) apart; remove weak seedlings to leave a single strong one growing in each station.

Hoe regularly to keep down weeds, but take care not to damage the parsnip crowns. Water well to ensure root development.

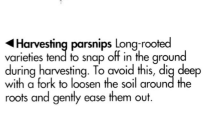

long-rooted parsnip

short-rooted parsnip

◀ **Harvesting parsnips** Long-rooted varieties tend to snap off in the ground during harvesting. To avoid this, dig deep with a fork to loosen the soil around the roots and gently ease them out.

Harvesting

Parsnips can be harvested as soon as the leaves die down in autum but a sharp frost improves their flavour. Use a garden fork to dig deep and loosen the soil so the roots are not damaged during harvesting.

Parsnips can be left in the ground and dug up as required, but lift the last roots in late winter or before the roots start to produce new leaves. Store them in a cool place, covered with soil.

Pests and diseases

The pest most likely to attack parsnips is the celery fly; spray with dimethoate to discourage it. Parsnip canker is the most common disease; there is no chemical treatment – grow short-rooted varieties or those known to be resistant to the disease.

VARIETIES TO CHOOSE

Parsnips
'Avonresister' – short roots; canker-resistant; early-maturing.

'Cobham Improved Marrow' – medium roots; canker-resistant; white, smooth-skinned.

'Dobies Exhibition' – long roots for deep soil; fine exhibition variety.

'Dobies Intermediate'– short-rooted early variety suitable for less deep soils.

'Gladiator' (F1 hybrid) – heavy cropper; smooth, white roots; good canker-resistance.

'Hollow Crown Improved' – long, well-shaped roots for deep soil.

'Tender and True' – long roots; canker-resistant; smooth-skinned.

'The Student' – slender, tapering roots; creamy flesh.

'White Gem' – short-rooted; smooth-skinned; canker-resistant.

Hamburg Parsley
'Omega' – long, smooth, creamy-skinned roots.

Salsify
'Giant' – reliable, long, well-flavoured roots.

'Sandwich Island' – long, smooth-skinned, tapering roots.

Scorzonera
'Russian Giant' – long, black-skinned roots; delicate flavour.

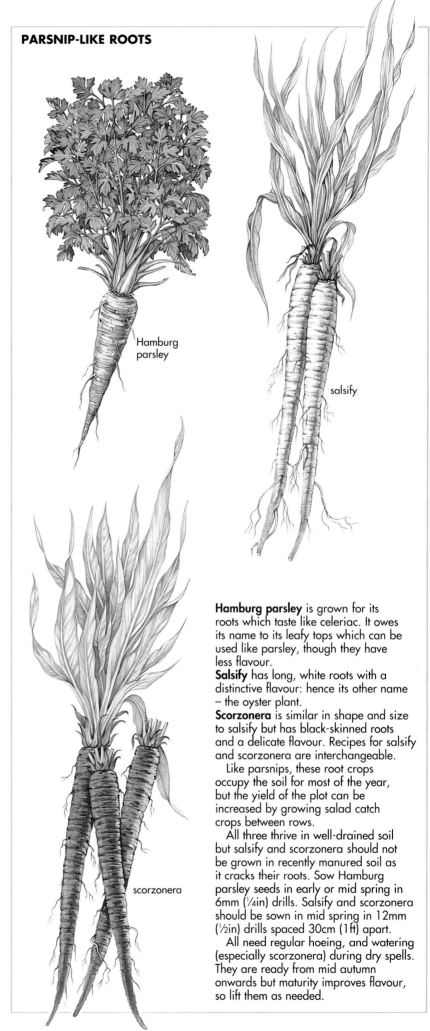

PARSNIP-LIKE ROOTS

Hamburg parsley

salsify

scorzonera

Hamburg parsley is grown for its roots which taste like celeriac. It owes its name to its leafy tops which can be used like parsley, though they have less flavour.

Salsify has long, white roots with a distinctive flavour: hence its other name – the oyster plant.

Scorzonera is similar in shape and size to salsify but has black-skinned roots and a delicate flavour. Recipes for salsify and scorzonera are interchangeable.

Like parsnips, these root crops occupy the soil for most of the year, but the yield of the plot can be increased by growing salad catch crops between rows.

All three thrive in well-drained soil but salsify and scorzonera should not be grown in recently manured soil as it cracks their roots. Sow Hamburg parsley seeds in early or mid spring in 6mm (¼in) drills. Salsify and scorzonera should be sown in mid spring in 12mm (½in) drills spaced 30cm (1ft) apart.

All need regular hoeing, and watering (especially scorzonera) during dry spells. They are ready from mid autumn onwards but maturity improves flavour, so lift them as needed.

PEAS

**Freshly picked garden peas have a superb
flavour. They need a fair amount of attention and take up
a lot of space, but are well worth the effort.**

There are two main types of garden peas. Hardy, round-seeded peas are sown in late autumn or early spring for picking in late spring and early summer; the wrinkled type (formerly known as marrow-fat), which have a much sweeter flavour, are less hardy, and are sown in the open from early spring until mid summer, for harvesting from early summer onwards.

Other varieties of garden peas include the sugar peas – subdivided into mangetout and snap peas – and petit pois. They are grown in the same way as early and maincrop garden peas, from sowings made in spring, but are picked when the seeds have only just begun to develop. They are cooked and eaten whole, pods and all.

The usual way of classifying peas is according to the time it takes from sowing until picking. First earlies mature in about 12 weeks; second earlies take 13 to 14 weeks; and maincrop varieties take 14 to 16 weeks.

With successive sowings from late winter until early summer, peas can be ripening from early to late summer and into autumn.

Depending on the variety, peas grow to heights ranging from 45cm to 1.8m (1½ft to 6ft). The taller types produce roughly two or three times as many peas as the small (dwarf) types.

Peas are prone to a number of pests and diseases and yield a comparatively small crop, considering the amount of space they take up. Yet they are well worth growing, since the flavour of freshly picked garden peas is so much finer than that of either fresh or field-grown peas grown for freezing on a commercial scale. This is because the sugar in peas begins turning into starch the moment the pod is picked.

Planning the crop

Peas grow best in rich, well-drained but moisture-retentive soil. Good drainage is particularly important for early varieties, as the seeds will rot in cold, wet soil.

Dig the plot at least three or four weeks before sowing, working in two buckets of well-rotted garden compost or farmyard manure to the sq m/yd. A week before sowing, rake in a top-dressing of general fertilizer at 50-75g per sq m (2-3oz per sq yd).

One packet of seed is usually sufficient for a 4.5m (15ft) long row, but the yield will depend on the pea variety and the growing conditions – dwarf early peas yield a smaller crop than the same number of maincrop varieties.

Growing peas

If you plan to grow a number of rows, make the distance between the rows the same as the full-grown height of the crop. First early varieties and dwarf varieties reach a height of 45cm (1½ft), while the later maincrops can grow as high as 1.8m (6ft).

You should also allow for a reasonable distance between peas and any neighbouring crop. Onions, beetroot or lettuces, for example, can be grown successfully only 45cm (1½ft) from a row of tall maincrop peas on the southerly or sunny side. But about double this space will be needed on the shady side.

Use a swan-neck hoe or a short-handled onion hoe to draw out flat-bottomed drills 10cm (4in) wide and 4-5cm (1½-2in) deep. In spring and summer, sow the seeds 5-7.5cm (2-3in) apart in three staggered rows in the drills. Sow overwintering varieties rather more thickly to compensate for any losses in bad weather.

Pea seeds sometimes germinate poorly, or they may be dug up by mice. To fill gaps in the rows, sow extra seeds in small pots or spaced out in trays; transplant the seedlings when fully developed.

Reduce the risk of disease in overwintered crops by shaking the seeds in a bag containing a proprietary chemical seed dressing.

After sowing, level the surface by drawing the soil over the drills with the back of a rake and firm lightly.

'Kelvedon Wonder' (first early)

'Onward' (second early)

▲ **Pea classification** Peas are listed according to the time taken from sowing to picking. First earlies mature in about 12 weeks; second earlies take 13 to 14 weeks; and maincrop varieties 14 to 16 weeks. Catalogue classifications vary.

Immediately after sowing, protect the seed from birds by covering the rows with netting, black thread criss-crossed from sticks close to the ground, or with clusters of twigs.

Overwintered crops are more likely to succeed if they are protected with cloches until the following spring.

As soon as the seedlings are through, hoe on each side of the rows to get rid of weeds. When the seedlings are 7.5cm (3in) high, push in small, twiggy sticks to encourage the plants to climb. Do not delay in giving this support because plants left to straggle on the ground may be attacked by slugs and snails.

Once the plants are growing strongly, put in the final supports, which should be at least as high as the ultimate height of the plants. These final supports can be long, twiggy branches, wire criss-crossed between bamboo stakes, or netting tied firmly to posts at either end of the rows.

Make sure the peas get a constant supply of moisture. Water regularly during dry spells and give the rows a mulch of damp coir, leaf-mould, garden compost, or even black polythene.

Harvesting and storing

When the pods seem to have reached their full length, check daily to feel if the peas are swelling inside.

Aim to pick the pods when the seeds are well developed but before they are fully mature – about four weeks after the main flowering display. The pods at the base of the plants will be the first to ripen.

To harvest, pull the pod upwards with one hand while holding the stem with the other. With regular picking, more pods are likely to develop.

Harvest sugar peas and mangetout when the pods are about 5cm (2in) long and the seeds are only just beginning to develop inside. If you don't get many of these small pods from a single picking, store them in the refrigerator until you have enough to cook. Petit pois should also be picked when young, otherwise they lose their delicate and sweet flavour.

As soon as the plants are cleared of pods, cut the top growth down, and either put the roots on the compost heap or dig them into the soil. As they are rich in nitrogen, they help to improve fertility.

Surplus peas are excellent for freezing.

Pests and diseases

The most troublesome pests are bean seed fly, pea moth, pea thrips and pea weevils; seed dressings and chemical sprays can be effective. Early varieties are often the most susceptible. Diseases likely to affect peas include damping off, mildew, foot rot and grey mould. Crop rotation and good cultural practices reduce the incidence of soil-borne diseases.

SOWING AND SUPPORTING PEAS

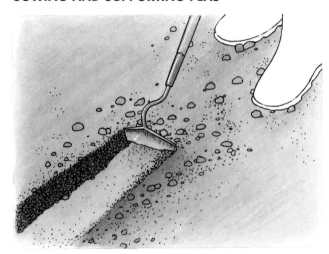

1 Using a swan-necked hoe or a short-handled onion hoe, draw straight and fairly shallow drills, 4-5cm (1½-2in) deep and 10cm (4in) wide. Use short, smooth motions and keep the depth even. Allow 60-120cm (2-4ft) between rows.

2 Sow the seeds 5-7.5cm (2-3in) apart in three staggered rows. Overwintering varieties should be sown rather more thickly, to compensate for any possible losses. After sowing, gently draw the soil over the drills with a rake and firm it.

3 Short, twiggy sticks will start the peas climbing. Insert the twigs when the young plants are about 7.5cm (3in) high. Don't delay providing support: plants sprawling over the ground may be attacked by slugs.

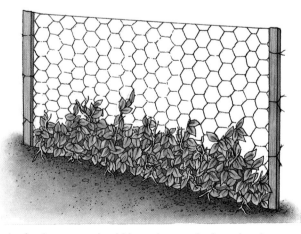

4 The final supports should be at least as high as the ultimate height of the plants. Use wire or plastic mesh tied to posts, wire criss-crossed between bamboo stakes or long, twiggy branches. Water regularly during prolonged dry spells.

VARIETIES TO CHOOSE

First early
'Feltham First' – rounded; large pointed pods 10cm (4in) long; 45cm (18in) plants.

'Kelvedon Wonder' – wrinkled; thin, pointed; 7.5cm (3in) pods; 45cm (18in); heavy yields, good for freezing.

'Little Marvel' – wrinkled; sweet and juicy; pods produced in pairs; 50cm (20in); can be grown as petit pois.

'Meteor' – rounded; heavy cropper; curved pointed pods; 45cm (18in).

Second early
'Cavalier' – wrinkled; heavy cropper, pods in pairs; sweet flavour; mildew resistant; 60-75cm (2-2½ft).

'Hurst Green Shaft' – wrinkled; pods 11cm (4½in) long, with 9-11 peas; heavy cropper; resistant to mildew; 75cm (2½ft).

'Onward' – wrinkled; blunt-ended, dark green pods; heavy cropper with good disease resistance; height about 60cm (2ft).

Maincrop varieties
'Alderman' – wrinkled; popular, heavy-cropping pea; long, thick pods; 1.5cm (5ft).

'Greenshaft' wrinkled; heavy crops; 10-12.5cm (4-5in) pods in pairs; resistant to mildew; good for freezing; 75cm (2½ft).

'Senator' – wrinkled; reliable cropper; pods in pairs; suitable for small gardens; 90cm (3ft).

Petit Pois
'Waverex' – heavy cropper; blunt pods; tiny sweet peas; height 45cm (18in).

Mangetout
'Oregon Sugar Pod' – slightly curved, fleshy pods, 10-11cm (4-4½in) long; pick young; 1-1.2m (3½-4ft).

Snap peas
'Edula' – curved pods; can be grown unsupported, or on short sticks or netting; 75-100cm (2½-3ft).

'Sugar Snap' – thick, fleshy pods, stringless when young; use as mangetout or allow seeds to mature; 1.5-1.8m (5-6ft) tall.

First early 'Kelvedon Wonder'

Mangetout 'Oregon Sugar Pod'

Maincrop 'Greenshaft'

Snap pea 'Edula'

MANGETOUT

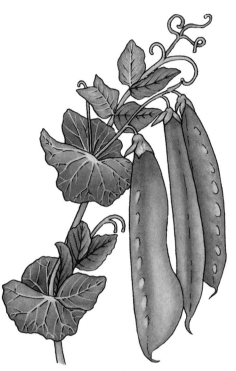

▲ **Mangetout** Also known as sugar peas, mangetout are cooked and eaten whole. They are easier to grow than ordinary garden peas. Pick the pods young, before the seeds start to swell.

Mangetout are also known as snow peas, sugar peas, eat-all and Chinese peas. They are similar to ordinary garden peas, but the pods are bright green, more tender, thin-skinned and usually stringless. The whole pod is eaten, either cooked or raw.

Once considered a gourmet food, mangetout have become very popular; they are readily available, at a price, from supermarkets and good fruit and vegetable shops; but as with ordinary peas, it's far better to grow your own.

Mangetout should be picked while they are still very young, and cooked whole. Sugar snap peas are grown and used like mangetout; the pods can also be left for the peas to swell, without any loss of the sweet flavour.

Planning the crop
Like ordinary peas, mangetout prefer rich, well-drained soil. Dig the plot over several times before sowing, working in two buckets of compost or well-rotted manure to the sq m/yd. A week before sowing, sprinkle a top-dressing of general fertilizer at 50-75g per sq m (2-3oz per sq yd) over the soil and rake it in.

Growing mangetout peas
Sow the seeds in double rows in spade-wide trenches, 5cm (2in) deep and 5-7.5cm (2-3in) apart each way. The trenches should be as wide apart as the height of the fully grown plants.

A first sowing produces pods two months later. Sow when the soil has started to warm up, in late spring or mid spring in mild areas. Two further sowings can be made, at monthly intervals.

Protect the seed from birds by covering the rows with netting, black thread or twigs. As soon as the seedlings are growing strongly, insert tall twiggy sticks for support. Net the pods at a later stage, as they will be equally vulnerable to attacks by birds.

Water the crop well in dry weather, and give an occasional mulch of moist coir, leaf-mould or garden compost.

Harvesting
Harvest the mangetout pods while they are still very young and before the peas in the pods begin to smell. Pick the pods in the same way as ordinary peas, pulling upwards while holding the stem secure.

ASPARAGUS PEAS

◄ **Asparagus peas** Related to garden peas, but half-hardy, asparagus peas cannot be sown until late spring. The plants have distinctive winged pods and a bushy, sprawling growth habit.

The asparagus or winged pea takes its name from the asparagus-like flavour of the pods, which are cooked whole. It looks quite different from other garden peas, having a bushy, sprawling habit and four wavy flanges, or wings, on the pod. There is only one variety of asparagus pea.

Planning the crop
Asparagus peas grow best in well-drained fertile soil in a sunny position. In the autumn or winter before sowing, prepare the bed by digging in some well-rotted manure or garden compost. Before sowing, dress the soil with a general fertilizer at 50g per sq m (2oz per sq yd).

A 6m (20ft) row will provide regular pickings for a family of four during late summer.

Growing asparagus peas
Asparagus peas are not frost hardy, and sowing should be delayed until all danger of frost has passed. In mild, sheltered gardens, seeds can be sown towards the end of May. Make the drills 5cm (2in) deep. If more than one row is required, space them 45cm (18in) apart. Sow two seeds in stations 20cm (8in) apart – remove the weaker seedling if both germinate.

In cold regions, such as the north of England, sow the seeds 2.5cm (1in) deep in pots of seed compost in a greenhouse or cold frame, or on a sunny window-sill indoors, at the beginning of May. Plant the seedlings out 20cm (8in) apart in early summer when the danger of frost has passed.

A second sowing can be made a few weeks later to give a succession of peas. Support the plants with twiggy sticks.

Harvesting and storing
Pick the pods when they are only 2.5-4cm (1-1½in) long. If they are allowed to grow longer, they become stringy and lose their delicate flavour.

Go over the plants daily, because regular picking will help to maintain supplies and encourage fresh crops.

Pests and diseases
Asparagus peas can suffer from the same pests as peas, though they are generally disease-free.

PEPPERS AND CHILLIS

Brilliantly coloured sweet peppers and hot chillis can be grown in the greenhouse or in sheltered beds outdoors.

Sweet peppers, or capsicums, are relatives of the tomato and require similar growing conditions. Although not true climbing plants, the brittle stems need support. The plants are grown under glass in temperate climates, though in a good summer they can be grown outdoors in mild southern areas, with the help of barn cloches or tall-sided cold frames.

The large fruits are often harvested green, but will ripen to yellow or through orange to red, depending on the variety. Flavour is not affected by colour.

Chillis are a form of capsicum, but are smaller and hot and fiery. They are grown in the same way as sweet peppers.

Planning the crop

Grown outside, sweet peppers need fertile soil, which is moist but well drained, and a sunny, sheltered site, preferably a bed against a south-facing wall.

Enrich the soil with well-rotted manure or garden compost during winter digging and keep it well watered. Rake in 50g per sq m (2oz per sq yd) of a general fertilizer before planting.

For greenhouse cultivation, prepare 23cm (9in) pots of potting compost, use grow bags or dig well-rotted garden manure into the greenhouse border.

Sowing and planting

Plant four to six outdoor plants or two to three greenhouse plants for a crop of 12 to 20 fruits – more in a good summer.

Growing under glass Sow seeds in a pan of seed compost in early spring, at a temperature of 16-18°C (61-64°F). When the seedlings are large enough to handle, prick them out individually into 7.5cm (3in) pots of potting compost.

Grow the plants at a daytime temperature of 16-27°C (61-81°F), and don't let the temperature fall below 7°C (45°F) at night. In southern areas, greenhouse crops should not need artificial heat after late spring.

Make a final potting into 23cm

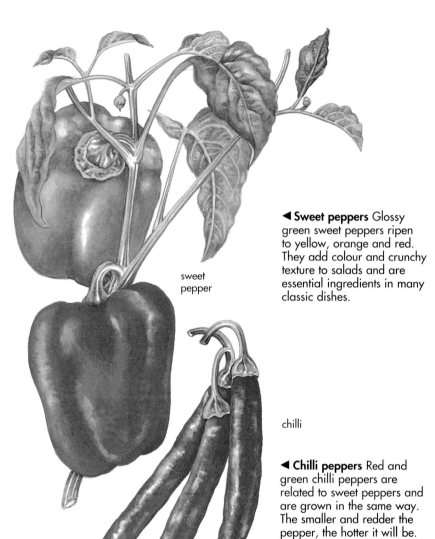

sweet
pepper

◄ **Sweet peppers** Glossy green sweet peppers ripen to yellow, orange and red. They add colour and crunchy texture to salads and are essential ingredients in many classic dishes.

chilli

◄ **Chilli peppers** Red and green chilli peppers are related to sweet peppers and are grown in the same way. The smaller and redder the pepper, the hotter it will be. Remove the seeds and blanch the chillis in boiling water before chopping them and adding them to curries and casseroles.

GROWING GREENHOUSE PEPPERS

1 When the plants are 15cm (6in) high, pinch out the growing points. Each plant should be supported by a cane inserted in the pot or the soil.

2 Spray the plants daily when in flower to help distribute pollen and to discourage red spider mites. Give liquid feeds every 10 days when fruits appear.

(9in) pots of a proprietary potting compost. Alternatively, set the plants 45cm (1½ft) apart in the greenhouse border.

Support the plants with 1m (3ft) canes inserted in the pot or soil and tie the plants to the canes with ordinary string. They should not grow much taller than 1m (3ft). Shade the glass in hot, sunny weather.

Growing outdoors Raise the plants under glass as already described. In late spring, harden the plants off gradually in a cold frame, then plant them out 45cm (1½ft) apart, in a warm sheltered spot, in early summer. Tie them to canes for support.

Looking after the crop

Syringe the flowers daily with water to help distribute the pollen. When the plants are 15cm (6in) high, pinch out the growing points to encourage branching.

Apply liquid fertilizer every 10 days after the first fruits appear. In the greenhouse, spray daily to keep the atmosphere moist and to discourage red spider mites. Keep the plants well watered, in the greenhouse and outdoors.

Harvesting and storing

Green peppers will be ready for picking in mid or late summer in the greenhouse, and in late summer or early autumn outside. They can be left to ripen to red or yellow.

Pests and diseases

Greenhouse plants may be attacked by whitefly and red spider mite. They are also vulnerable to grey mould.

Sweet pepper 'Bell Boy'

Sweet pepper 'Gypsy'

Chilli pepper 'Apache'

VARIETIES TO CHOOSE

Sweet peppers

'Ace' (F1 hybrid) – early and prolific; suitable for growing under glass, or outdoors.

'Bell Boy' (F1 hybrid) – prolific; suitable for glass and outdoors; thick-walled fruit maturing to red.

'Californian Wonder' – reliable cropper; green-red, mild flavour.

'Canape' (F1 hybrid) – early; suitable for outdoor culture; deep green fruits, turning bright red.

'Gypsy' (F1 hybrid) – early; slightly tapered fruits, yellowish green ripening to deep red.

'Redskin' (F1 hybrid) – dwarf plants for greenhouses, patios and window-sills; green bell fruits mature to bright red.

'Salad Festival' – mixed colours, green, purple or cream fruits ripening to red and gold; squat or long and narrow in shape.

Chilli peppers

'Apache' – prolific; for window-sills, patios or under glass; medium hot fruits ripen to red.

'Chilli Cayenne' – thin green pods ripen from yellow to red; very hot; 5-7.5cm (2-3in) long.

'Chilli Serrano' – very hot; best under glass; fruits 4cm (1½in) long.

POTATOES

Few vegetables can compare in flavour with home-grown new potatoes – and they don't take up a lot of space.

Potato varieties are grouped according to when they are lifted. There are three groups – first early (ready from early to mid summer), second early (from mid summer to early autumn) and maincrop (lifted in autumn and stored for winter use).

Within these three groups, potatoes may be round, oval or kidney-shaped, with red, white or yellow skins. The flesh may be white or yellow and the texture either floury or waxy.

If you have plenty of room, grow all three types of potatoes. With limited space, grow a small crop of early (new) potatoes only, for eating in summer when they are expensive in the shops. Apart from their kitchen use, a potato crop helps to clear the ground of weeds and releases nitrogen into it; and they mature early enough for later crops, such as cabbages and leeks, to take their place.

Sprouting seed potatoes

Potatoes of all types are grown from small tubers (seed potatoes) – it is advisable to buy them from a reputable nursery as stock certi-fied to be free of virus diseases. They are usually labelled as first or second earlies, or maincrops.

In mid to late winter, set the seed potatoes in trays or egg boxes with the rose end uppermost – this is the end with the most eyes, from which the sprouts grow. Place the trays in a cool but frost-free, light but not sunny room or greenhouse.

In about four to six weeks the potatoes will have sprouted (chit-ted). They are ready for planting when the purple-green sprouts are sturdy and 12-25mm (½-1in) long. Sprouted in this way, the potatoes have a longer growing season and produce a heavier crop.

Soil and site preparation

Potatoes grow reasonably well in most soils, although a well-manured soil is best.

In the autumn or winter before planting, dig the ground well, working in compost or well-rotted manure at the rate of a bucketful per sq m/sq yd. Two weeks before planting, apply a general fertilizer at a rate of 50-75g per sq m (2-3oz per sq yd).

▲ **New potatoes** The unique flavour and firm texture of early potatoes are achieved only with earthing up, so that light is excluded from the developing tubers. Lift early potatoes when the tubers are the size of a hen's egg. Harvest maincrops in autumn.

Potatoes grow best in an open site – they grow spindly in shade. To avoid the build-up of eelworm, don't grow potatoes on the same site in consecutive years.

Planting

Plant first early varieties such as 'Arran Pilot' between early and mid spring, second earlies such as 'Nadine' in mid spring and main-crop potatoes such as 'Desirée' towards the end of April.

Use a hoe to make drills 15cm (6in) deep and 60cm (24in) apart for earlies, and 75cm (30in) apart for maincrop varieties. Alternatively, plant potatoes in holes 15cm (6in) deep with a trowel.

Set the sprouted tubers in the drills 30cm (12in) apart for earlies, and 38cm (15in) apart for maincrop potatoes. Place them carefully with the sprouts upper-most. Return the soil to the drill, taking care not to damage the sprouts. Draw up enough soil to make a slight ridge over the line of planted potatoes.

POPULAR POTATO VARIETIES

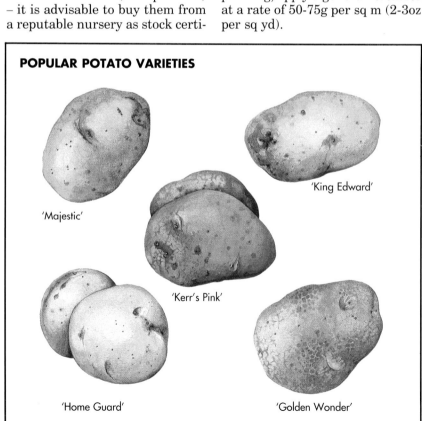

'Majestic'

'King Edward'

'Kerr's Pink'

'Home Guard'

'Golden Wonder'

GROWING POTATOES

1 To sprout seed potatoes, place tubers upright in trays or egg boxes in mid to late winter. Make sure the end with the most eyes is uppermost. Keep the trays in a cool, light place for four to six weeks or until the young sprouts are about 12-25mm (½-1in) long.

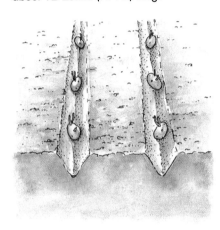

2 Plant the sprouting potatoes in drills 15cm (6in) deep, in rows 60cm (24in) apart for earlies, and 75cm (30in) apart for maincrops. Set early potatoes 30cm (12in) apart and maincrop varieties 38cm (15in) apart. Cover with a shallow ridge of soil.

3 Begin earthing up potatoes when the top growth is 23cm (9in) high. Break up the soil between the rows with a fork and apply a general compound fertilizer at 25g per sq m (1oz per sq yd). Use a draw hoe to draw soil up around the stems of the plants, making a ridge about 15cm (6in) high.

Looking after the crop

As the first shoots appear, increase the height of the soil ridge as protection against late spring frosts.

When the potato plants are 23cm (9in) high, scatter a general fertilizer between the rows, carefully following the manufacturer's instructions. Earth up the plants, using a draw hoe to draw up the soil from between the rows. This increases the amount of soil over the roots and encourages them to spread and form tubers. It also reduces the risk of potatoes being exposed to light and becoming green and poisonous.

As a bonus, the frequent moving of soil during the cultivation of potatoes helps rid the vegetable plot of annual weeds.

If it is dry, water early potatoes frequently during late spring and early summer. Water maincrop potatoes well when the tubers are the size of marbles – scrape away a little soil to check their size from time to time. Continue earthing up maincrop potatoes until the foliage meets between the rows, and then shade the tubers.

Spray maincrop potatoes once a fortnight with either mancozeb or Bordeaux mixture to prevent potato blight.

Harvesting

In sheltered areas, the earliest potato varieties will be ready for lifting at the beginning of early summer – several weeks before other, colder districts.

As a rough guide, you should be able to harvest a few early potatoes about 12 to 14 weeks after planting. Maincrop potatoes take at least 20 weeks to mature fully and be ready for storing.

Early potatoes To gather a few new potatoes, brush away a little bit of soil with your hands from the side of a ridge. Remove any potatoes that are the size of a hen's egg.

Replace the soil over the smaller tubers and leave them to grow. After two to three weeks – towards the end of early summer or the beginning of mid summer –

▼ **Lifting potatoes** Use a garden fork to prise plants out of the ground and dislodge all the tubers. Early potatoes, ready after about 12 weeks, can be followed by winter vegetables.

they will have doubled in size and be ready for lifting. Lift only as many as you need at the time.

When lifting potatoes, insert the fork straight into the ground at least 15cm (6in) away from the stems to avoid spearing the tubers. Lift the complete plant and throw it between the rows in a single action.

Maincrop potatoes Once the foliage has turned brown and withered in autumn, leave the tubers in the ground for a further 10-14 days for the skins to harden. A slight frost will not harm them.

Test one or two potatoes by rubbing the skin with your thumb. If the skin of the tuber doesn't rub off, the crop is ready for lifting and storing.

Storing maincrops

On a dry day, lift maincrop potatoes and leave them on the surface to dry for a couple of hours. Check the tubers and store only healthy ones in a cool, dry, frost-free place. Put them in light-proof but ventilated containers, such as boxes or paper sacks, or pile them on a dry floor and cover with straw. They should keep until the following spring.

Never store any damaged or diseased potatoes – they will infect all the others nearby. Check the stored potatoes every few

weeks and remove any that show signs of turning rotten. Use the potatoes before the eyes start growing white sprouts; discard any with green flesh.

Potatoes can also be stored in the ground in a clamp. Put a layer of straw over a patch of levelled soil and pile the potatoes on top, up to a height of 90cm (3ft). Cover the mound with a 15cm (6in) layer of straw and then a similar layer of soil, leaving a trench around the clamp to drain excess moisture.

Keep the top of the mound open for about a week to allow for sweating. Then cover completely with soil, leaving a 10cm (4in) thick tuft of twisted straw passing through the soil at the top as ventilation for the tubers.

As potatoes are needed, open one end of the clamp, making sure to seal it properly again with soil to protect against frost.

Alternative cultivation methods

Potatoes can be grown under black polythene – this does away with the laborious earthing up process. Plant the tubers as before and cover with polythene sheeting. Anchor it at the edges with stones. When the shoots start pushing against the polythene, cut holes in it to allow the sprouts to grow through.

▲ **Potatoes on the flat** Eliminate the earthing-up process by growing potatoes under black polythene sheeting. Make slits in the polythene for the top growth to grow through.

When the potatoes are ready – most will be near the surface – remove the polythene sheeting and begin lifting. Gather potatoes of the right size and replace the polythene until the remainder have reached harvesting size.

Alternatively, grow potatoes in plastic barrels; they are purpose built and ideal where space is limited. Three or four potatoes are planted in the barrel, and as the shoots grow, more potting compost is added until the barrel is full. The tubers are then left to grow to maturity. This growing method is more suitable for a small crop of early potatoes than for a maincrop.

Pests and diseases

The most common pests of the potato are aphids, potato cyst eelworm, wireworm and slugs. Chemical controls are rarely effective although slugs and snails can be deterred with baits, and aphids with systemis insecticides.

The diseases most likely to occur are potato blight, scab and leaf roll and mosaic viruses. Crop rotation and good cultural practices can minimize these problems, and several varieties are certified as being completely free of specific diseases.

◄ **Potato barrel** Where space is limited, grow potatoes in purpose-built plastic barrels or improvise your own using dustbins with holes drilled in the base, and with crocks in the bottom for drainage. Plant three or four potatoes in each container and gradually fill with more compost as the plants grow.

VARIETIES TO CHOOSE

First early

'Arran Pilot' – kidney-shaped; white flesh; heavy cropper which does well in light soil; prone to dry rot.

'Home Guard' – round; white flesh; good on heavy soil; sensitive to blight and drought.

'Maris Bard' – oval; white flesh; early cropper; good disease resistance.

'Pentland Javelin' – oval; white flesh; heavy cropper; resistant to scab and a common strain of eelworm.

'Sutton's Foremost' – oval; white flesh; good cropper with good flavour; resistant to drought, but prone to blight.

'Vanessa' – round to oval; red-skinned; firm creamy-white flesh; good cropper.

Second early

'Baillie' – round tubers; firm flesh; some disease resistance.

'Maris Peer' – oval; white flesh; good cropper; some resistance to scab and blight; needs moist soil.

'Nadine' – oval; white-skinned; heavy, reliable yields.

'Stroma' – oval; large; red-skinned; yellow flesh; heavy cropper.

'Wilja' – oval; pale yellow flesh; heavy cropper; resistant to blight.

Maincrop

'Desirée' – oval; pale yellow flesh; heavy cropper; resistant to drought, but common scab is a problem.

'Golden Wonder' – kidney-shaped; yellow flesh; moderate cropper; prone to blight, but resistant to scab.

'Kerr's Pink' – round; white flesh; good on heavy soil; prone to scab; can be grown as second early.

'King Edward' – kidney-shaped; creamy flesh; heavy cropper; prone to blight and drought, but resistant to scab.

'Majestic' – kidney-shaped; white flesh; prone to blight and scab, but resistant to drought.

'Maris Piper' – oval; creamy flesh; excellent cropper; resistant to eelworm, but troubled by scab, slugs and drought.

'Pentland Crown' – oval; pale yellow flesh; heavy yields; stores well; resistant to scab.

'Pink Fir Apple' – oval; yellow flesh; irregularly shaped tubers; fair cropper; sensitive to drought; good new-potato flavour.

First early 'Maris Bard'

Maincrop 'Desirée'

Second early 'Wilja'

Maincrop 'Pink Fir Apple'

153

RADISHES

Quick growing and disease free, radishes take up little space and can be grown for summer or winter use.

There are two main types of radish. Summer varieties – usually small – are used in salads, while larger winter radishes (225g/½lb or more in weight and red, black or white in colour) are cooked like turnips. Summer radishes are particularly quick to mature and can be grown for most of the year if protected by frames or cloches during winter.

For a continuous supply of radishes throughout summer, sow the equivalent of a 2.5m (8ft) row every three or four weeks. A single packet of seeds should be enough for three sowings.

Preparing the site

As they are not in the ground for more than a few weeks, summer radishes do not need a deeply dug plot. However, they do grow better – especially in hot weather – in fertile, moisture-retentive soil; dig well-rotted compost into the top 7.5-10cm (3-4in) of soil at the rate of a bucketful per sq m/yd. Well-drained soil is essential for the first sowing under glass in early to mid winter. Winter radishes grow best in soil manured for a previous crop.

In spring, rake the soil to a fine tilth and make the first sowing in a sheltered, sunny spot. In summer, however, choose a shaded position to prevent the plants from going to seed prematurely.

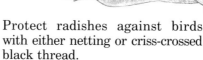

long-rooted white summer radish

round-rooted summer radish

long-rooted summer radish

winter radish

Protect radishes against birds with either netting or criss-crossed black thread.

Summer radishes

Make the first sowings in a cold frame or under cloches from early to mid winter. Place cloches in position two weeks before sowing to warm the soil and prevent excessive wetness. Sow seeds thinly in 5mm (¼in) deep drills about 15cm (6in) apart.

Do not sow seeds thickly or the plants will produce foliage at the expense of roots – the seeds should be about 12mm (½in) apart in the drills. Keep the soil moist to maintain growth.

From early spring, sow outdoors at the spacing described above. Regular sowings at three-week intervals will ensure a continuous supply of tender radishes. Don't sow too many at once – if

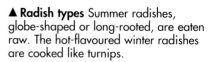

▲ **Radish types** Summer radishes, globe-shaped or long-rooted, are eaten raw. The hot-flavoured winter radishes are cooked like turnips.

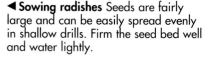

◄ **Sowing radishes** Seeds are fairly large and can be easily spread evenly in shallow drills. Firm the seed bed well and water lightly.

◄**Catch crops** Quick-growing radishes are ideal for growing between slower-growing vegetables such as cabbages. They are out of the ground before the other crop is large enough to be affected.

If radishes are attacked by flea beetles – small holes in the leaves – dust or spray with derris or pirimiphos-methyl.

left in the ground for more than a week or two after maturing, the roots become woody and lose their crispness and flavour.

Winter radishes

Sow the large-rooted winter varieties from mid summer to late summer. Sow seeds in drills 1cm (½in) deep and 30cm (12in) apart. Thin the young plants to 20cm (8in) apart when large enough to handle. Always keep the soil well watered in dry weather or the plants will not make enough growth in autumn.

Harvesting and storing

Summer radishes should be harvested as needed while they are young and tender. Throw any unwanted plants on to the com-post heap. The roots of winter radishes can be left in the ground until required, but the crowns can be covered with a protective layer of straw or bracken. Alternatively, lift them in mid autumn and store in boxes of sand in a cool, airy place. Throughout winter check stored radishes regularly; discard any that show signs of either rot or mould.

Pests and diseases

Flea beetles eat the leaves of young plants, particularly during hot spells in late spring; dust plants with HCH or derris. Winter crops are vulnerable to wire-worms and cutworms. Treat the seed drills with diazinon + chlor-pyrifos prior to sowing and keep weeds down.

VARIETIES TO CHOOSE

Summer varieties

'Cherry Belle' – round, bright scarlet; remains crisp longer than most varieties.

'French Breakfast' – long-rooted, red and white; crisp and mild.

'Long White Icicle' – long-rooted, white; crisp, nutty flavour.

'Pink Beauty' – globe-shaped; pink; crisp, distinctive flavour.

'Scarlet Globe' – round, all-red; quick-maturing from early spring sowing.

'Sparkler' – round; bright scarlet tipped white; crisp and sweet; ready in four weeks from sowing.

Winter varieties

'Black Spanish Long' – long-rooted, black-skinned, white-fleshed (must be peeled).

'Black Spanish Round' – round, black-skinned, white-fleshed (needs peeling).

'China Rose' – oval roots, deep rose colour, crisp white flesh.

'Mino Early' – long cylindrical white roots with a milder flavour than other winter varieties.

Summer radish 'French Breakfast'   **Winter radish** 'Black Spanish Round'

Summer radish 'Scarlet Globe'

SEAKALE

A perennial winter vegetable, seakale is grown for its succulent, delicately flavoured white shoots.

Seakale is a hardy perennial whose blanched leaf-shoots make an excellent winter delicacy. A double row of seakale, 6m (20ft) long, will provide shoots from late autumn right through to mid spring if successive methods of forcing are used. Seakale needs a permanent site and produces crops, from the second year onwards, for up to five years in a well-tended bed. It should not be confused with seakale beet, a spinach-like leaf vegetable.

Soil and site preparation

Seakale grows best on sandy loam containing plenty of lime, though it will succeed in most soils. In autumn, dig in a bucketful of manure or compost per sq m/yd.

Before planting or sowing in spring, rake in a compound fertilizer at 50g per sq m (2oz per sq yd).

Planting and sowing

Growing seakale from seed takes two years to produce edible shoots. Alternatively, seakale crowns (main roots) or thongs (root cuttings) are sometimes available from nurseries.

Seakale thongs are the side roots of plants dug up in autumn for forcing. They are cut into sections 10-15cm (4-6in) long, tied in bundles and placed under a 7.5cm (3in) layer of sand in a cold frame for the winter.

By early spring, the thongs will have developed buds at the straight-cut top end; rub off all but the strongest bud, which will form a new shoot. Plant in prepared ground in late spring in rows 45cm (1½ft) apart. Set individual crowns or thongs 5cm (2in) below ground level and 60cm (2ft) apart. Cover with topsoil.

Water and feed the plants regularly, and mulch with coir or well-rotted manure in late spring. Remove flowering stems as soon as they appear and discard them.

Seakale from seed Sow seeds in early to mid spring, 12mm (½in)

▶ **Seakale 'Lily White'** The only available variety, 'Lily White' is a heavy cropper with pure white, well-formed, tasty shoots.

▼ **Forcing seakale** Terracotta jars which cut out light are used to blanch seakale shoots. In winter the shoots will be ready for picking in 4-5 weeks.

SEAKALE THONGS

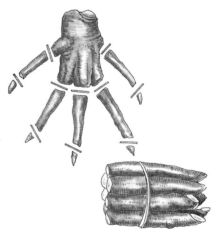

Take root cuttings (thongs) from fleshy side roots of plants lifted in autumn for forcing. Choose roots about 7.5-15cm (3-6in) long and pencil-thick. Make a straight cut across the top and a sloping cut at the bottom for later identification. Tie the thongs in bundles and store in sand until spring.

OUTDOOR CULTIVATION

1 In early to mid spring, rub off all but the strongest bud from each thong and, using a trowel, plant 60cm (2ft) apart with 45cm (1½ft) between the rows. Set the thongs with their tops 5cm (2in) below soil level.

2 In summer, hoe away weeds and remove flower stems as soon as they appear, or they will reduce the plant's strength and diminish the crop. Water and feed plants regularly. In autumn remove the yellowing foliage.

3 In early winter, cover plants with upturned flower pots 23-25cm (9-10in) in diameter. Pile straw or leaves around the pots. In mid winter, raise the temperature by replacing the leaves with fresh, rotting manure.

deep in prepared ground. When the seedlings are large enough to handle thin them out to 15cm (6in) apart and leave them to grow on for another year, allowing one bud only to develop on plants that are to be forced.

The following spring, transplant the young seakale plants, 60cm (2ft) apart, to a well-prepared permanent bed. In autumn, dress the bed with rotted garden compost and leave for another year before forcing.

Seakale is generally pest and disease free.

Forcing outdoors

Outdoor plants can be forced in mid to late autumn. Cover with flower pots 23-25cm (9-10in) in diameter. Pile straw or leaves around the pots. In mid winter raise the temperature by replacing the leaves or straw with fresh, rotting manure packed in a 30cm (1ft) layer around and over the pots.

Shoots forced during winter are ready for picking in five to seven weeks. Those forced in early spring are ready in three weeks.

For a final crop in mid spring, pile soil to a depth of 20cm (8in) over selected plants in autumn.

Fork around the roots of plants that have been forced, cover the crowns with about 2.5cm (1in) of soil, and allow them to grow again, for forcing again in winter.

Forcing indoors

Lift the main roots in mid autumn. Cut off side-shoots for planting out in mid spring, and tie them in bundles for overwintering in sand. Trim the crowns back to 15cm (6in) in length. Put three crowns in a 23cm (9in) diameter pot, fill with good soil, and water well.

Cover with an upturned pot of the same size and place in total darkness at a temperature of about 7°C (45°F). Increase to 13°C (55°F) once they start growing. In four to five weeks, the blanched shoots will be ready.

Lift more roots in early and mid winter and force in the same way. Shoots are ready when they are 13-18cm (5-7in) long.

Using and cooking

The blanched shoots are delicious when steamed like asparagus and served with butter. They can also be used raw in salads.

The leaves can be eaten raw in salads or cooked like spinach.

FORCING INDOORS

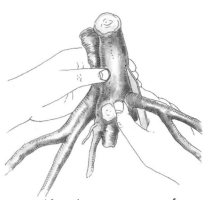

1 Start lifting the roots in autumn for forcing. Choose strong, healthy-looking roots and prepare them for propagation and forcing by trimming off the side roots or thongs to be stored in sand for planting in early spring.

2 Pack the crowns (main roots) which are to be forced in 23cm (9in) diameter pots of rich soil, with three crowns to a pot. Cover with an upturned pot of the same size and place in total darkness – a cellar is ideal.

3 Increase the temperature from about 7°C (45°F) to 13°C (55°F) as the forcing gets under way. The shoots are ready in four to five weeks. Lift more roots in early and mid winter and force for a continuous supply.

SPINACH

Leaf spinach and other similar types can be cropped throughout the year. Successive sowings ensure a steady supply of these nutritious vegetables.

Rich in iron and vitamins, spinach is quick and easy to grow in fertile, moisture-retentive but well-drained soil. New varieties are less prone to bolting (running to flower prematurely), and spinach-like vegetables (see opposite) are even easier to grow.

There are two types of true spinach – the round-seeded, which is generally harvested in summer; and the hardier, prickly-seeded variety that is grown for picking in winter and spring.

By successive sowing of summer and winter crops, you can enjoy fresh spinach throughout the year. If you are growing only one crop, freeze surplus leaves for later use.

Planning the crop
In order to produce large succulent leaves over an extended cropping period, summer spinach should be grown quickly, in good moist soil. It is ideal for growing as a catch crop between other more slower-growing vegetables. In hot, dry weather, summer spinach bolts rapidly; it benefits from shade cast by taller vegetables, such as rows of beans or peas.

Sow in soil that has been recently dressed with well-rotted manure or garden compost. Two weeks before sowing, rake in a general fertilizer at the rate of 50g per sq m (2oz per sq yd). Sow the seeds at three-weekly intervals to produce a constant supply of young leaves throughout summer.

Growing summer varieties
Sow round-seeded summer spinach in drills about 12mm (½in) deep from mid winter onwards or as soon as the soil is workable. Weak plants bolt more easily so sow thinly to encourage good-sized plants. Thin seedlings to about 7.5cm (3in) apart, then again to 15cm (6in) apart. The second thinnings can be cooked.

Water liberally, especially during dry spells, to reduce the risk of the plants running to seed. At least 10 litres per sq m (4 gal per sq yd) each week are necessary during prolonged dry weather.

Summer spinach 'Sigmaleaf'

Spinach doesn't grow well if the ground becomes too densely packed. Hoe carefully around the plants to break up the soil and remove any weeds.

Summer spinach is ready to pick about eight weeks after sowing, six weeks from sowings in early summer. Pick up to half the outer leaves, but no more, from each plant when they are not quite full-sized. Leave the rest for picking about three or four days later. Continue to pick the plants every three or four days until they stop producing.

Growing winter varieties
Sow seeds of the winter varieties from mid summer to early autumn for harvesting between mid autumn and mid spring. Sow as for summer spinach but choose varieties that are recommended for autumn sowing. Winter spinach grows best in a sunny site.

In cold areas cover the growing plants with cloches from mid autumn onwards. Hoe to break up the soil and remove all weeds.

Winter spinach takes about 10-12 weeks to mature. Pick only a few leaves from each plant at a time. Break or cut the stalks – don't tear them off or you will damage the plants and prevent later leaves from growing.

Harvesting
Spinach deteriorates rapidly after picking. Use it as quickly as possible while it's still crisp or freeze it at once.

Pick the spinach just before cooking, cut off the stalks and remove the midribs as well if they are coarse. Wash thoroughly in several changes of water until all traces of sand and grit have been removed. Drain well.

Pests and diseases
Spinach may be attacked by leaf aphids, slugs, snails and even birds.

Downy mildew – grey furry spots on the undersurfaces of leaves – can be prevented by proper thinning and watering. If it does occur, remove affected

SPINACH TYPES

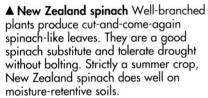

▲ **New Zealand spinach** Well-branched plants produce cut-and-come-again spinach-like leaves. They are a good spinach substitute and tolerate drought without bolting. Strictly a summer crop, New Zealand spinach does well on moisture-retentive soils.

▲ **Perpetual spinach** This perennial vegetable, also called leaf or spinach beet, bears spinach-like leaves. It is tolerant of both frost and drought, and can be harvested throughout the year. It occupies the ground for a long time and needs well-manured soil.

leaves and spray the remainder with a proprietary fungicide.

Spinach-like vegetables

Several other leaf vegetables resemble spinach; they are grown, harvested and used like true spinach varieties.

Spinach beet, also known as leaf beet or perpetual spinach, is a useful substitute for summer and winter spinach. It is a perennial and does not begin to run to seed until the second year, but produces a succession of fresh leaves over a long period.

Make drills 2.5cm (1in) deep and 23cm (9in) apart. Sow seeds thinly in mid spring for a summer and autumn crop, or in mid to late summer for a winter and spring crop. Thin the seedlings to 20cm (8in) apart. Keep the rows free of weeds, and water plants occasionally during dry spells.

Pick the leaves regularly as they become ready for use. Any coarse leaves should be picked and put on the compost heap.

Don't pick too many young leaves from autumn-sown spinach beet, as the plants should build themselves up before winter.

Seakale beet, or Swiss chard, is grown in the same way as spinach beet. Sow seeds in mid spring in good moist soil, and thin the seedlings gradually until they are 25cm (10in) apart. The plants produce large leaves which are cooked and treated like spinach, while the midribs or chards are a choice vegetable and can be cooked separately, like asparagus.

New Zealand spinach is not hardy and should not be sown until all danger of frost has passed. Soak the seeds overnight to aid germination and sow in drills 2.5cm (1in) deep in groups of two or three, spacing them 30-38cm (12-15in) apart with 1m (3ft) between rows.

Thin the seedlings to leave only the strongest in each group. These plants don't bolt but need plenty of watering to promote growth. Pinch out growing tips to encourage more laterals.

Harvest from early summer to early autumn by picking a handful of leaves from each plant. Plants produce more leaves if lightly but frequently picked. Gather the young shoot tips – each tip has two or three leaves.

SPROUTING SEEDS

**As a quick, cheap and nutritious food crop,
sprouting seeds can hardly be bettered – and they
can be grown on a kitchen window-sill.**

Mustard and cress are probably the most familiar of edible sprouting seeds, but there are many more – including mung beans (Chinese bean sprouts), adzuki beans, buckwheat, fenugreek, sunflower, chick peas and lentils, as well as various grains such as wheat, rice and rye.

Some sprouting seeds are available in seed packets from nurseries and large garden centres, while others can be bought from health food shops. Check that the seeds you buy are intended for eating – those sold for sowing in the ground to produce a crop may have been treated with seed dressings and other chemicals.

There are several different ways of growing sprouting seeds – all quick and easy and all requiring nothing more than a few

jam jars or trays, paper towels, muslin and elastic bands.

Most seeds will germinate at room temperature and can be grown in the kitchen on a window-sill. Some may need a few days in a warm airing cupboard and some require 'greening' to achieve their full flavour. Seeds can be eaten when they have 6-12mm (¼-½in) sprouts or when they have developed into small seedlings with one or more pairs of green leaves.

Whichever method you follow, first wash the seeds well and soak them overnight in lukewarm water. Then drain off the water, rinse the seeds thoroughly and put them in the sprouting container. During the next few days rinse the seeds again, once or more often every day, depending

on the variety and the dryness of the weather. Rinsing is essential to keep the seeds fresh and clean – otherwise they quickly deteriorate.

Sprouting in trays
This is the traditional method for growing mustard and cress. Put a thick layer of cotton-wool, flannel, paper towel or blotting paper in a seed tray or wide, flat plastic container. Spread the seeds thickly and evenly on top and press down lightly. Sprinkle thoroughly with lukewarm water and cover with brown paper or black polythene.

Keep the tray at a temperature of 10-16°C (50-61°F) and remove the cover when the seedlings are about 4cm (1½in) high. Put the tray on a window-sill and allow a few days for the seedlings to green up and expand fully before cutting. Keep them moist at all times. Use scissors to cut the crop when the white stems are about 5cm (2in) long – about 11-14 days after sowing. Daily rinsing is not necessary with mustard and cress.

Cress seedlings have a very strong, peppery tang, so you will need a smaller quantity of cress than of mustard – no more than a quarter of the total.

Sprouting in jam jars
Not all seeds can be grown successfully in a seed tray or pan – a jam jar is better when the seeds must be rinsed at least once a day.

You will need a jam jar, a square of muslin and an elastic band. Put the soaked and rinsed seeds into the jar and cover the opening with the muslin, holding it in place with an elastic band. Lay the jar on its side in a bowl with the open end pointing slightly downwards to help drainage; place the bowl in a dark corner or an airing cupboard.

Rinse the seeds at least once daily by removing the muslin and half-filling the jar with clean

◄ **Mung beans** Easy to sprout, nutty-flavoured mung beans are rich in vitamins and amino acids. They are ready for use after three to five days.

▲ Seeds for sprouting Easy-sprouting seeds include (from the top) fenugreek, sunflower, mung, alfalfa, soya and adzuki beans.

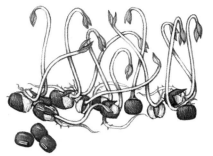

Adzuki beans

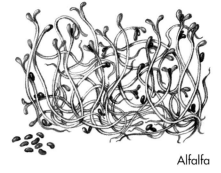

Alfalfa

water. Replace the muslin, swill the seeds around gently in the water, then pour the water away through the muslin cover. Another method is to empty the seeds into a sieve and rinse them under the cold tap, allowing them to drain thoroughly before putting them back into the jar.

Repeat the rinsing regularly until the seedlings have grown to a suitable length. If they require greening, leave the jar on a shady window-sill for a day or two. Empty the jar into a colander and rinse well before eating the seedlings.

Keeping the seeds in the dark will produce whiter, crisper sprouts, while those kept in the light will be softer and greener.

It is nearly always best to grow small quantities of seeds and use them regularly. Growing little and often will ensure that the sprouts are always fresh. However, sprouts can be kept in the fridge for a few days. Put them in a bowl of water or in a plastic bag and rinse them every day. Check for mould before eating.

What can go wrong
Seeds need heat and moisture if they are to germinate, but if conditions are too hot and humid, they can easily go mouldy. Always use clean containers, and don't neglect regular rinsing. Seeds that become mouldy or diseased will be discoloured and quickly develop a sour smell.

SPROUTING SEEDS

Adzuki beans
Grow in jars or trays. Rinse four times daily. Harvest after three to four days or when the crisp, sweet sprouts are 2.5cm (1in) long.

Alfalfa
Grow in jars. Rinse twice daily. Harvest after three to six days (including greening) or when 2.5-5cm (1-2in) long. Crisp and sweet, for eating raw or stir-frying.

Buckwheat
Grow in jars or trays. Rinse once daily. Harvest after two to three days or when the sprouts are 12mm (½in) long.

Chick peas
Grow in jars. Rinse four to five times daily. Harvest after three to four days or when 12mm (½in) long.

Cress
Grow in trays, moisten as necessary. Harvest after 11-14 days or when the seedlings are 5cm (2in) long.

Fenugreek
Grow in jars. Rinse once or twice daily. Harvest after four to seven days or when the sprouts are

7.5cm (3in) long. Spicy, rich in minerals and vitamins.

Lentils
Grow in jars. Rinse two or three times daily. Harvest after three or four days or when 2.5mm (1in) long.

Mung beans
Grow in jars or trays. Rinse three times daily. Harvest after four or five days or when sprouts are 5-7.5cm (2-3in) long.

Mustard
Grow in trays. Moisten as necessary. Harvest after eight to ten days or when the seedlings are 5cm (2in) long. (Start three days later than cress.)

Radish sprouts
Grow in jars. Rinse two or three times daily. Hot and spicy. Ready in three to five days.

Sunflower
Grow in jars. Rinse twice daily. Ready in two or three days when the sprouts are 12mm (½in) long.

Wheat
Grow in jars. Rinse two or three times daily. Harvest after two to five days or when 12mm (½in) long.

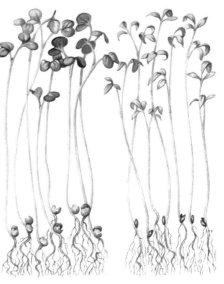

Mustard   Cress

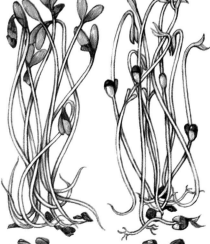

Fenugreek   Mung beans

SWEDES AND TURNIPS

**Swedes and turnips are usually winter
roots, while summer turnips provide delicious,
sweet-flavoured catch crops.**

Swedes and turnips are both root crops and members of the brassica family. The word swede is an abbreviation of 'Swedish turnip'. Swedes have sweet yellow flesh, and are hardier than turnips but need a longer growing period. Turnips are smaller and mainly white-fleshed. Harvested when no bigger than golf balls, they are tasty enough to be eaten raw. Swedes, too, taste sweeter and have a fine, tender texture if harvested young, before they develop woody cores.

Both swedes and turnips yield the best crop in northern, cool and moist areas, where they are staple winter vegetables. They have the same cultural needs – fertile, well-limed soil that is moisture-retentive; on hot, dry soils, the top growth is susceptible to mildew and the roots become tough and fibrous.

Swedes are sown in late spring and early summer and make a good autumn and winter crop as they can be left in the soil and lifted when needed.

Turnips can be sown in summer for an autumn crop, but early varieties are also available for sowing in spring and for harvesting in early summer when they are small and tender.

Turnips can also be sown in autumn and their tops cut and eaten as a nutritious spring vegetable. The overwintered roots, though, are less tasty than younger ones although they are good in casseroles and stews.

Cultivation

Both vegetables are sown in the bed where they are to crop. Swedes need open ground, but quick-growing summer turnips make a useful catch crop between slower growing vegetables, such as parsnips, as they are ready for lifting six to eight weeks after sowing. They need rich, well-manured soil so that they grow quickly and without check.

Early turnips should be grown in soil manured the previous season – fresh manure makes the

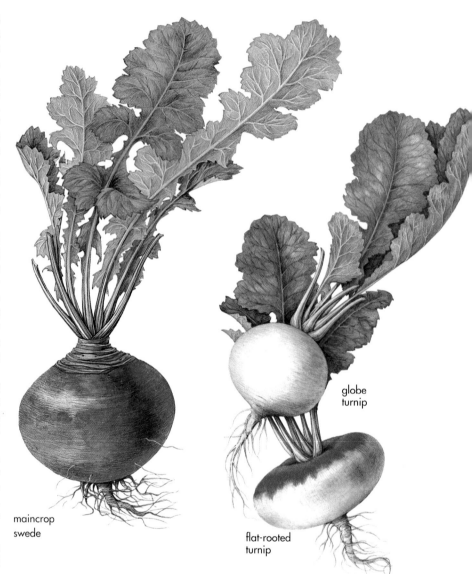

maincrop
swede

globe
turnip

flat-rooted
turnip

roots split. Dig the ground thoroughly, then dust the surface with 75g (3oz) of super-phosphate, 50g (2oz) of sulphate of ammonia, and 25g (1oz) of sulphate of potash to each sq m/yd. Do this about a week before sowing and rake the fertilizers into the top soil.

Sow the first early turnips in early mid spring and repeat every three weeks until early mid summer. Sow 12mm (½in) deep in rows 30cm (1ft) apart. Thin the seedlings when they are large enough to handle, and again about three weeks later to 15cm (6in) apart.

Swedes and maincrop turnips for autumn and winter use require ground that has been

cleared of an early crop. Lightly dig over the plot, and hoe in a fertilizer dressing similar to that recommended for summer turnips.

Sow swedes in late spring or early summer, in drills 12mm (½in) deep and 38cm (15in) apart. As soon as the first true leaves appear, thin the seedlings to stand 7.5cm (3in) apart. About three weeks later thin the seedlings again, to 15cm (6in) apart.

In mid summer make drills 2cm (¾in) deep and 30cm (1ft) apart and sow maincrop turnips thinly. Thin as for swedes. For both crops, hoe regularly to keep down weeds, and in dry weather water at the rate of 9 litres per sq m (2 gal per sq yd) each week.

Swede 'Acme Purple Top'

Maincrop turnip 'Veitch's Red Globe'

Maincrop turnip 'Golden Ball'

VARIETIES TO CHOOSE

Early turnips
'Milan White' – very early; flat top; white delicate flesh; suitable for forcing.

'Purple Top Milan' – white flesh with purple top; flat-shaped roots; very quick maturing; ideal for growing in frames and cloches.

'Snowball' – globe; white skin; mild flavoured, tender white flesh; rapid grower.

'Tokyo Cross' (F1 hybrid) – globe; smooth, white skin; six weeks to full maturity; can be sown as late as early autumn.

Maincrop turnips
'Golden Ball' – globe; tender, yellow flesh; small tops; keeps well; suitable for late sowing.

'Green Globe' – globe; good for spring greens; pure white flesh.

'Veitch's Red Globe' – medium-sized, flattish roots; bright red top; white flesh.

Swedes
'Acme Purple Top'– purple top; large globes; ready to lift from early autumn; sweet, orange flesh.

'Best of All' – purple skin; globe; very hardy – reliable variety for overwintering and storing.

'Marian' – purple skin; globe; bred for resistance to club root and mildew; yellow flesh; good yields.

'Western Perfection' – purple-topped roots; yellow flesh; quick-growing; ready from early autumn on.

Spring green turnips should be sown at the end of summer. Make drills 12mm (½in) deep and 7.5cm (3in) apart. Do not thin the seedlings. Harvest the tops when they are no more than 20cm (8in) high. If you cut them at 10-15cm (4-6in) high, they will sprout again and produce several crops.

Harvesting and storing
Pull summer turnips when they are about the size of golf balls –

any larger and they become fibrous – and use them within a few days.

Maincrop turnips are lifted and stored around the middle of autumn. Swedes can be left in the ground over winter and lifted as required – they taste sweeter the younger they are.

Gently prise the roots out of the ground with a fork and avoid bruising them.

A few swedes can be lifted and stored, in case the ground freezes

hard. Twist the leaves off sound roots and stack the roots on a bed of dry sand or soil in a box, covered with more sand or soil. Put the box in a cool, dry, frost-proof shed.

Pests and diseases
Flea beetles can be a serious pest to seedlings; dust them with derris or HCH.

Club root, mainly prevalent on badly-drained soils lacking in lime, can ruin crops.

163

SWEETCORN

Fresh, home-grown sweetcorn cobs are delicious and the attractive tassel-like flowers look decorative in the garden.

Sweetcorn is a half-hardy annual, also known as maize, corn-on-the-cob and Indian corn. Although it is native to South America, the quickly maturing hybrid varieties can be grown successfully in most parts of Britain, even during poor summers. One or two cobs should be produced by each plant, depending on weather and soil conditions.

Planning the crop

Sweetcorn needs a sunny, sheltered position, and a well-drained and fertile soil. A slightly acid soil is an advantage, and liming is unnecessary before sowing or planting out.

During the winter before planting, enrich the bed with well-rotted garden compost or farmyard manure, at the rate of one bucketful per sq m/ yd. A couple of weeks before planting or sowing, rake in an all-purpose fertilizer such as Growmore at the manufacturer's recommended rate.

Sweetcorn should be grown in a block rather than in long rows. This arrangement makes it easier for the light, airborne male pollen to reach the female flowers.

Each plant bears male and female flowers. The male flowers grow at the tops of the plants and the silky female flower tassels hang from the tops of the immature cobs.

Growing sweetcorn

Sweetcorn can be sown directly in the open ground in late spring, but seeds that are given an early start under glass are more likely to succeed, especially if the summer turns out to be poor.

Sowing

Sow the seeds in pots under glass in mid spring and plant the seedlings outdoors in late spring after hardening off. Alternatively, sow them directly in open ground under cloches in mid spring: put the cloches in position a couple of weeks in advance to warm up the soil before sowing. The ground temperature should be 10-13°C (50-55°F) for rapid germination. It is also possible to buy strips of young sweetcorn plants for planting out in late spring.

Under glass, sow the seeds two at a time and 12mm (½in) deep in 6.5cm (2½in) pots or plug trays filled with moist seed compost – it is important not to disturb the roots.

Cover the pots with newspaper and glass and keep them covered until the seeds germinate. Maintain a temperature of 16-18°C (61-64°F).

If the seeds are being germinated indoors, enclose the pots in plastic bags and place them in a warm airing cupboard. As soon as the seeds have germinated, remove the top growth of the weaker of

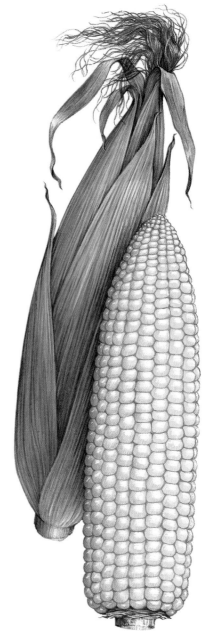

▲ **Corn-on-the-cob** Home-grown sweetcorn is often superior to shop-bought produce – its tender succulent kernels taste sweet rather than starchy.

SOWING AND HARVESTING

1 Sow the seeds, two at a time, in individual pots in mid spring. As soon as the seeds have germinated, remove the weaker of the two seedlings.

2 Remove any side-shoots from the base of developing plants to direct all energy into cob production. Pinch them out when they are about 15cm (6in) long.

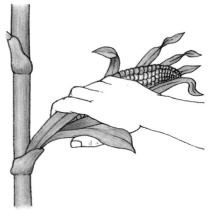

3 The cobs are ready for harvesting when the kernels start to turn pale yellow. Twist the cobs away from the plants or snap them outwards.

the two seedlings in each pot (taking care not to disturb the roots) and move the pots into full light.

When the young plants are about 15cm (6in) tall, harden them off in a cold frame. Plant them out in late spring, or once the danger of frost has passed. Set dwarf varieties about 30cm (1ft) apart each way, and taller plants about 38cm (15in) apart each way, in short rows 60cm (2ft) apart in a square block arrangement.

Sowing outdoors Sow seeds in groups of three under cloches in mid spring, setting each group 30-38cm (12-15in) apart. Once the seedlings have developed, remove the two weakest from each group. Hoe to keep down weeds but be careful not to damage the stems of the plants.

Water the young plants during dry spells. Once the flowers have appeared, water freely in dry weather to ensure good cob quality and yield. Leave the cloches in position until the plants touch the top but remove the end panes.

Alternatively, sow the seeds in

VARIETIES TO CHOOSE

'Conquest' (F1 hybrid) – early; long, well-filled cobs with sweet golden kernels.

'Dickson' – early; vigorous plants recommended for cool northern areas; sweet, crisp-textured cobs.

'Earlibelle' (F1 hybrid) – early; long, well-filled cobs; good cropper, even in poor summers.

'Early Xtra Sweet' (F1 hybrid) – early to mid-season cropper; very sweet flavour. Grow it on its own, as cross-pollination with another variety will spoil the flavour.

'Kelvedon Glory' (F1 hybrid) – early; heavy cropper; 15-18cm (6-7in) cobs of good flavour.

'Sugar Boy' (F1 hybrid) – late-maturing; long deep yellow cobs; grow away from standard varieties.

'Sundance' (F1 hybrid) – early to mid season; vigorous even in cool weather; heavy cropper with sizeable, well-filled cobs.

'Two's Sweeter' (F1 hybrid) – especially sweet-flavoured; bicoloured cobs of white and golden kernels.

open ground in late spring, in the same way as for seeds under cloches: sow more deeply, at 2.5-4cm (1-1½in). Net the plot against birds. The seedlings will take several weeks to appear while those started under glass will already be growing strongly. Sowing directly in the open ground is feasible only in sunny and sheltered gardens.

Once the sweetcorn is growing strongly, give all plants a regular and plentiful supply of water and a weekly feed of liquid fertilizer. Hoe carefully to keep down weeds, and on windy sites tie young plants to canes.

Remove any side-shoots that grow from the base of a plant, pinching them out when they are about 15cm (6in) long.

Harvesting
The cobs will be ready for harvesting in late summer or early autumn, when the tassels have

▲ **Cob pollination** The silky female flower tassels are pollinated by male flowers at the top of the plants.

withered and turned dark brown.

To test for maturity, pierce a grain with your fingernail: when ripe, it should exude a creamy (not watery) liquid.

Twist the cobs off the plant to remove them, and eat or freeze immediately. They become dry and lose their flavour if stored.

Pests and diseases
Bean seed fly may attack seedlings, which wilt and collapse at ground level. Prevent attacks by dusting seed drills with pirimiphos-methyl prior to sowing. Destroy affected seedlings.

Ornamental varieties
Some varieties of sweetcorn have variegated foliage or coloured cobs. These ornamental varieties are not edible, but make an attractive display in bedding schemes and herbaceous borders. The ripe cobs can be dried and used as winter decoration.

▲ **Harvesting** Sweetcorn cobs are ready for picking when the flower tassels have shrivelled and turned dark brown.

Sweetcorn 'Kelvedon Glory'

TOMATOES

The sweet juicy flavour of home-grown tomatoes is incomparable. They crop from early summer, under glass and in the open, in patio grow bags and window-sill pots.

Tomatoes are the gardener's most economical crop. Given the correct growing conditions, they will produce consistently good yields. They can be grown in the greenhouse or in the open, and range from tall cordon types to bush tomatoes and dwarf and trailing varieties. The fruits vary from large, irregularly shaped beefsteak tomatoes through medium-sized globe or plum-shaped types to small cherry-like fruits.

Most nurserymen divide tomatoes into three groups – greenhouse tomatoes; outdoor and greenhouse types; and outdoor (bush) tomatoes. It is advisable to choose seeds and buy seedlings that are suitable for the intended growing method.

All tomatoes are half-hardy plants; under glass they can be grown in cold greenhouses or, for earlier crops, in heated greenhouses. Outdoors, planting should be delayed until all danger of frost has passed.

Soil and site preparation

Tomatoes are greedy feeders and need a rich, moisture-retentive soil, whether in the open or in the greenhouse border.

For outdoor tomatoes, dig in well-rotted manure or compost at the rate of one bucketful per sq m/yd. Before planting, rake in 75g per sq m (3oz per sq yd) of a general fertilizer.

In a greenhouse border, improve drainage on heavy soil or where tomatoes have been grown previously by digging in straw or a bucketful of organic matter or peat substitute per sq m/yd.

Outdoor tomatoes grow best in a sunny, sheltered position such as a south-facing wall.

Sowing

For planting outside, sow seeds in early April; for growing in a cold greenhouse, sow in late March; and for growing in a heated greenhouse, sow in January.

Sow seeds about 2.5cm (1in) apart in seed boxes or trays of seed compost. Alternatively, use 7.5cm (3in) pots, sowing a couple of seeds in each. Cover with 6mm (¼in) of compost and water well.

Cover the boxes or trays with a sheet of paper and place in a propagator, or drape them with polythene bags and place in an airing cupboard.

Check for germination after about four days. As soon as the seedlings begin to push up through the compost, remove the covering and transfer the seedlings to better light.

When two true leaves have formed, prick the seedlings out into 7.5cm (3in) pots of potting compost. Reduce pot-grown plants to one strong seedling per pot.

To make life much easier, you can bypass the sowing stage and buy ready-grown plants from nurseries and garden centres, although the choice of varieties is

▼ **Tomato varieties** Numerous seed selections are available offering fruits that range from a large beefsteak size to miniature cherry tomatoes. Some are perfectly round, others squat or plum-shaped, and colours vary from golden and yellow through orange to bright scarlet – some are even striped.

'Moneymaker'

'Big Boy'

'Yellow Perfection'

not as great as with seeds. Choose sturdy, dark green plants about 20cm (8in) high.

Outdoor tomatoes

Plant out the seedlings – home-grown or bought – in the prepared bed, grow bag or container by late spring or early summer when night frost is no longer a threat. Water the pots, then knock each plant out gently.

In open ground, set the plants 45cm (1½ft) apart, allowing 60cm (2ft) between rows of dwarf and bush varieties, and at least 75cm (2½ft) between rows of cordon varieties. The top of the soil ball should be about 12mm (½in) below ground level.

In grow bags, plant two to four seedlings, depending on variety. A 23cm (9in) pot, patio container or hanging basket will accommodate one seedling.

For dwarf and bush-type toma-toes, spread black polythene or a layer of straw over the ground to deter slugs and snails and to keep the fruits off the soil.

Cordon types need staking: push a 1.5m (5ft) garden cane or stake just outside the soil ball and

PRICKING OUT AND PLANTING OUT

1 As soon as two true leaves have fully developed, prick out the seedlings into 7.5cm (3in) pots of potting compost. Hold the seedlings gently by the leaves and firm the compost around the stem.

2 When the young plants are 15-20cm (6-8in) high and the danger of frost is past, plant them out in a prepared bed. Set them 45cm (18in) apart with the soil ball 12mm (½in) below ground level.

as the plant grows, tie it to the stake at approximately 30cm (12in) intervals. Remove side-shoots often. There is no need to stake or pinch out side-shoots on dwarf, bush and trailing varieties.

Water plants frequently in dry weather and, once small tomatoes have started to form on the first truss of flowers, feed once or twice a week with a liquid tomato

fertilizer, following the manufac-turer's instructions.

Stop further growth on cordon varieties by pinching out the top of the plants when small tomatoes have formed on the fourth truss. Continue to remove side-shoots.

Outdoor crops can be advanced a couple of weeks by setting the plants under cloches in the middle of late spring. Position the cloches over the prepared bed a fortnight before planting out.

Greenhouse tomatoes

In a cold greenhouse, the seedlings can be planted out at the beginning of late spring. Space the plants 38-45cm (15-18in) apart in the border and, if space allows, in staggered rows 60cm (2ft) apart. Water the pots well beforehand.

In a heated greenhouse, plant out seedlings in early spring. Maintain a minimum night tem-perature of 10-13°C (50-55°F).

Grow bags and pots can be set out on the floor and on the staging of the greenhouse.

Support all plants with tall stakes and secure them at regular intervals. Alternatively, tie slack string under a leaf joint near the base of each plant and attach it to the greenhouse roof. As the plants grow, twist the stems carefully around the strings.

◄ **Grow bag cultivation** Tomatoes can be grown successfully in grow bags indoors or outside. If you want large fruit, grow two plants in each bag. For heavier yields of smaller fruits grow four in each bag. It is important to water and feed frequently.

TYING UP AND PINCHING OUT

1 Tie each plant to a stake at 30cm (12in) intervals. Wrap the string twice round the stake and loop it loosely round the plant stem, allowing space for the stem to thicken.

2 On cordon tomatoes, remove all side-shoots appearing in the leaf axils when they are about 2.5cm (1in) long. Pinch them out with your finger and thumb or cut them off with a clean, sharp knife.

3 When a cordon tomato has formed four trusses outdoors and six trusses in the greenhouse (or has reached the roof), pinch out the growing tip, leaving two leaves above the top truss.

Remove side-shoots regularly, and pinch out the top of the stems when the plants have reached the top of the greenhouse or when they have formed at least six trusses.

Water the plants regularly, at least once a day if they are in grow bags or a pot. When some tomatoes have formed on the lowest truss, start feeding with a liquid fertilizer, following the manufacturer's recommendations. Ventilate the greenhouse during the day and provide shading in high summer.

Ring culture is a growing method which saves the trouble of replacing the soil in the greenhouse border and helps to reduce the incidence of soil-borne diseases. Rings are bottomless pots made from bituminous felt; they are filled with sterilized potting compost and placed on a 15cm (6in) deep bed made up of free-draining aggregate of crushed stones and clinkers of weathered ashes. The tomato plants, one to each ring, send roots down into the aggregate, which must be watered thoroughly every day. Liquid feed only is applied to the compost in the rings once the first flower truss has formed.

Harvesting

In the open, the crop should be ready for picking from late sum-

▶ **Greenhouse tomatoes** Grown as single-stemmed cordons, greenhouse tomatoes must be supported with stakes and the plants tied in loosely at 30cm (12in) intervals.

Alternatively, tie string from the base of each plant to the greenhouse roof and twist the stem around it.

Cordon 'Sweet 100'

Bush 'The Amateur'

Cordon 'Ailsa Craig'

mer to early autumn. In an unheated greenhouse, you can pick tomatoes from mid summer onwards, and in a heated greenhouse from early summer.

Pick tomatoes as they ripen. Hold the tomato in your hand and press the stalk with your thumb to break it neatly at the joint just above the fruit.

Before the first frosts arrive cut any remaining green trusses and lay them on a window-sill indoors to ripen.

Alternatively, wrap individual tomatoes in paper and place them in a drawer. You can speed up the process by putting a ripe tomato in with them.

Pest and diseases

The most common pests of tomatoes are aphids, glasshouse whitefly and red spider mites. Biological control can be effective.

Tomatoes are also affected by various diseases and disorders (although outdoor tomatoes are less susceptible), including grey mould, greenback, tomato leaf mould, leaf roll, foot rot, magnesium deficiency and some virus diseases. Maintain good greenhouse hygiene and disinfect or fumigate the house annually.

VARIETIES TO CHOOSE

Outdoor

'Marmande' – cordon; large, irregularly shaped beefsteak tomatoes; good flavour.

'Pixie' – dwarf; heavy cropper of small fruits; ripens quickly.

'Red Alert' – bush; good cropper of small tomatoes; early maturing.

'Sweet 100' – cordon; heavy cropper of small, cherry tomatoes.

'The Amateur' – bush; heavy cropper of medium-sized tomatoes; early maturing.

'Tumbler' – bush; specially bred for hanging baskets and patio pots; good yields of bright red cherry tomatoes.

'Yellow Perfection' – cordon; early maturing; golden-yellow tomatoes.

Outdoor or greenhouse

'Ailsa Craig' – cordon; reliable cropper of medium-sized tomatoes; early maturing; susceptible to greenback.

'Alicante' – cordon; heavy cropping; early maturing; red fruits; resistant to greenback and mildew.

'Gardener's Delight' – cordon; heavy cropper of medium to small-sized tomatoes; sweet tangy flavour.

'Moneymaker' – cordon; heavy, widely grown cropper of medium-sized tomatoes.

'Tigerella' – cordon; good cropper of medium-sized tomatoes with red and golden stripes; early maturing; resistant to greenback.

Greenhouse

'Big Boy' – cordon; large beefsteak tomatoes, each as much as 450g (1lb).

'Dombello' – cordon; large golden-yellow beefsteak tomatoes; early maturing under cold glass; high disease-resistance.

'Golden Boy' – cordon; globe-shaped yellow tomatoes of good size; resistant to greenback.

'Primato' – cordon; large round fruits; good keeping quality; good disease-resistance.

'Shirley' – cordon; heavy crops of medium-sized red tomatoes; early maturing; resistant to leaf mould, virus disease and greenback.

Cordon 'Yellow Perfection'

Cordon 'Gardener's Delight'

Cordon 'Big Boy'

WATERCRESS

**Tasty and nutritious, watercress will thrive
in the vegetable garden if the soil is kept constantly
moist with fresh, clean water.**

Watercress grows wild on the banks of streams and in ditches at the edges of fields – but contamination by liver fluke, a parasite associated with sheep and cows, can mean that wild watercress is unfit for human consumption.

Watercress can, however, be grown easily in the vegetable garden, although frequent watering with fresh, clean water is necessary for a healthy crop. The leaves have a delicious and distinctive mustard-like flavour and contain both iron and vitamin C.

There are two types available: one has bronze-green leaves while the other has dark green leaves. The bronze-green type is hardier and has a slightly more pungent flavour. Both are perennial and can be raised from seeds or cuttings.

Planning the crop

Choose a damp, slightly shady patch of the vegetable garden which is within easy reach of fresh mains water.

▲ **Watercress** Native to Britain, watercress grows wild near streams. The leaves can be eaten raw or cooked and have a delicious mustard-like flavour. They are highly nutritious, containing both iron and vitamin C. When growing watercress in the vegetable garden, choose a damp, shady spot which is within easy reach of fresh mains water.

Prepare the ground by digging a trench 23cm (9in) wide and 60cm (2ft) long. Mix a bucketful of moisture-holding organic matter – such as well-rotted manure, garden compost or coir – with the soil in the bottom of the trench, smoothing it down to 7.5cm (3in) below the surrounding soil level. Fill in with topsoil when the time comes for sowing or planting in spring.

For a smaller crop, grow watercress in shallow boxes such as seed trays, lined with polythene to retain moisture, or in tubs or pots placed in large bowls containing fresh clean water. Fill the container with potting compost.

Cultivation

Sow watercress by sprinkling the seeds in the prepared trench, tray or pot from mid to late spring. Water the soil thoroughly beforehand or the seeds will not germinate. When the seedlings are large enough to handle, thin them until they are 15cm (6in) apart.

A second sowing can be made in late summer for a final crop. Cover with cloches for protection against frost in early autumn.

◄ **Salad greens** For a small crop, grow watercress in a pot placed in a large bowl of fresh water. Alternatively, use a shallow box such as a plastic seed tray and line it with polythene so that it will retain moisture without leakage.

Remove the covering on mild days to give the plants plenty of fresh air.

Alternatively, take cuttings from healthy plants bought from a greengrocer in late winter to early spring. Stand them in jars of water and keep on the kitchen window-sill. As soon as roots appear, plant cuttings 15cm (6in) apart in the prepared trench, tray or pot. Make successive plantings to prolong harvesting.

Watercress plants can only be grown in soil that is continuously damp – so keep the trench well watered, taking care to firm the plants in so that they are not washed away.

To encourage plants in a tray to establish, cover with a polythene bag to increase humidity and keep the tray out of direct sunshine.

Remove flower heads as soon as they appear since they reduce the plants' leaf growth.

In well-prepared soil, watercress plants should need no extra feeding, but if the leaves get smaller towards the end of the season, feed with a liquid fertilizer of high nitrogen content to encourage sturdier growth.

Harvesting

Start picking watercress as soon as the plants are established. From cuttings, this can be as early as three or four weeks after planting.

Regular cropping will encourage plants to grow a fresh supply of new stems. Take care, however, not to remove too many leaves during the first few months after sowing as this can weaken the plants.

Picking can continue into autumn, when the plants in trays or pots can be brought indoors or placed in a cold greenhouse to extend the season further.

Pests and diseases

Home-grown watercress is usually free from pests, although plants may sometimes be attacked by virus diseases. Destroy any badly diseased plants and replace with virus-free stock.

Use watercress to garnish savoury dishes. It is also delicious when made into soup.

LAND CRESS

▲ **Land cress** A good substitute for watercress, land cress can be harvested within eight weeks of sowing. Six to eight plants will provide a constant supply of tasty salad leaves.

Land cress is also commonly known as American cress or winter cress. It is very similar in appearance to watercress, but the leaves are smaller and have a less delicate flavour.

Land cress is a useful and economical plant to grow since as few as six to eight plants will provide a constant supply of salad leaves during the summer months, as well as during winter.

Preparing the ground

A moist, shady position is suitable for land cress. Prepare the ground by adding well-rotted manure or garden compost to the soil at the rate of one bucketful per sq m/yd. Alternatively, grow in 18cm (7in) pots filled with potting compost.

Cultivation

Land cress is hardy and able to overwinter so that successive sowing will give year-round supplies.

Sow the seed in shallow drills 6mm (¼in) deep and 23cm (9in) apart in early spring for summer use. Water the prepared bed very thoroughly before sowing. Three weeks later thin the seedlings to stand 20cm (8in) apart. Make successive sowings to prolong harvesting.

Keep the ground well watered and mulch with well-rotted manure or garden compost, or with moist coir.

Make a final sowing in early autumn for winter use, preferably in a cold frame or under cloches to protect against frost.

Alternatively, sow three or four seeds to each pot and remove all but the strongest when the seedlings are large enough to handle. Keep in partial shade and water regularly.

Harvesting

The first pickings can be made about eight weeks after sowing. Pick the outer leaves first, leaving the centre to produce more. As the plants get older, discard the tougher, outer leaves and pick the new, tender leaves that grow from the centre. Remove flower heads as soon as they appear.

Pests and diseases

The pests most likely to occur are slugs and snails, which are best destroyed with slug bait.

▼ **Moist shade** Most vegetables thrive in an open sunny site, but land cress develops the best flavour in cool, moist shade where little else will grow.

WILD FOOD

**Wild fruits, salad leaves and mushrooms are still
plentiful and can be picked from the countryside and hedgerows
sited well away from major traffic routes.**

To supplement cultivated fruit and vegetables, it's worth gathering some of the wild plants normally considered to be weeds. This will enable you to include a wide range of intriguing and delicious flavours in your cooking. Be sure to collect such food from sites where the air is pollution-free – plants and fungi growing on the waysides of busy roads are best left alone. Pick fruits, flowers and leaves with care so that the area is not deprived of its beautiful natural flora.

Wild fruits
In autumn, hedgerows, woods and moorland provide a rich harvest.
Bilberry (*Vaccinium myrtillus*) is an attractive moorland plant, related to the blueberry. It is a bushy shrub with bright green leaves, found on heaths and moors throughout Britain.

Fresh bilberries are sharp but refreshing eaten with sugar and

elder

cream. They are delicious in pies, tarts and crumbles, especially when combined with apples, and add fine flavour to jams and jellies.
Crab apple (*Malus sylvestris*) is a deciduous tree found in woods, hedges and scrubland. It flowers in late spring and the small apples which follow are at their best in early autumn. They are too tart for eating, but are excellent for jelly-making.

▼ **Crab apples and hawthorn** Growing wild on the edges of woods and in hedges and scrubland, crab apples produce their fruits in autumn. They are used for jellies and wine-making. The young hawthorn leaves have a pleasantly nutty taste and can be included in mixed salads.

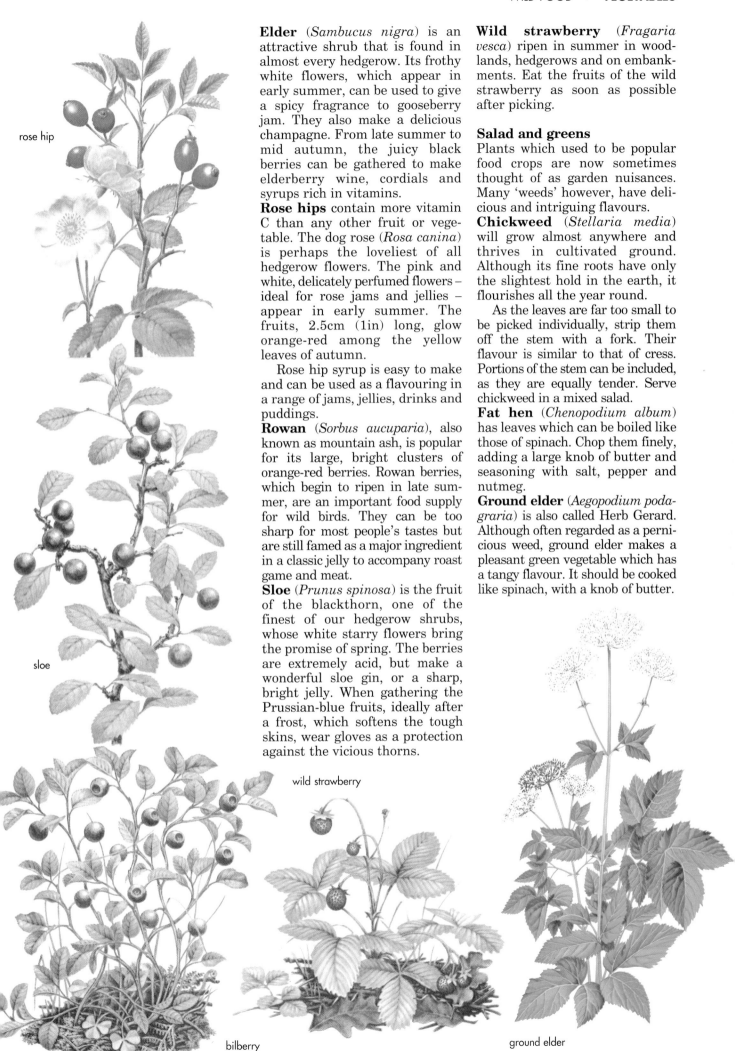

rose hip

sloe

Elder (*Sambucus nigra*) is an attractive shrub that is found in almost every hedgerow. Its frothy white flowers, which appear in early summer, can be used to give a spicy fragrance to gooseberry jam. They also make a delicious champagne. From late summer to mid autumn, the juicy black berries can be gathered to make elderberry wine, cordials and syrups rich in vitamins.

Rose hips contain more vitamin C than any other fruit or vegetable. The dog rose (*Rosa canina*) is perhaps the loveliest of all hedgerow flowers. The pink and white, delicately perfumed flowers – ideal for rose jams and jellies – appear in early summer. The fruits, 2.5cm (1in) long, glow orange-red among the yellow leaves of autumn.

Rose hip syrup is easy to make and can be used as a flavouring in a range of jams, jellies, drinks and puddings.

Rowan (*Sorbus aucuparia*), also known as mountain ash, is popular for its large, bright clusters of orange-red berries. Rowan berries, which begin to ripen in late summer, are an important food supply for wild birds. They can be too sharp for most people's tastes but are still famed as a major ingredient in a classic jelly to accompany roast game and meat.

Sloe (*Prunus spinosa*) is the fruit of the blackthorn, one of the finest of our hedgerow shrubs, whose white starry flowers bring the promise of spring. The berries are extremely acid, but make a wonderful sloe gin, or a sharp, bright jelly. When gathering the Prussian-blue fruits, ideally after a frost, which softens the tough skins, wear gloves as a protection against the vicious thorns.

Wild strawberry (*Fragaria vesca*) ripen in summer in woodlands, hedgerows and on embankments. Eat the fruits of the wild strawberry as soon as possible after picking.

Salad and greens

Plants which used to be popular food crops are now sometimes thought of as garden nuisances. Many 'weeds' however, have delicious and intriguing flavours.

Chickweed (*Stellaria media*) will grow almost anywhere and thrives in cultivated ground. Although its fine roots have only the slightest hold in the earth, it flourishes all the year round.

As the leaves are far too small to be picked individually, strip them off the stem with a fork. Their flavour is similar to that of cress. Portions of the stem can be included, as they are equally tender. Serve chickweed in a mixed salad.

Fat hen (*Chenopodium album*) has leaves which can be boiled like those of spinach. Chop them finely, adding a large knob of butter and seasoning with salt, pepper and nutmeg.

Ground elder (*Aegopodium podagraria*) is also called Herb Gerard. Although often regarded as a pernicious weed, ground elder makes a pleasant green vegetable which has a tangy flavour. It should be cooked like spinach, with a knob of butter.

wild strawberry

bilberry

ground elder

Sorrel (*Rumex acetosa*) looks very much like a small dock. Its pointed, spear-shaped leaves are among the first green shoots of spring, while its deep red flowers lend colour to many roadside verges and hedgerows from early to late summer.

The leaves have a sharp taste and one or two, finely chopped, are a welcome addition to a salad. The common use for sorrel is to make it into a sharp, green sauce; it also makes a fine soup.

Stinging nettle (*Urtica dioica*) thrives in rough, nitrogen-rich soil. Wear gloves to gather the tender leaves in spring, when the plants are no more than 20cm (8in) high. To serve as an accompanying vegetable, wash the leaves and cook them gently – without water – for 20 minutes, chop finely and rub through a sieve. Nettle soup, too, is delicious.

Field/woodland mushrooms
Despite their bizarre appearance, many wild mushrooms and other fungi make tasty additions to a

blewit

wood hedgehog

cep

sorrel

stinging nettle

morel

chanterelle

chickweed

wide range of dishes.

Blewit, also known as blue legs, (the name deriving from the blue/violet stems) is normally used to give body to soups and stews. The most popular form is the meadow or field blewit (*Tricholoma saevum*) which can be found growing in clusters in rough pasture from mid autumn to well after the early frosts. The caps are irregular and flattish, curling under at the edges.

Cep or Cèpe de Bordeaux (*Boletus edulis*) have caps which closely resemble old-fashioned buns. The underside is a mass of yellowish pores like sponge rubber and this must be removed with a spoon before preparing the rest.

Colour changes in fungi denote poison. When picking ceps, break a small piece off each cap. If the flesh remains firm and white, they are true ceps. But if any colour change occurs, you have probably gathered some other species. Some of these are inedible, and one, devil's boletus (*Boletus satanas*), is poisonous. However, it is also recognized by a blood-red stripe at the base and pores of a similar colour on mature caps.

Chanterelle (*Cantharellus cibarius*), also known as the egg mushroom because of the vivid, egg-yolk colouring of its flesh, is one of the most popular of all edible fungi. It flourishes from late spring to mid autumn in mixed and coniferous woodlands.

Perhaps the most distinctive feature of this attractive fungus is its scent, closely akin to ripe greengages or apricots. The flavour, too, resembles that of apricots.

Morel mushrooms (*Morchella esculenta*) are popular for their delicate, aromatic flavour, and are unusual among fungi in that they grow only in spring. They are generally found on light soil near trees and hedgerows, and grow best on damp, warm days. Pick morels only when they are young.

Parasol mushrooms (*Lepiota procera*) are generally found in colonies on the edges of woods, in grassy clearings and on roadsides, from summer to late autumn and are easily recognised from their shape.

The shaggy parasol (*Lepiota rachodes*) grows in similar places and closely resembles its relative, except that it is shorter and sturdier. Both varieties are delicious when cooked like field mushrooms.

Shaggy cap or shaggy ink cap (*Coprinus comatus*) favours areas of mown grass rather than meadowland, and can be found from early summer to late autumn on road verges, well-established lawns and playing fields.

Pick only the young mushrooms before the gills blacken and dissolve into an inky liquid.

Wood hedgehog (*Hydnum repandum*) is so called because it belongs to the only group of fungi that possesses spines instead of gills. It flourishes in woodland from late summer to late autumn and is at its best when young.

Wild flowers for flavour

Spring flowers add colour to finished dishes, but pick them sparingly and only from large colonies. Never uproot wild flowers.

Broom (*Cytisus scoparius*) bears gold flowers which create an early summer blaze of colour on sandy heathlands throughout Europe.

The buds can be gathered in spring and packed into jars with vinegar or salt. Pickled in this way, they can be used as an alternative to capers.

Primrose (*Primula vulgaris*) flowers can be crystallized and stored in jars to be used as decoration for cakes and confectionery.

Sweet violet (*Viola odorata*) appears in early spring under hedgerows and in shady woods. The flowers may be violet-mauve or white.

The young, tender leaves impart a delicate flavour to soups and salads. The flowers may be crystallized like primroses or steeped in syrup or hot, white vinegar as a flavouring for drinks and puddings.

broom

sweet violet

primrose

INDEX

ACKNOWLEDGEMENTS

Photographer's credits
A-Z Botanical Collection Ltd 38 (br) /Elsa Megson 104(tl); Bernard Alfieri 137; Gillian Beckett 25; Biofotos 23, 136; Pat Brindley 83(br), 101(tr), 125, 131(bl); Eric Crichton 24(tl), 26, 33, 96(c), 99(t), 103(t), 107(t), 107(b), 141(bl), 155(bc), 156; Eaglemoss (Graham Rae) front cover; Mr Fothergill's Seeds Ltd 101(cr); Brian Furner Horticultural Pictures 24(tr), (Marion Furner) 82, 101(tl), 129(tr), 135(cr), 146(t), 163(tl), 163(cl), 165(cl), 165(b), 170; Garden Picture Library (Geoff Dann) 2-3, (Michael Howes) 141(l); Rob Herwig 91(c), 115(r); Marijke Heuff 72(t); Neil Holmes 8; Lamontagne 6, 20-21, 46, 76, 85, 105, 135(b), 171; S & O Mathews 4-5, 141(c); Ken Muir 72(b), 74(b), 75(tr), 75(bl); Natural Image (Bob Gibbons) 172, (P Wilson) 53; Clive Nichols back cover; Photos Horticultural 16,

28, 31(l), 32, 39(t), 39(cr), 39(b), 40, 47, 49(bl), 49(br), 50, 55, 59, 61, 69, 73, 74(t), 75(tl), 78, 81, 83(bl), 87, 89, 91(br), 92-93, 94(bl), 96(b), 118, 127(br), 131(t), 135(t), 141(r), 146(b), 153(cl), 153(bl), 160, 167, 168, 169(bc), 169(br); Harry Smith Collection 18, 24(b), 31(r), 37, 39(cl), 42, 49(bc), 63, 65, 67, 71, 75(br), 91(bl), 94(br), 99(c), 99(b), 104(tr), 104(c), 104(b), 107(c), 110, 111, 113(tl), 115(l), 120, 126, 127(bl), 129(bl), 130, 131(bc), 131(br), 133, 135(cl), 142, 146(c), 149(t), 151, 152, 153(cr), 153(br), 155(bl), 155(br), 161, 163(br), 165(cr), 169(t), 169(bl); Suttons/Dobies Group, Hele Road, Torquay 90, 113(cl), 149(cr), 149(bl); Elizabeth Whiting Associates 154, 155(t).

Illustrators
David Ashby 52(b), 53; Elisabeth Dowle 12-15, 51, 52(t), 60(r), 66(t), 86(b), 87, 97-98, 100(t), 119(b), 123, 130, 136-137, 148(t), 156-157, 158; Will Giles 73(tr),

74; Christine Hart-Davies 10-11, 27, 29, 43-44, 45(tr), 45(br), 48(br), 49(t), 88(tr), 106(bl), 122(b); Nigel Hawtin 23-24, 34, 45(cr), 45(bl), 48(bl), 62-64, 70-71, 145, 147(t), 164(b); Dee Mclean 79-80; Reader's Digest 1, 28, 35, 38, 46, 48, 50, 56, 60(l), 75, 86(t), 102(t), 103(b), 108(t), 113, 121, 126, 142-143, 144, 147(b), 159, 161, 162, 170-171, 172-175, (David Baxter) 54(t), 105(t), 116, (Leonora Box) 124, 154, (Shirley Ellis) 114(tr), 138, 140(tr), 164(t), (Colin Emberson) 20, 22, 25, 26, 30(t), 36(t), 68(r), 82, 106(r), 110, 119(t), 120, 122(r), 132, 150(b), 166, (Charles Pickard) 19, (Basil Smith) 92, 134(t), (Norman Weaver) 128; Ann Winterbotham 105(c), 105(b); Claire Wright 17-18, 21, 30(b), 31, 36(b), 54(b), 55, 57-58, 66(b), 67, 68(bl), 69, 84-85, 88(bl), 89, 93, 100(b), 102(b), 108(b), 109, 111-112, 114(bl), 117, 125, 127, 134(b), 139, 140(bl), 148(b), 150(t), 151, 167-168.

Typesetting SX COMPOSING, ESSEX; Printing & Binding PRINTER INDUSTRIA, GRÁFICA S.A. BARCELONA
Separations COLOURSCAN OVERSEAS CO PTE LTD, SINGAPORE; Paper PERIGORD-CONDAT, FRANCE

53-014-1